Copyright in Cyberspace 2

QUESTIONS AND ANSWERS FOR LIBRARIANS

GRETCHEN McCORD HOFFMANN

D1403025

NEAL-SCHUMAN PUBLISHERS, INC.

NEW YORK   LONDON

Published by Neal-Schuman Publishers, Inc.
100 William Street, Suite 2004
New York, NY 10038

Printed and bound in the United States of America

The paper used in this publication meets the minimum requirements of American National Standard for Information Sciences—Permanence of Paper for Printed Library Materials. ANSI Z39.48–1992. ∞

PLEASE READ THIS:
We have done our best to give you useful and accurate information on copyright law. But please be aware that laws and precedents are constantly changing and are subject to different interpretations. The information presented here does not substitute for the advice of an attorney. You have the responsibility to check all material you read here before relying on it. Of necessity, neither Neal-Schuman nor the author makes any warranties concerning the information in this book or the use to which it is put.

"This publication is designed to provide accurate and authoritative information in regard to the subject matter covered. It is sold with the understanding that the publisher is not engaged in rendering legal, accounting or other professional service. If legal advice or other expert assistance is required, the services of a competent professional person should be sought." *From a Declaration of Principles adopted jointly by a Committee of the American Bar Association and a Committee of Publishers.*

Library of Congress Cataloging-in-Publication Data

Hoffmann, Gretchen McCord.
    Copyright in cyberspace 2 : questions and answers for librarians / Gretchen McCord Hoffmann.
        p. cm.
    Includes bibliographical references and index.
    ISBN 1–55570–517–0 (alk. paper)
    1. Copyright and electronic data processing—United States. 2. Fair use (Copyright)—United States. 3. Cyberspace. I. Title.
    KF3030.1.ZH644 2005
    346.7304'82—dc22

                                                                2004018238

Contents

Foreword by Mary Minow   v
Preface   vii
Acknowledgments   xi

Part I: Copyright fundamentals in cyberspace
1 History and purpose of copyright law   3
2 Overview of copyright law   15
3 Fair use: is it all it's cracked up to be? and other pockets
   of protection for librarians   27
4 Some Internet basics   43
5 Recent copyright legislation   51

Part II: Applying copyright in cyberspace
6 Hyperlinks and framing   59
7 Browsing and caching   69
8 Using digital images   81
9 The dark side of the DMCA   93
10 File-sharing   101
11 Non-copyright issues   107
12 I'm the good guy: what can they do to me?   113

Part III: Specific library applications
13 Liability for content provided on the Internet and as
   Internet access provider   121
14 Interlibrary loan and resource sharing   127
15 Electronic reserves and class-based Web pages   135
16 Library instruction and distance education   147
17 Licensing   155
18 Writing a copyright policy   163
19 Librarians as representatives of libraries and library users   169

Part IV: Sourcebox
A Selected excerpts from the Copyright Act of 1976
   (17 U.S.C. 101 *et seq.*)   183

B   Copyright Term Duration   209
C   The Conference on Fair Use: Educational Fair Use Guidelines
    For Digital Images   211
D   The Conference on Fair Use: Fair Use Guidelines For Electronic
    Reserve Systems   221
E   Code of Ethics of the American Library Association   225
F   The Conference on Fair Use: Fair Use Guidelines for
    Educational Multimedia   227
G   American Library Association Model Policy Concerning
    College and University Photocopying for Classroom,
    Research and Library Reserve Use   237
H   Agreement on Guidelines for Classroom Copying in
    Not-for-Profit Educational Institutions   245
I   How to get permission to use copyrighted material   249
J   How to protect your work   251
K   Resources: organizations   255
L   Resources: publications   257
M   Resources: Web pages   259
N   Glossary   261

Index   267

About the author   271

Foreword

I first met Ms. Hoffmann at a Texas Library Association conference and was instantly drawn to her. We are both librarians who went to law school, a rarity. Most people I know who have both degrees had the good sense to leave the law and go to library school. Having experience working in libraries gave Gretchen a grounding that she put to good use — writing the first edition *of Copyright in Cyberspace* while she was still in law school.

This new edition is an even stronger call to action to librarians than the first. The last chapter exhorts us to get involved in the law-making process and *do something!* The best part is that Ms. Hoffmann readies us for action by explaining complicated copyright issues in language that anyone can understand.

She brings us to "The Dark Side of the DMCA," which sounds ominous. It is. The Digital Millennium Copyright Act (DMCA) affects libraries profoundly, yet its complicated wording keeps most of us from understanding what is at stake. *Copyright in Cyberspace 2* tells us in plain language that library copying is at stake — copies we make for lending, for archival purposes, for distance education, and more.

Content control by copyright owners has expanded greatly over recent years — licensing, encryption, digital restrictions management systems. The legal system adds additional layers, and librarians must unwrap each layer to get access to traditional library materials, which now take the form of electronic books, online periodicals, digital music files, and more.

Fittingly, this second edition greatly expands the discussion of licensing. Like Ms. Hoffmann, I also find that many librarians assume they have no control over the content of licenses they sign and don't pay attention to the terms. Ms. Hoffmann explains that many of the terms are negotiable and gives a useful checklist of what to look for in a licensing agreement.

Copyright in Cyberspace 2 also gives the most thorough treatment on writing a copyright policy I've ever seen. I had a draft copy and showed it to librarians at a recent workshop I conducted. Chapter 18 was practically gobbled up before my eyes. Librarians were taking fast and furious notes. Why are librarians writing or updating their policies at such a brisk pace? Because new laws give libraries some protections from lawsuits...*if the li-*

braries have certain elements in their copyright policies. Ms. Hoffmann explains these elements, tells us what the policy should say, and gives practical advice on who should be involved in writing the policy. This is essential reading for both the library and the library's attorney.

It is precisely this level of nitty-gritty detail that truly educates the reader about today's rapidly shrinking user rights. Librarians in the trenches who read this book will better understand why they can no longer access materials the public needs. To lobby legislators, librarians are best equipped when they bring specific examples of public information that is locked up.

Ms. Hoffmann closes by reenergizing us with Mahatma Ghandi's words, "You must be the change you wish to see in the world." This book shows us the way.

Mary Minow, J.D., A.M.L.S.
Library Law Consultant
LibraryLaw.com

Preface

Librarians are the last line of defense against the efforts of publishers to sacrifice the right of the people to know on the altar of profit.
Professor Ray Patterson

In the four years since *Copyright in Cyberspace: Questions and Answers for Librarians* was published, much in the world of copyright and cyberspace has changed. Some of the changes have been good, some not so good, and some almost good but not quite what we need them to be. Among the things that remain unchanged is the need for librarians to be knowledgeable about copyright law and to get involved in making law and policy that addresses copyright issues. By doing these two things, librarians will help uphold one of the central purposes of libraries: open access to information.

Like its predecessor, *Copyright in Cyberspace 2: Questions and Answers for Librarians* is designed as a basic guide for librarians who need to understand and apply copyright law to information obtained from and/or transmitted through the Internet. *Copyright in Cyberspace 2* achieves three important goals:

1. It provides a general understanding of copyright law as it relates to the librarian's use of the Internet;
2. It offers an awareness of the issues that the Internet brings to bear on copyright law, the fact that many of these issues remain undecided, and that how they are decided is of the utmost importance for the future of libraries and library users; and
3. It inspires a sense of responsibility for helping our society and its decision makers to resolve those issues.

An increased emphasis has been placed in this new edition for library and information professionals to become a voice in the copyright debate. If librarians do not become active in these debates, libraries will no longer be able to provide free access to information.

Copyright in Cyberspace 2: Questions and Answers for Librarians is divided into four parts. Part I, "Copyright Fundamentals in Cyberspace," provides the basic information needed to understand how the Internet as a communications medium affects the application of copyright law to content. Chapter 1 describes the history and purposes of copyright law, while Chapter 2 provides an overview of various current copyright laws by discussing what can be copyrighted, how to obtain copyright protection, and the possible limitations of these rights. Fair use is discussed in Chapter 3, followed by Internet basics in Chapter 4. Chapter 5 examines recent copyright legislation, such as the Digital Millennium Copyright Act and the TEACH Act.

Part II, "Applying Copyright to Cyberspace," applies copyright law to various aspects of using the Web and analyzes what may or may not be legal. Chapter 6 answers questions on hyperlinking and framing; Chapter 7 covers browsing; and Chapter 8 is devoted to digital images. Each of these chapters includes new information on important legal updates. Chapter 9 is entirely new and discusses "The Dark Side of the DMCA." (Digital Millennium Copyright Act). It explores what many consider to be misuses of the act and what this means for libraries. Likewise, Chapter 10 is also new. It explains the hot issue of file-sharing and the significance to librarians of recent legal actions taken by some aggressive copyright owners. Chapter 11 explains noncopyright issues, including the implications of trademarks, words used as logos, deep linking, and how these issues share a similar, though not exact, relationship with copyright. Chapter 12 looks at the potential exceptions and damages today's courts might impose upon the "good guys" (like libraries) and the increasing likelihood of a library being sued for infringement.

Part III, "Specific Library Applications," covers copyright in librarians' day-to-day use of the Internet. Chapter 13 covers the library's liability for copyright infringements as both content provider and as an Internet service provider. When the first edition of *Copyright in Cyberspace* was published, this was a very new part of statutory law, and the intervening four years have provided some glimpses at how courts will interpret and apply the law. Copyright considerations related to interlibrary loan and resource sharing; electronic reserves and classroom copying requirements, Web pages, and library instruction and distance education are covered in Chapters 14, 15, and 16. Chapters 17 and 18 are entirely new and address licensing — among the most questioned issues on today's library listservs—and implementing copyright policies — an increasingly important issue for librarians because of the requirements and implications of the TEACH Act, DMCA, and ever more aggressive copyright owners policing uses of their works. The last chapter in Part III emphasizes the dire need for librarians to become true activists in the copyright arena and provides some guidance for to how to go about doing so.

Throughout Parts I–III you will find new sideboxes with specific copyright-related questions and brief answers. Although the answers may often vary depending on the specific situation, these sideboxes attempt to highlight some of the questions I am most frequently asked at workshops and programs.

Part IV, "Copyright Information Sourcebox," presents a wealth of documents that reference librarians can use to properly develop and administer copyright policies and procedures. The first of the fifteen sources, "Selected Excerpts from the Copyright Act of 1976," (17 U.S.C. 101 *et seq.*) provides the significant excerpts of the copyright statute. This section also includes copyright term durations, fair use guidelines, and a model policy statement from the American Library Association. In addition, there are many "how-to" sources providing information on obtaining permission for copyrighted material, protecting your own work, and representing the needs of your library. The Sourcebox continues with helpful resources from organizations, publications, and Web pages. It concludes with an all-new glossary perfect for referencing terms or finding out more about specific topics that come up in your day.

Copyright in Cyberspace 2 is written in such a way that you need not read it from beginning to end. If you feel grounded in the basics of how the Internet works, for example, you might skip Chapter 4. If your library is looking at using the Internet for electronic reserves, you can skip to Chapter 15. However, do keep in mind that if you have questions as you read, they are likely answered in other chapters because many of the topics are interrelated.

I hope that *Copyright in Cyberspace 2: Questions and Answers for Librarians* will increase your knowledge about copyright law in general and strengthen your ability to apply copyright law to new information environments. I also hope that it will make clear to you how imperative it is for each and every one of us to become involved in the copyright discourse, and that it will provide you with useful direction in how to go about doing so. All of these things — greater knowledge, enhanced abilities, and re-energized commitment to your profession — will be of great benefit to all of those you serve.

Acknowledgments

Once again, I am indebted to many people for their roles in helping this book come about.

I again must thank the many librarians whose questions and comments have resulted in new material in this edition and have made clear that so many of the same challenges are faced by all types of librarians. I am grateful to those who sent me their questions and concerns on various listservs, to those who contributed to my thought process through their participation in my workshops and programs, and to those with whom I have worked on individual bases.

I continue to be indebted to those who have taught me much about writing, including Professor Wayne Schiess of the University of Texas School of Law, Myrtis McCord, and others who have unofficially edited my work.

I would like to thank those who have contributed greatly to my knowledge of the subject matter of copyright law in the cyber arena, in particular R. Anthony Reese, Thomas W. Gregory Professor of Law at the University of Texas School of Law; Neil W. Netanel, Arnold White & Durkee Centennial Professor of Law at the University of Texas School of Law; and my numerous colleagues within the legal arena.

Again, I save the best for last: my eternal gratitude to my husband, Peter Briggs Hoffmann, for his unending support and encouragement, especially during trying times.

PART I

Copyright fundamentals in cyberspace

1

History and purpose of copyright law

At each turn ... during the 210-year history of American copyright law ..., copyright's adaptation to a new technology was a rocky one, and there were those who argued that copyright simply could not be adapted to fit the new technology. (Merges et al., 1997: 323)

There is nothing new under the sun. (Ecclesiastes 1:9)

Knowing a little about the history of copyright law helps us to appreciate its intricacies and complexity and to understand its purpose. Understanding the purpose behind the law, in turn, helps in understanding the law itself. I have found that many people who criticize the very application of copyright law to the cyberworld, who make arguments that copyright should not apply to the Internet, or who argue that "information wants to be free," often do not understand either the purpose of copyright law or what it really protects. Likewise, the growing movement to increase the control of copyright owners over the use of their works often reflects an ignorance of the purpose of copyright protection. With just a general understanding of both, you'll be one step ahead of many Internet users.

The U.S. Constitution proclaims the purpose of copyright law: "to promote the Progress of Science and the useful Arts," followed by the means of achieving the purpose: "by securing for limited Times to Authors and Inventors the Exclusive Right to their respective Writings and Discoveries." (U.S. Constitution, art. I, sec. 8, cl 8). The fundamental purpose of modern copyright law, then, is to ensure the continuing expansion of the body of human knowledge. Our society has deemed a two-pronged approach essential to achieving this purpose: (1) granting authors exclusive proprietary rights to their works in order to encourage further creations; and (2) limiting authors' control over their works to the extent necessary to allow others to access and thereby build on those works. The greatest challenge that faces copyright law is to balance the two oppositional prongs in such a way that its fundamental purpose is indeed realized. The courts and legislatures try to achieve this balance by creating specific exemptions for limited and specific actions and by applying the fair use doctrine to address situations not covered by exemptions. It is interesting to note that the needs on each side of this scale reflect two broad values that have played vital roles throughout American history: on one side, protection of private property and the right of every member of American society, no matter his position, to own private property; and, on the other side, the fundamental right of every member of American society to better himself and his position in life through education. Maintaining such a balance, however, is easier said than done. Accordingly, copyright law is a continually developing doctrine, constantly reacting to new developments in technology.

You won't be surprised to hear that the original copyright law was a reaction to the development of the printing press. The rise of the ability to copy works quickly and cheaply and to distribute them widely, quickly, and cheaply led to the need to protect the rights of the creators of those works. (Does that sound familiar? How often have you heard it said that the Internet creates problems for authors because of the ability it gives us to copy works quickly and cheaply and to distribute them widely, quickly, and cheaply?) Major advances in technology have always led to changes in copyright law. For example, the development of player pianos led to copyright protection for music for the first time, and the development of the Internet and digital technology were the impetus behind the Digital Millennium Copyright Act. Finding the balance is a continuing challenge, because the development of new technology will always outpace the law's ability to respond.

What *is* copyright, anyway?

Copyright is actually a "bundle" of rights giving the copyright owner control over various uses of his works. These rights will be discussed in detail in Chapter 2, but include the rights to reproduce, distribute, make derivatives of, and publicly perform and display the work. Copyright law provides several exceptions to these rights, however, which represent the other side of the balance—the need to allow some access to and use of the works. These are discussed in detail in Chapter 3.

How did copyright law begin?

As is true for much of American law, copyright law finds its roots in the British legal system. Before mass publishing began, the majority of the British population was illiterate and uneducated. Those authors and artists who produced works did so not for mass consumption, but for the very limited aristocratic class. They were rewarded by the patronage system: Rather than being

> Q Isn't copyright all about protecting the "rights" and ownership of the author?
>
> A No! American copyright law has always emphasized the need to balance the rights of the author with the need for a democratic society to have access to information. We give rights to the author to encourage production of works, and we protect the ability to access information in order to encourage a free flow of ideas. Both are necessary to meet the rationale for copyright law as stated in the Constitution: "To promote the Progress of Science and useful Arts."
>
> Unfortunately, in recent years, many copyright owners seem to have forgotten—or have chosen to ignore—the access side of the balance. Strong and aggressive movements are well under way to truly make copyright law all about the copyright owner. Now more than ever, it is absolutely essential for librarians to stand up as a voice for information users and their rights.

paid for each work they produced, they were supported by aristocrats, many of whom were interested in acquiring artistic works that they could then dedicate to the monarch and so achieve recognition for themselves. (Gasaway and Wiant, 1994)

The invention of the printing press in 1476 coincided with the reign of the Tudors, from 1485 to 1603. The printing press was a valuable tool for the Tudor period, which was marked by the Renaissance, an emphasis on education, and the rise of a middle class. Mass publishing became one more piece of the social mosaic. Although publishers and book vendors became wealthy from the new technologies, authors seldom saw much, if any, reward. Making matters worse for authors, the publishing industry thrived on piracy. (ibid.) Copyright, however, was a response not to a concern for authors' rights, but to the government's reaction to the power created by the printing press: The monarchy was terrified by the possibilities for political and religious rebellion created by the widespread dissemination of heretical writings.

The government's response was, in 1534, to require authors to obtain both a license and approval from official censors before publishing a work. (Leaffer, 1995) In 1557, the Stationer's Company, a guild for publishers and book vendors, was created to fulfill the role of censor and was given a monopoly on publishing. Only members of the guild could publish, and they could publish only works approved by the guild. (Gasaway and Wiant, 1994)

By the early eighteenth century, however, when its license to control publishing expired (Leaffer, 1995), the 150-year-old guild had suffered from years of rampant piracy. (Gasaway and Wiant, 1994) The members petitioned parliament for help and then became victims of the adage: "Be careful what you ask for." The result was the first modern copyright law. Remarkably, the Statute of Anne, passed by Parliament in 1710, recognized not only the rights of authors but also the concept of a public domain. (Leaffer, 1995) Where the Stationer's Company had owned perpetual rights to works it published, author's rights in their own works were limited. Under the new law, copyright in already published works was given a term of twenty-one years; newly published works were protected for fourteen years, which term was renewable for another fourteen years if the author was still alive. The Statute required registration with the Stationer's Company in order for a work to be protected. In later years, a requirement of posting a copyright notice on all registered works was added; at this point, "innocent infringement" became impossible. (Gasaway and Wiant, 1994)

Despite the revolutionary nature of the rights bestowed by the Statute of Anne, the law was still quite limited in scope. For starters, it applied only to written works. Thus, piracy remained a serious problem for artists. Eventually, as a result of great pressure from individual artists, Parliament passed the Engraver's Act of 1735, which gave the same rights to artists as those given to authors by the Statute of Anne. (ibid.)

What about American copyright law?

Most of the original American colonies adopted their own Copyright Acts. Nonetheless, the framers of the Constitution considered the issue important enough to incorporate into the constitution of the new nation. The United States Constitution provides that "Congress shall have Power to . . . promote the Progress of Science and the useful Arts, by securing for limited Times to Authors and Inventors the Exclusive Right to their respective Writings and Discoveries." (U.S. Constitution, art. I, sec. 8, cl 8) Although no further guidance for establishing copyright law is given in the Constitution, such as defining what should be included in the "exclusive rights" granted to authors, the wording of the copyright clause makes clear the intent of granting those rights: (1) to promote the growth of the body of human knowledge by (2) protecting the rights of authors.

One of the first acts of the new Congress was to pass the Copyright Act of 1790. The Act was modeled after the Statute of Anne and granted protection to authors of maps, charts, and books for an original fourteen-year period, renewable for an additional fourteen years if the author survived the first term. (Leaffer, 1995) Over the course of the nineteenth century, the scope of the Act was expanded by amendments to include protection for prints, musical compositions, dramatic works, photographs, artistic works, and sculpture. (Merges, 1997)

When did modern copyright law begin?

The Copyright Act was first overhauled in the early twentieth century. The Copyright Act of 1909 made several substantial changes to copyright law. First, it expanded the scope of copyright law to cover "all writings of an author." (*Copyright Act of 1909, U.S. Code*, vol. 17, sec. 4 (1909)) It also doubled the term of protection from two fourteen-year terms to two twenty-eight-year terms (as under the previous Act, the first term was renewable upon expiration of the first only if the author survived). Finally, whereas the previous act had established the beginning of protection at the moment of *registration*, under the 1909 Act, protection began at the moment of *publication*. Like the original Act, unpublished works were not protected. (Leaffer, 1995) Also unchanged from the first act were the requirements to register a work with the U.S. Copyright Office and deposit copies of the work with the Library of Congress. (Gasaway and Wiant, 1994)

What is the law now?

Like the original Copyright Act of 1790, the 1909 Act was amended several times to adapt to a changing world. Finally, in 1955, Congress authorized a revision of the Copyright Act, which, after twenty years of work, finally culminated in the Copyright Act of 1976. The fact that Congress worked on the revision for twenty years might lead one to believe that the resulting Act would be concise, logical, and well crafted. But consider the fact that twenty years equals ten Congresses.

It is also both instructive and entertaining to know how the statute developed. Although the process in general is not unusual when new laws are written, the extremity of the process in the case of drafting the Copyright Act is. Copyright protection was, of course, of great interest to various types of parties: copyright owners, publishers, the entertainment industry, library associations, educational institutions, and consumer advocates, to name a few. When the revision was authorized in 1955, these interested parties began to lobby Congress to ensure that their interests and the interests of those they represented were addressed in the new law. Given both the complexity of the subject matter and of the interests involved, Congress at some point more or less threw up its hands and said to the lobbyists, "Go away, write a bill you can all live with, and bring it back to us." Which is not to say that Con-

---

Trends in copyright law

Looking at the development of copyright law reveals several trends, including the following:

- Increase in the term of copyright protection
- Expanded categories of works that may be copyrighted
- Lessened formalities required to acquire copyright protection
- Increased complexity in the law as it attempts to respond to increasing complexity in technology
- Overall, an attempt by powerful copyright owners to make a "land grab" for all they can get, taking advantage of new technologies and copyright law's inability to address those technologies.
- On the other hand, these aggressive actions have, to some extent, led to an increase in recognition of the needs of "special" groups, such as libraries and educational institutions. This recognition is due solely to the actions of individuals and professional associations in taking active roles in the debate accompanying changes to the law, and it is imperative that librarians become ever more involved in these debates.

---

gress had no role in the content of the Act of course, but this was the basic process for the first major round of drafting it. So you see how very real a role library lobbyists played in the drafting of the Copyright Act. This is the prime example of how extremely important it is for librarians to become active in representing their users' needs. I shudder to think about what our current copyright law would look like if ALA and other library organizations had not been part of that process.

Indeed, each successive revision seems to be more complex than the last, but this is also a reflection of the increasing complexity of the world in which copyright moves. Like both Copyright Acts before it, the 1976 Act has been subject to a variety of amendments in attempts to adapt copyright law to an ever more rapidly changing world. Unfortunately, the current state of the Copyright Act suffers from even more complexity as a result of almost thirty years of often highly political amendments.

The rest of this book is devoted to discussing the intricacies of what currently is and is not covered by copyright protection and what exactly that protection means. The next chapter gives a broad overview of these issues. Here, I will simply describe some of the substantial changes made by the 1976 Act.

First, and perhaps most importantly, publication is no longer required to obtain copyright protection. A work is protected from the moment it is first "fixed in a tangible medium of expression." (*Copyright Act of 1976, U.S. Code*, vol. 17, sec. 102(a) (1999)) Second, the Act changed the term of copyright law from two 28-year terms to life of the author plus fifty years (for works made for hire, which are essentially works with corporate authors, and anonymous or pseudonymous works, the term was 75 years from publication or one hundred years from creation, whichever is less). (ibid., sec. 301)

The new Act covered a broad range of subject matter. A non-exclusive list includes literary, musical, and dramatic works; pantomimes and choreographic works; pictorial, graphic, and sculptural works; motion pictures and audiovisual works; sound recordings; and architectural works. (ibid., sec. 102) The rights of a copyright owner are specified as the right to reproduce, prepare derivative works, distribute copies, and publicly perform and display the work. (ibid., sec. 106) Specific limitations to these rights are also laid out, including, for the first time, an attempt to codify the fair use doctrine. (ibid., secs. 107–112) Until the 1976 Act, fair use had been developed slowly by the courts. Fair use is discussed further in Chapter 3.

Important aspects of the law that did not change, and which later caused problems, included the requirements of placing a copyright notice on a work and registering a work in order for it to be eligible for copyright protection.

What significant changes have occurred since 1976?

The Congresses writing the 1976 Act recognized the need to establish a flexible law that could be adapted to unforeseen changes in technology as painlessly as possible. A clear example of this attempt is the definition of "copies": "material objects . . . in which a work is fixed by any method *now known or later developed*, and from which the work can be perceived, reproduced, or otherwise communicated, *either directly or with the aide of a machine or device*." (ibid. sec. 101 (emphasis added)) Nonetheless, as we will see, some changes in technology were so unforeseeable in 1976 that the Act was only partly successful in meeting this goal.

Technology is one of two major forces behind amendments to copyright law. The other is the increasingly important international nature of copyright law. Even before the Internet, international law was a major concern for copyright. Think of all you've heard or read about bootleg CDs and cassette tapes made in Asia, imitation Rolexes sold in Times Square, and knock-off name-brand clothing. The Internet, of course, thrusts us up to an entirely new level, since pretty much everything that goes on the Internet is immediately international in scope.

How do governments deal with these issues, given that copyright law is not at all the same from country to country?

Treaties are agreements between governments stating that signatories will follow certain regulations specified in the treaties, subject to whatever penalties may be laid out in the specific treaty. In some cases, penalties involve lack of recognition of each other's goods; for example, a treaty may state that if a signatory does not meet the treaty requirements, its own authors' copyrights will not be recognized in other member countries. In other cases, penalties focus on trade regulations; if signatories do not abide by the rules of the treaty, they may be sanctioned with trade restrictions.

Two treaties have resulted in major changes to the 1976 Copyright Act: the Berne Convention for the Protection of Literary and Artistic Works ("the Berne Convention") and the Agreement on Trade-Related Aspects of Intellectual Property Rights ("TRIPS"). The United States joined both treaties to ensure greater international protection to its authors and inventors. The Berne Convention required the elimination of formalities such as requiring notice and registration. As a result, the Copyright Act was amended in 1988 to do away with the requirement of placing a copyright notice on a work and registering a work with the Copyright Office. (Although registration is no longer required for protection, a work must be registered before filing suit for infringement, and registration confers significantly greater damages on copyright owners whose works have been infringed. See Chapter 12 for further discussion.) Joining TRIPS led to the Digital Millennium Copyright Act, discussed further in Chapter 5, which addresses a range of issues and problems created by the digital world.

Finally, another major change recently made to copyright law is the Sonny Bono Copyright Term Extension Act, passed in 1998, which extends the term of copyright by twenty years, to life of the author plus seventy years. For anonymous and pseudonymous works and works made for hire, the term is ninety-five years from first publication or 120 years from time of creation, whichever is shorter. (ibid. sec. 302)

What is "intellectual property," and how does it compare to copyright?

The concept of intellectual property is actually pretty simple, but the terminology in the field is often used—or misused—in confusing ways. At the risk of sounding overly simplistic, I want to put forth some definitions that are worth thinking about for a moment, even though you already know what the words mean. *Black's Law Dictionary* defines *property* as "that which belongs exclusively to one person . . . an aggregate of rights which are guaran-

Q What can I do to ensure that the rights of my library as an institution and my library users, as well as my rights as an individual, are acknowledged and addressed in future copyright law?

A First of all, you should have a general understanding of copyright law and how it affects your library, your users, and you. That's the purpose of this book. Next, you should keep up with what's going on in Congress and the courts concerning copyright issues. Finally, part of your duty as an information professional is to make your voice heard to decision makers. You can do this through the American Library Association, among other organizations. Chapter 19 provides a list of ways in which you can keep abreast of issues and also discusses how you can be an active player in decisions that affect your institution and your users.

teed and protected by the government . . . ownership." *Webster's* defines *intellect* as "the capacity for understanding and knowledge." *Intellectual property*, then is exactly what it sounds like: It is specific knowledge or understanding, or the expression thereof, that is owned by a particular person or persons. It encompasses ideas, writings, artwork—basically any form of knowledge or understanding.

In the legal world, "intellectual property" refers to three very specific and very different types of federal protection—or exclusive rights in—different subject matter: copyright, trademark, and patent. (To a more limited extent, intellectual property can be protected by some state laws as well, such as the law of trade secrets.) Obviously, copyright is the subject matter of this book. Copyright protection allows the owner of a copyright in a work to prevent others from making particular uses of that work. A trademark, in a nutshell, is anything that can be used to identify the source of a particular product that is sold in commerce; for example, a logo like the Nike swoosh, or a name like Neal-Schuman Publishers. Trademark protection allows the owner of the trademark to prevent others from using that same trademark or one that is confusingly similar on the same or very similar products. Trademarks are discussed in Chapter 11. Patents protect ideas, such as formulas, recipes, and designs. The owner of a patent can prevent anyone else from making the particular good that implements his idea. For example, if I own a patent for a new cancer drug, I can use the legal system to prevent others from making a drug using that same formula (though only for a limited time).

Keep in mind that each type of intellectual property protection has certain requirements; not every idea can be patented, for example. To some ex-

---

One more reason why librarians must become activists

The Copyright Act of 1976 was essentially written by lobbyists with vested interests (including several professional library organizations) in the outcome of the process and then presented to Congress for it to hone. By some estimates, the RIAA spends over four million dollars a year in lobbying activities, and the MPAA even more. Nationwide, lobbyists in all areas reported spending almost 25 percent more in 2003 than in 2002. The voices of copyright owners are being heard loud and clear; who will voice the needs of information users?

---

tent, the types of protection may overlap. As is discussed later, it may be possible to protect a logo with both copyright and trademark. But the types of protection are very different, as noted above. Copyright, then, is one type of intellectual property.

Conclusion

One way to address gaps that develop over time in any law is to amend the law as each new issue presents itself. Sometimes this works well; at other times, the amendments become so numerous that the result is a piecemeal law, a hodgepodge of band-aids. It has been argued that our current copyright law is rapidly approaching this point and is ripe for a new revision. The same problem that has led to this situation, however—the remarkably rapid pace of technological development—also argues against moving too soon in rewriting the law as a whole. Almost any professional working with the Internet on a regular basis would agree that we have a long way to go before the development of the Internet and its myriad possible uses "shakes out" enough to offer some consistency in the cyberworld. Rewriting the Copyright Act in the midst of such a dramatic paradigm shift would be pointless. And perhaps dangerous, given the impossibility of predicting even the capabilities of new, yet unknown technology.

Meanwhile, we must manage, and sometimes struggle, with the law in its current state, constantly asking ourselves what changes are necessary and worthwhile in a constantly changing arena. As information professionals, we also must keep in mind that part of our responsibility is to help others, *especially those making our laws*, to understand how to make these judgments and how to recognize the difference between knee-jerk reactions and well thought-out plans. The emotional and continual reaction to the easy availability of pornography on the Internet and the question of filtering in libraries and educational institutions is a good example of both the difficulty in recognizing this difference and the crucial need for librarians to take part proactively in these discussions.

Bibliography

Copyright Act of 1976, U.S. Code, vol. 17 (1999).

Gasaway, Laura N. and Sarah K. Wiant. 1994. *Libraries and Copyright: A Guide to Copyright Law in the 1990s.* Washington, D.C.: Special Libraries Association.

Leaffer, Marshall. *Understanding Copyright Law.* 2nd ed. 1995. New York: Matthew Bender.

Merges, Robert P., Peter S. Menell, Mark A. Lemley, and Thomas M. Jorde. 1997. *Intellectual Property in the New Technological Age.* New York: Aspen Law & Business.

U.S. Constitution, art. I, sec. 8, cl 8.

2

Overview of copyright law

To recognize and understand some of the quagmires of copyright issues involving the Internet, you should first be familiar with a few basics of copyright law. Copyright is considered by many in the legal arena to be one of the most complicated areas of law. And it certainly doesn't come any easier to those without legal training! This chapter barely dips into the subject, giving you just enough to introduce the basic ideas behind copyright and to explain your rights and how to avoid violating the rights of others. Several excellent guides to copyright are available, many of them targeted specifically to librarians and educators. My favorites are listed in Sources I and J.

What does copyright protect?
Written words are only the tip of the copyrightable-works iceberg. Anything that meets the following four requirements is eligible for copyright protection:

1. an expression
2. that is an original work of authorship
3. with a modicum of creativity
4. and that is (a) fixed in a tangible medium of expression, whether now known or later developed and (b) from which the work can be perceived, reproduced, or otherwise communicated, whether directly or with the aid of a machine or device (*Copyright Act of 1976, U.S. Code*, vol. 17, sec. 101; *Feist Publ'ns, Inc. v. Rural Tel. Serv. Co., Inc.*, 499 U.S. 340 (1991)).

This means that musical works, audio recordings, movies, artwork, dances, dramatic works, and even architecture can be protected by copyright.

Let's take a closer look at the requirements and what they mean in the cyberspace arena.

1. Expression
Copyright protects expressions, as opposed to ideas. Einstein could claim copyright protection in the book *Meaning of Relativity*, in which he explains

> **Q** Does providing the appropriate credit and citation allow a librarian to copy something for library use?
>
> **A** No. Plagiarism has nothing to do with copyright law. Although they may seem similar at first glance in that an infringer is "stealing" someone else's work, they differ in several ways. One may infringe a copyright without claiming to be the author of a work. Likewise, one may commit plagiarism with a work not protected by copyright.

his discovery—i.e., expresses his idea—but he could not claim copyright protection in the actual idea of relativity. Keep in mind that the fundamental purpose of copyright law is to encourage the growth of the body of human knowledge. If we could copyright ideas, one person would have almost total control over the use of that idea for years. Aside from the impracticality of this notion, we fear the potential results of severely limiting access to knowledge rather than providing means by which we can build on knowledge. Conversely, by protecting the *expression* of ideas, we reward the creator of the idea for making his idea available to the public, where society can then benefit from it, in part by using it.

2. Original work of authorship

"Original" for copyright purposes does not mean something that no one has ever thought up before. Rather, it means original to that author, as opposed to being copied from another source. Thus, the idea of telling a tragic story of star-crossed lovers has been around at least since Ovid told the story of Pyramus and Thisbe, but each original telling of that idea can be copyrighted; even had they all been written at the same time, Ovid could have copyrighted his story, Shakespeare could have copyrighted *Romeo and Juliet*, and Irving Shulman could have copyrighted *West Side Story*.

3. Modicum of creativity

Even if a work is created by the author and has not been copied from elsewhere, it must exhibit a "modicum of creativity." Although "modicum" is nowhere defined, it turns out to be pretty minimal. Facts themselves cannot be copyrighted, since they are, by definition, not subject to different modes of expression. I can say that it was extremely hot yesterday, you can say yesterday was a scorcher, Jane can say it was hotter than a polar bear in a pepper patch. These expressions may be based on fact, but they are not facts. But there's only one way to say it was 102 degrees outside; this is a fact.

> Q Can a faculty member show her class a video checked out from the library?
>
> A Only if the film is "a regular part of the systematic instructional activities." Recall that the right to publicly perform a work is one of the exclusive rights of the copyright owner. A work is performed publicly when performed "at a place open to the public or at any place where a substantial number of persons outside of a normal circle of a family and its social acquaintances is gathered." Thus, performance anywhere in a school—whether library, classroom, or auditorium—would constitute a public performance.

However, the actual presentation of facts may exhibit the "modicum of creativity" necessary to be protected by copyright, because, as the United States Supreme Court stated in a landmark case concerning the creativity requirement, "the author typically chooses which facts to include, in what order to place them, and how to arrange the data so that readers may use them effectively." (*Feist Publ'ns, Inc. v. Rural Tel. Serv. Co., Inc.*, 499 U.S. 340 (1991)) Thus, a white pages phone book would not be copyrightable, because the author has listed everyone in a given area, rather than using his discretion to choose whom to list, and has listed them in the most obvious order and arrangement (alphabetically). In contrast, the *Physicians' Desk Reference (PDR)* is copyrightable. Although all of the information it contains is factual, the authors chose what to include, how to organize it, and how to present it. The facts contained in the *PDR*, however, are not themselves copyrightable.

4. Fixed in a tangible medium of expression, whether now known or later developed, from which the work can be perceived, reproduced, or otherwise communicated, either directly or with the aid of a machine or device

The phrase "now known or later developed" is often cited as evidence that Congress intended to write copyright laws that would be applicable throughout unpredictable changes in technology. Nonetheless, the fixation requirement has become problematic and has caused some controversy when applied to the cyberworld.

Consider, for example, e-mail. E-mail is seldom intended to be permanent and is often used for communications that would have been made by phone a few years ago. We tend to think of e-mail as being rather ephemeral. However, even when the individual recipient of an e-mail deletes it as soon as

Section 110(1) of the Copyright Act, however, provides an exception to this right for the public performance of a lawfully made copy of a work "by instructors or pupils in the course of face-to-face teaching activities of a non-profit educational institution, in the classroom or similar place devoted to instruction." One of the most frequent complaints I hear from school librarians is that teachers want to check out movies to show their classes just to kill time, not for true instructional purposes. Because this seems to be such a common problem, let's go to the trouble of breaking down the elements of this exception:

- "Teaching activities" are defined as those that involve "systematic instruction" and specifically do *not* include performances, regardless of their "cultural value or intellectual appeal, that are given for the recreation or entertainment of any part of the audience." So those Friday afternoon everyone's-tired-and-wants-to-go-home-including-the-teacher performances very clearly do not fit into the exception and would constitute an infringement of the copyright in the movie.
- A classroom or "similar place devoted to instruction" would include a library, gymnasium, studio, or even auditorium *if* the facility is being used as a classroom for systematic instructional activities. So while an auditorium might qualify for the exception if a specific class is being taught there, it would not for a movie shown during a school assembly, pep rally, ceremony, or sporting event.
- The copy shown must be lawfully made. This would exclude copying a program or movie from television.
- The "face-to-face" requirement is not literally interpreted; it is intended to exclude transmissions from outside the classroom location, but as long as the instructor and pupils are in the "same building or general area," the exemption applies. Keep in mind the "teaching activities" requirement, though. The performance must be related to the systematic instruction of all the students viewing it.
- The nonprofit educational institution requirement means that the institution must be "primarily and directly involved in education." Thus, foundations, associations (like ALA), etc. would not be allowed the exemption. "Nonprofit" is meant to exclude schools, like dance studios, and language schools; private, nonproprietary schools charging tuition and fees to meet operating expenses would be allowed the exemption.

> The only difference between showing a movie rented from a video store and showing a video checked out of the library is the issue of whether, when renting the video, one enters into a license agreement not to publicly perform the work. Although this situation is slightly more risky than the above, the bottom line is that the analysis should come down to whether the performance meets the Section 110 requirements.

she has read it, several copies have been made during the short life span of the message. Many systems create a copy of a message in a "sent mail" folder when the sender transmits it. Copies are made during the transmission of the message. A copy is made when the message arrives on the recipient's server. In common systems currently being used, the recipient creates a copy on her own computer by downloading the message from the server. Each of these copies resides in a tangible medium—a hard drive, a server, a CD-ROM. Thus, even though we may not intend e-mail to be around long enough to take advantage of it, e-mail is certainly copyrightable matter.

How do I get copyright protection for my works?

Very few formalities must be met to "copyright" a work.[1] If the work meets the conditions discussed above, it is copyrighted at the moment of fixation, i.e., at the moment of creation. Publication is not required to protect a work by copyright (though at one time it was), nor is the display of any type of notice, such as © or "Copyright 2004, ABC Press." You are not required to register your work or to deposit a copy of your work with the Copyright Office or anyone else in order to receive copyright protection.

The lack of formal requirements has substantial implications for copyright in cyberspace, with the bottom line being: You cannot tell by looking at a work whether or not it is protected by copyright. For this reason, it is very important to assume that everything you see is protected, unless you know otherwise.

Although not required, registering the copyright in a work with the United States Copyright Office and displaying a copyright notice on the work have valuable benefits. Displaying a notice gives other users notice that your work is protected by copyright and, hopefully, will discourage infringement. Second, you must register your work with the Copyright Office to be able to file a federal claim of copyright infringement, should your rights be violated. Indeed, the damages you can receive should your copyright be infringed are significantly greater if the copyright is registered before the infringement occurs. Infringement and damages are discussed in more detail in Chapter 12.

Who owns the rights in the works I create?

In some circumstances, the individual who creates a work is not considered to be the owner of the copyright in that work, or even the author of the work. The work-made-for-hire doctrine states that for "a work prepared by an employee within the scope of his or her employment," the employer is deemed to be the author of the work and therefore the copyright owner as well, unless there is an express agreement to the contrary. (*U.S. Code*, sec. 101) Defining the relationship as employee/employer is based on analysis of the following factors: (1) the hiring party's right to control the matter and means of the project's progress; (2) the skill involved; (3) the source of instrumentalities and tools; (4) the location of the work; (5) the duration of the parties' relationship; (6) whether the hiring party can assign additional projects to the other; (7) the hiring party's control over working hours; (8) the method of payment, provision of employment benefits, and treatment of taxes; (9) the hired party's role in hiring assistants; and (10) whether the hiring party is in business in general, and specifically whether the work in question is a regular part of that business. This means that the institution for whom you work owns the copyrights in those beautiful Web pages you sweated over, absent an agreement to the contrary. In academia, for example, it is common for the institution to allow faculty to retain the copyright in the works they create.

What if my library hires outside sources to create copyrightable works for the library?

Note that the above is *not* true for independent contractors, unless the created works fall into certain limited categories *and* the employer and contractor execute an agreement specifying that the works are to be considered works made for hire. (*U.S. Code*, Sec. 101) The categories of works for which this is true are (1) a contribution to a collective work; (2) a contribution to a motion picture or other audiovisual work; (3) a translation; (4) a supplementary work (defined as "a work prepared for publication as a secondary adjunct to a work by another author for the purpose of introducing, concluding, illustrating, explaining, revising, commenting upon, or assisting in the use of the other work, such as forewords, afterwords, pictorial illustrations" by Sec. 101 of the *U.S. Code*); (5) a compilation; (6) an instructional text; (7) a test; (8) answer material for a test; or (9) an atlas. (Note the strange selection of categories here;—this is a prime example of the weird outcomes that sometimes result from the lobbying part of the legislative process.)

This part of the work-made-for-hire doctrine is extremely important for libraries that hire anyone in a relationship other than traditional employee/

> Q If a book is out of print, does that mean it is no longer pro-
> tected by copyright?
>
> A No. The only correlation between a work being out of print and
> its being in the public domain is that the more time goes by, the
> more likely it is that a work will fall into both categories. Copyright
> protection now lasts for the lifetime of the author plus seventy years.
> Very few books stay in print that long. Nor does the fact that a work
> is out of print somehow grant permission to make uses that would
> otherwise infringe a work still in print.

employer. If your library hires an outside contractor to create your Web site for example, the library will not own the copyright in the Web site unless a written agreement is executed transferring copyright from the creator to the library. Because the creator is not an employee of the library creating the site in the course of his or her regular duties, and because the Web site does not fall into one of the nine quirky categories listed above, an agreement must be in place actually assigning the rights in the Web site to the library.

What rights are included in copyright protection?

Copyright protection consists of four basic categories of uses. The owner of a copyright in a work has the *exclusive* rights to:

1. reproduce, or make copies of, the work
2. prepare derivative works based on his work (such as writing a sequel or making a movie based on a book)
3. distribute copies of the work to the public
4. publicly display and perform the work
   (*Copyright Act of 1976, U.S. Code*, vol. 17, sec. 106 (1999))

That these rights are exclusive means that no one else other than the copyright owner has the legal right to make copies or to distribute copies of the work (or to prepare derivative works or publicly display or perform the work) without the permission of the copyright owner.

Each of these rights applied to the Internet creates results and issues that differ from those in the "real" world. For example, debate exists over what constitutes a copy in cyberspace. Do end-users make copies when they simply browse the Web? If so, does that mean each time we look at a Web page we are potentially infringing the copyright of that Web page? Questions also

> **Q** Is there a trend or movement towards implementing a global copyright law or standard?
>
> **A** To some extent, yes, there is a movement towards international adoption of a body of copyright law. International treaties have always been an important part of copyright law. In modern times, as we feel the world shrinking around us, international treaties become increasingly important. Various provisions of the current U.S. Copyright Act are the direct result of obligations the U.S. took on when acceding to various treaties. For example, the anti-circumvention provisions of the Digital Millennium Copyright Act were in part due to the requirement in the WTO Copyright Treaty requiring signatories to implement law protecting against circumvention of copyright protection technology. However, copyright law does differ from country to country—sometimes in significant ways—and will continue to do so into the foreseeable future.

exist regarding what constitutes a derivative work in cyberspace. Some copyright owners have argued in court that a derivative of their work is created when someone else links to their work using frames, because the original Web page now appears quite differently than when the copyright owner created it. What about distribution and display? Does linking to a page constitute public distribution? Does providing access to the Web in a public place, like a library, constitute public display of individual pages? If so, who is responsible for that display: the end-user, the library, the Internet service provider, or the original author of the page?

None of these questions has easy or straightforward answers. (Otherwise, there would be no need for this book.) All of them are important questions, the resolution of which will affect all Internet users. Each will be discussed further in relation to particular types of Web usage.

How long does copyright protection last?

Under current copyright law, the exclusive rights of a copyright owner last for the lifetime of the author plus an additional seventy years after his death. Like so much else in copyright law, the duration of the rights has changed periodically as copyright law has been revised. The result is that different works have different terms of copyright protection, depending on when they were created or published. See Source B for an overview of the copyright term for works created or published at different times.

Q Aren't all government documents in the public domain?

A Not exactly. Section 105 of the Copyright Act states that "copyright protection under the title is not available for any work of the United States Government." A *work of the United States Government* is defined as "a work prepared by an officer or employee of the United States Government as part of that person's official duties." As every government documents librarian knows, the Government Printing Office publishes many works that are not "prepared by an officer or employee of the United States Government." Such works would therefore be protected by copyright. In addition, the Copyright Act does not preclude protection for works created by state governments. Many state governments do exempt from copyright protection works created by their employees in the course of performing their official duties. However, this is up to each state and does indeed differ from state to state.

What are the limitations and exceptions to these rights?

Several limitations to the above enumerated rights exist. Probably the single most important limitation for libraries is that of fair use, codified in Section 107 of the Copyright Act. (ibid., sec. 107) Fair use will be discussed in some depth in Chapter 3. For the moment, it is important to know that what constitutes fair use is not clearly defined and that fair use is a defense. Contrary to popular belief, it is not correct to say that any use made by a library or for non-commercial purposes is allowed by the fair use doctrine. This is made clear by the fact that the Copyright Act includes other exceptions specifically for libraries, such as limited exceptions for photocopying. If all library uses were considered fair use, there would be no need for these exceptions.

One exception that is particularly important to libraries, although libraries are not specifically mentioned in this section of the statute, is the first sale doctrine, found in Section 109. (ibid., sec. 109) This rule states that the owner of a particular lawfully made copy is entitled to dispose of that copy however he wishes and to publicly display (but not perform) the copy without the need to obtain permission from the copyright owner. The first sale doctrine thus allows libraries to lend books to users; to sell old copies at book sales; and to create exhibits using copyrighted works.

Some of the more recent copyright legislation limits not the rights of copyright owners but the liability of Internet service providers ("ISPs"). Why should this be important to libraries? Because under this section of the Copyright Act, an ISP is defined as "a provider of online services or network access, or the operator of facilities therefor." (ibid., sec. 512(k)(1)(B)) Clearly, libraries providing access to the Internet may be considered an ISP under the Copyright Act. This section, which will be discussed in greater depth in Chapter 11, limits the liability of ISPs for the infringing activities of their users *if* the ISP meets certain requirements. Without it, or for ISPs who do not meet the requirements, it is entirely possible for an ISP (read "library") to be held criminally liable when one of its users violates copyright law.

How do I avoid getting in trouble?!

There are three categories of copyright violation: direct infringement, contributory infringement, and vicarious infringement. Direct infringement is the most obvious: If you violate one of the exclusive rights of the copyright owner, say by making copies of a protected article and distributing them to everyone attending your conference presentation on the topic, you have directly infringed the copyright in the article and may be subject to various remedies, including damages of up to $30,000 per work infringed, or, if the infringement is "willful," up to $150,000 per work infringed.

It is very important to know that direct infringement has no knowledge requirement. In other words, ignorance is no excuse. However, in the case of "innocent infringement," damages may be reduced to as little as $200. The term "innocent infringement" is really a misnomer; an infringement has actually occurred, and the infringer acted on purpose. However, if the infringer "was not aware and had no reason to believe that his or her acts constituted an infringement of copyright," the reduced damages may apply. Note that a copyright notice displayed on a work may invalidate any argument that the infringing act was "innocent."

Contributory infringement occurs when you knowingly induce, cause, or contribute to someone else's direct infringement. Does providing links on your library Web site to Web pages at another site that contain infringing material, thereby "knowingly inducing" users to access the infringing page, constitute contributory infringement? Possibly.

Vicarious infringement occurs when you have the right and ability to control the infringing activity and you have an obvious and direct financial interest in the activity. Seldom will a situation occur in a library to which vicarious infringement may be applied.

How to keep safe? Assume everything you see is protected by copyright, unless you know otherwise. If your desired use does not fit within one of the delineated exceptions, including fair use, get permission from the copy-

---

One more reason why librarians must become activists

"By vesting copyright owners with control of any reproduction or transmission of their works . . . and any transfer of that work to, from, or through any other computer, the Draft Report [released ten years ago, in 1994, by the Clinton Administration's Information Infrastructure Task Force] recommendations would . . . give the copyright owner the exclusive right to control reading, viewing or listening to any work in digitized form. . . . Nor is anyone else clamoring to volunteer. The general public's interest in copyright legislation is diffuse; a grass-roots revolt of copyright users seems unlikely. Interest groups with copyright on their agendas have a long history of dropping their opposition to copyright amendments of general application in return for narrow provisions addressing their specific concerns." (Jessica Litman, *The Exclusive Right to Read,* 13 CARDOZO ARTS & ENT. L.J. 29 [1994]).

---

right owner before doing anything. (See Source I for further discussion on getting permission to use protected works.)

What happens to me or my library if we are found liable for infringement?

This is the subject of Chapter 12. For the moment, suffice to say that it is highly unlikely that you or your library would ever get to this point. As a general rule, should a copyright owner think that you are infringing his work, he will almost always send you a cease-and-desist letter. First, you will contact your institution's legal counsel. Together, you will consider whether you think your use actually is infringing or is allowed under fair use or one of the exemptions. If you think not, you will probably either cease and desist in using his work, or work out an agreement to use it. Even if a lawsuit is filed, seldom do copyright infringement situations actually make it to the courtroom. If that should happen, however, it is possible that your use will be excused under an exemption or the defense of fair use. Should, against the odds, your library be found liable for infringement in a court of law, the damages—or fines—are almost solely at the discretion of the judge. For "innocent infringement," a fine may be as little as $200. For willful infringement, it may be as much as $150,000. As unlikely as it is that you or your library would actually be found liable for infringement in a court of law, the consequences of it ocurring are a clear motivation for obeying the law!

Notes

1. The word "copyright" is often used as a verb, as in "I want to copyright my work." This can be misleading, because it implies that one must take some action before one's work is protectable by copyright. Although this used to be the case, it no longer is.

Bibliography

Copyright Act of 1976, U.S. Code, vol. 17, secs. 101, 102, 106, 109(a), 109(c), and 512(k)(1)(B).

Feist Publ'ns, Inc. v. Rural Tel. Serv. Co., Inc., 499 U.S. 340 (1991).

3

Fair use: is it all it's cracked up to be? and other pockets of protection for librarians

For librarians and other educators and public servants, the fair use doctrine may be one of the most confusing aspects of copyright law. Certainly it is one of the more complicated components of copyright law, according to almost anyone's standards. Unfortunately, it is human nature to try to simplify complex issues so that we can better understand them and deal with them. In the world of fair use, this often results in dangerous and widespread assumptions. Too many people in various educational and nonprofit arenas assume that any use of a copyrighted work made for educational purposes, or even more generally for noncommercial purposes, constitutes fair use. Unfortunately, nothing in copyright law is that simple.

What is the fair use doctrine?

Fair use is the epitome of the copyright balancing act—balancing the rights of owners of copyright with those of users of protected works. Fair use is a judicially created doctrine, born out of not legislation, but the courts. Which implies that the courts began to recognize that, in some cases, carrying out the letter of the law violated the spirit of the law. In other words, in some situations, it is more fair *not* to follow the law. When would this be the case? Recall that the purpose of copyright law is "to promote the progress of science and the useful arts;" we can consider this the "spirit" of copyright law. When following the law literally, as written, negates this purpose, the letter of the law conflicts with the spirit of the law. To deal with such situations, the American legal system applies "rules of equity," which, very broadly stated, often means that the legal system will choose to apply the spirit of the law despite the fact that it conflicts with the letter of the law. Such is the fair use doctrine.

The fair use doctrine allows one to use copyrighted works without obtaining permission of the owner if the use meets certain criteria, which are meant to determine whether promoting the progress of science and the useful arts is better served by allowing the use, despite copyright protection for the work. A fair use may involve any of the exclusive rights of the copyright owner. The tricky part comes in attempting to create a flexible doctrine. Somewhat obviously, making a determination like this can be a very subjective process. Knowing this, the courts, and later Congress, attempted to create a doctrine that will allow only those uses that really should be allowed in order to be fair and equitable. Keep in mind that each fair use is a denial of what would otherwise be rights belonging to copyright owners under the law. It would be extremely difficult to write a fair use law in very specific terms, stating precisely what type of copying is and is not allowed, so that all copying meant to be allowed is, yet no one can take advantage of the language of the law. Thus, in attempting to be flexible and allow subjective decisions, the fair use doctrine is somewhat unclear at times.

Although the general principle of fair use can be seen in British case law dating back to the eighteenth century, the milestone case decided in 1841 that gave us our current vision of fair use. The defendant in *Folsom v. Marsh* had copied letters written by George Washington to include in a biography on Washington, but, rather than copying from the original letters, he had copied from the reproduction of those letters in a multi-volume biography written by the plaintiff. The Circuit Court of Massachusetts stated:

> In short, we must often in deciding questions of this sort, look to the nature and objects of the selections made, the quantity and value of the materials used, and the degree in which the use may prejudice the sale or diminish the profits, or supersede the objects, of the original work. (*Folsom v. Marsh*, 9 F. Cas. 342 (C.C.D. Mass. 1841))

The courts relied on this statement for over one hundred years, until the very criteria cited here were codified in Section 107 of the Copyright Act of 1976. The fact that fair use was originally developed by the courts, those who sat on the front line of deciding copyright infringement issues, and survived in the courts for many years, suggests that fair use is a doctrine born of a widely recognized and accepted need.

How are fair use judgments made?

The first thing to note is that fair use judgments are made on a case-by-case basis. This means there are no stringent rules that say, for example, as long as you copy less than 10 percent of a book, your use is fair. Each use is evaluated on its own. The guidelines for making this evaluation, however, are enunciated in Section 107 of the Copyright Act.

Q Doesn't the "first sale doctrine" mean a librarian can do what ever she wants with one particular copy of a book or other work?
A Not exactly. The first sale doctrine, Section 109 of the Copyright Act, allows the owner of a particular copy of a work to dispose of that copy however he pleases. Thus, when a library purchases a book, it can lend it to whomever it chooses. When it is no longer appropriate for the collection, the library may then sell the book at a book sale. Libraries and educational institutions can even loan or rent computer programs, though no one else can. Section 109 also allows the owner of a particular copy to publicly display that copy.

Types of uses

The preface to Section 107 provides a nonexclusive list of illustrative uses that *may* be considered fair use: criticism, commentary, news reporting, teaching, scholarship, and research. This list serves only as an example of the types of uses likely to be determined to be fair. It is not inclusive, so other uses also may be considered fair. Just as importantly, it does *not* mean that those uses listed will always be fair.

The statute then sets out four factors that must be considered in determining whether a use is fair. The case-by-case analysis of these four factors *must* be made for every claim of fair use. The court *may* also consider other factors, but that seldom happens.

Factor 1: Purpose and character of the use

The purpose and character of the use factor looks at whether the use is (1) commercial or for a nonprofit educational purpose and (2) transformative. Nonprofit educational uses are more likely to be fair uses, because they are more likely to support the purpose of copyright law—contributing to the body of human knowledge—and less likely than commercial uses to harm the copyright owner. A transformative use is one that changes the original work in some way, as opposed to flat-out copying it. If a use "adds something new, with a further purpose or different character, altering the first with new expression, meaning, or message," the use is more likely to be fair. (*Campbell v. Acuff-Rose Music*, 510 U.S. 569) This, too, can be traced back to the question of balancing the purpose of copyright law with the interests of the copyright owner: An exact copy of a work is more likely to mean a lost sale to a copyright owner, whereas a transformative use is more likely to further the advancement of the arts.

The case from which we take the "transformative" language serves as a good example of both what is meant by a transformative use and the tension inherent in trying to define a transformative use when it is also a commercial use, as opposed to any other commercial use. In *Campbell v. Acuff-Rose*, the rap music group 2 Live Crew had recorded a parody of "Pretty Woman," the classic Roy Orbison song. The group used the original music and repeated the phrase "pretty woman," but otherwise used entirely different lyrics, as the following stanza exemplifies:

Roy Orbison Original
Pretty Woman, won't you pardon me,
Pretty Woman, I couldn't help but see,
Pretty Woman, that you look lovely as can be
Are you lonely, just like me?

2 Live Crew Version
Big hairy woman, you need to shave that stuff,
Big hairy woman, you know I bet it's tough,
Big hairy woman, all that hair it ain't legit,
'Cause you look like 'Cousin It'

The Supreme Court noted that creating transformative works, because they are new works, furthers the purpose of copyright law. It then turned to the discussion of parodies specifically, which are a good example of a transformative use, and explained how parodies may further the public good: They provide "social benefit, by shedding light on an earlier work, and, in the process, creating a new one." Thus, even a commercial use may be a fair use if the use serves a public good with which copyright law is concerned.

Note that a work that is transformative will almost always by definition be derivative as well. Fair use allows uses that would otherwise infringe any of a copyright owner's rights, including the right to create derivative works. However, creating a derivative work creates a new avenue for exploitation of the exclusive rights. Allowing others to create derivative works deprives the copyright owner of those opportunities. Thus, there is some potential conflict between the two considerations under this factor: A commercial work is less likely to be fair use, but a transformative work is more likely to be fair use.

Factor 2: Nature of the copyrighted work
In determining the nature of the protected work, courts usually consider whether the work is factual or creative. Recall that a work must show a "mo-

> Q Can my library digitize older materials for preservation and ar-
> chival purposes?
>
> A Assuming a work is still protected by copyright, one may make
> copies for archival purposes within certain limitations. The digi-
> tal reproduction must not be distributed or otherwise made available
> to the public outside of the library premises. For unpublished works,
> the item being reproduced must be part of the library's collection;
> only three copies are allowed for purposes of "preservation and se-
> curity or to deposit for research use in another library." For published
> works, the library must have determined, "after reasonable effort,
> that an unused replacement cannot be obtained at a fair price;" only
> three copies may be made of a published work for the purpose of
> replacing a lost, stolen, damaged, or deteriorating copy.

dicum of creativity" to be protectable by copyright. Pure facts cannot be protected. However, many factual works, such as a biography, or even a collection of statistics, include much original work as well as facts. In a biography,
original work would include the language the author chooses to tell the story.
In a statistical collection, the selection and organization of the facts may be
sufficiently original to allow copyright protection. Protecting factual works
encourages the publication and dissemination of hard knowledge. At the same
time, however, we consider the ability to access and use works of hard knowledge to be more important to education and society, and thus to the progress
of science and the arts, than the ability to access and use purely fictional
works. Therefore, courts are more likely to judge use of a factual work to be
a fair use than use of a purely fictional work.

Courts also consider whether a work is published or unpublished. Usually, an unpublished work will be given stronger protection than a published
work. One could argue that this is a case of giving more importance to the
author's rights than to the importance of public access to works. On the other
hand, one could argue that an author needs such protection to encourage him
to produce works. Without such protection, another party could potentially
"scoop" the author, so that even if the use would otherwise be fair, such as
for commentary purposes, the author is still in danger of losing valuable compensation for his work. Such was the situation in the defining case concerning unpublished materials, *Harper & Row, Publishers, Inc. v. Nation
Enterprises.* (471 U.S. 539) The Supreme Court ruled that publication by *The
Nation* of a relatively small portion of an unpublished biography of Gerald

Ford, in which Ford discussed his pardon of Richard Nixon, was not a fair use. The holding focused on the unpublished nature of the work.

In *Harper & Row*, the reporters responsible for the story had apparently gotten access to the manuscript through questionable means. In comparison, the Second Circuit Court of Appeals held that use in a biography of significant portions of J.D. Salinger's unpublished letters was not a fair use, despite the fact that they were publicly accessible in the special collections of various libraries. (*Salinger v. Random House, Inc.*, 811 F.2d 90 (2d Cir. 198)) Again, the court focused on the unpublished nature of the works, interpreting *Harper & Row* as stating that no use of unpublished works could be fair use. The same court two years later, however, found uses of a smaller amount of personal letters and journals to be a fair use. (*Wright v. Warner Books, Inc.*, 953 F.2d 731 (2d Cir. 1991))

Congress finally stepped into the debate in 1992 and amended Section 107 to add: "The fact that a work is unpublished shall not itself bar a finding of fair use if such finding is made upon consideration of all the above [fair use] factors." (*Copyright Act of 1976, U.S. Code*, vol. 17, sec. 107 (1999)) In doing so, Congress emphasized again that no single factor is determinative and that judgments of fair use are to be made on a case-by-case basis.

Factor 3: Amount and substantiality of the portion used in comparison to the work as a whole

As you might guess, the smaller the portion of the work taken, the more likely the use will be considered fair. However, even taking proportionately tiny portions of a work may constitute infringement, if the portion taken is important enough to the work as a whole.

No distinct guidelines are given, however, for what that ratio should be, since different proportions will be appropriate for different uses. The key inquiry is: Has the user taken more than is necessary to meet his needs? Many librarians write book reviews for publication in professional journals. Consider in this context how your needs vary. If you are commenting on the author's political view in general, you might not actually need to quote any of the text, or you might quote only a few lines to make the point of the vehemence of his views. On the other hand, if you are commenting on a poet's use of repetition, you might need to quote several lines of a poem to make your point.

Even taking a very small portion of a very large work, however, may not satisfy the fair use analysis if the portion taken constitutes "the heart" of the work. Going back to the case of *Harper & Row*, the Supreme Court held that copying only 300 words of a 200,000-word manuscript (or .0015 percent) was not allowable, because the words taken constituted "the heart of the book." (*Harper & Row, Publ'r, Inc. v. Nation Enter.*, 471 U.S. 539 (1985)) The Court gave the following explanation for this judgment:

> A *Time* editor described the chapters on the pardon as "the most interesting and moving parts of the entire manuscript." The portions actually quoted were selected by Mr. Navasky as among the most powerful passages in those chapters. He testified that he used verbatim excerpts because simply reciting the information could not adequately convey the "absolute certainty with which [Ford] expressed himself," or show that "this comes from President Ford," or carry the "definitive quality" of the original. In short, he quoted these passages precisely because they qualitatively embodied Ford's distinctive expression. (ibid.)

Note that the very same rationale could be used by the author to argue that he needed precisely the portion of the work that he took in order to convey his point. This is yet another example of the complexity associated with fair use determinations, due in large part to the subjective nature of the determination. In this case, the fact that *The Nation* scooped Harper & Row, the book publisher, may have played a subjective role in the Court's final holding of infringement.

Factor 4: Effect on the potential marketplace for the work

The fourth factor is often given greater weight than the other three. The inquiry here is: How great was the effect of the use on the potential market for the work? The rationale behind this factor relates directly to the purpose of copyright: If the copyright owner's ability to sell his work is significantly impaired, so is the incentive basis for copyright protection.

Several aspects of this factor should be noted. First, the focus is on *potential* market harm, not actual harm. In other words, would unrestricted and widespread use of the type the defendant has made harm the marketability of the work?

It is also important to note that the defendant need not actually be selling copies of the work to harm a potential market. *Harper & Row*, discussed above, is a good example of that. The defendant magazine was not distributing copies of the original work—recall that only very small portions of the work had even been copied—but the importance of the pieces copied were held likely to damage the market for the entire work, since the copied portions were considered to be the portions of most interest to the buying public. Thus, even though copies may be used for nonprofit purposes, the

Q Aren't all library and educational uses considered to be fair use?

A No! Fair use is determined by the application of four criteria to any and every case in which a defendant claims his use is fair. Nonprofit institutions, libraries, and educational institutions get no break per se. Many uses by the groups will be fair, but only because their uses tend to be more likely than many to meet the requirements of fair use. It is important to understand that there are no guarantees at all under the fair use doctrine. Decisions of fair use are made on an individual, case-by-case basis.

possibility of market damage still exists. Indeed, as the following discussion makes clear, in some cases, even the ease with which one may be able to purchase a work, or access to it, has been taken into consideration in evaluating the fourth factor.

Pulling it all together for libraries

As you may have noticed, the four fair use factors interrelate. Nonetheless, it is important to analyze each factor separately from the others. *American Geophysical Union v. Texaco* (60 F.3d 913 (2d Cir. 1994)), with which many librarians are already familiar, is a good example of how the factors interrelate. It also provides a look at how subjective and individual each fair use analysis is. In that case, the court analyzed the behavior of one scientist, with both parties agreeing that his behavior was to be considered an example of the type of behavior common within the corporation of Texaco. Issues of a journal, *Catalysis*, to which Texaco held three subscriptions, were circulated to scientists at Texaco. The scientist in question, Chickering, copied articles he thought might be of use later and kept them in a file.

In considering the first factor (purpose and character of the use) the court noted that Chickering had made the copies for his own convenience and had never even used five of the seven articles copied. It then acknowledged that photocopying those articles could serve legitimate purposes, such as allowing Chickering to carry the article with him into the lab to avoid risk of damaging the original journal. Had such purposes dominated, the court said, the first factor might tilt in favor of Chickering. However, the fact that the copying was done for "archival purposes," superceding the original rather than transforming it, and that it contributed to Texaco's efforts to develop profitable products, the plaintiff publishers won the first factor test.

The court held the second factor (nature of the work) to favor the defendant Texaco, based on the predominantly factual nature of the works.

The third factor (amount and substantiality of the copied portion compared to the work as a whole) was held to favor the plaintiffs, since the articles were copied in their entirety. Notice that the court looked at each *article* as an individual work, not a journal *issue* or *volume*. As the court noted, each article was individually authored and enjoyed individual copyright protection as an original work of authorship.

Finally, we come to the fourth factor (effect on the potential market for the work). This is where the fun starts and is the portion of the fair use analysis of most interest to librarians. The court began by noting that there is "neither a traditional market for, nor a clearly defined value of," individual journal articles. (ibid.) Rather than personally marketing their journal articles, authors sell their rights to publishers, who produce and market the work in exchange for paying royalties to the author. In academia, however, authors are much more likely to be motivated by nonfinancial rewards, such as prestige. The profits made from journals, then, act as an incentive for publishers to produce and disseminate the information; such dissemination—not monetary profits—is the author's incentive for writing. Thus, the court rationalized, "evidence concerning the effect that photocopying individual journal articles has on the traditional market for journal subscriptions is of somewhat less significance than if a market existed for the sale of individual copies of articles." (ibid.)

The court's attention then turned to "the significance of the publishers' establishment of an innovative licensing scheme for the photocopying of individual journal articles." Even though the plaintiff publishers had not established their own mechanism for direct sale and distribution of individual articles, "they have created, primarily through the CCC [Copyright Clearance Center], a workable market for institutional users to obtain licenses for the right to produce their own copies of individual articles." (ibid.) In one of the most significant statements in the case, the court stated that the right to seek payment for a particular use can be related to the ease with which such a payment may be made. In other words, were there no CCC, the court might have given this factor to the defendants; even if the plaintiffs had some sort of ethical right to payment, if there was no realistic way for the user to make that payment, the use may have been judged fair.

Finally, the court noted that its holding applies only to "the institutional, systematic, archival multiplication of copies," not to copying for personal use. (ibid.)

Obviously, the *Texaco* case provides some important lessons for libraries.

The CCC provides a mechanism for getting permission for the use of thousands of journals. On the other hand, keep in mind that the availability of the CCC was only one part of the *Texaco* court's analysis of only one of the fair use factors. The fact that you may be able to license use of a work through the CCC does not necessarily mean that to use it without doing so would not constitute fair use.

Are any guidelines out there to help interpret what actions might qualify as fair uses?

As a matter of fact, yes, there are. It is important to keep in mind, however, the distinction between law and guidelines. Guidelines are not law. They are guiding principals that have been written in an effort to help the user interpret and apply the law, usually by someone other than the lawmakers.

It is also important to know the intent behind the guidelines discussed here. Some of this background will be discussed in more detail in the context of the particular sets of guidelines, but in general, keep in mind that the guidelines are meant to delineate the *minimum* amount of copying or other use that should be allowed. Unfortunately, courts sometimes consider the guidelines as the *maximum* use allowed. Indeed, many of the guidelines discussed here have been criticized for this very reason. So the way to approach use of the guidelines is to know that although there is no guarantee that a use falling within the guidelines will be considered a fair use, you have a very good argument that it will be. On the other hand, uses that go beyond the guidelines may also be considered fair use, though taking this position may be somewhat riskier.

Other guidelines are discussed in further chapters devoted to the subject matter of the guidelines, such as the Conference on Fair Use Guidelines for Electronic Reserve Use.

Classroom copying

The House Judiciary Committee included in its report to Congress on the 1976 Copyright Act an "Agreement on Guidelines for Classroom Copying in Not-For-Profit Education Institutions With Respect to Books and Periodicals" (Congress is fond of long titles). The stated purpose of these guidelines is to "state the minimum standards for educational fair use." The Report goes on to warn that things may change in the future, including how much copying will be permissible for educational purposes, as well as what types of copying may and may not be permissible. Finally, the Report emphasizes that the guidelines are not meant to limit permissible copying; copying beyond that described in the guidelines may meet fair use.

> Q Aren't the fair use criteria well enough established that I can tell which of my uses will be fair and which won't?
>
> A There is no guarantee under fair use. The criteria used to judge fair use are completely subjective. There are no concrete guidelines, such as any use for research purposes is fair, or any copying of less than 5 percent of a book is fair. Each determination is made based on the facts of that specific case. This means that you can never be certain beforehand whether a court would consider your use to be fair. For this reason, it is best to act conservatively if your use of a work is not explicitly covered by other exceptions.

The complete text of the guidelines is provided in Source H. In a nutshell, the guidelines suggest that, for research purposes, or for use in teaching or preparation for teaching, one copy may be made by or for a teacher of: a book chapter; a journal article; a short story, short essay, or short poem; or a chart, diagram, drawing, cartoon, or picture from a book, periodical, or newspaper. Multiple copies for classroom use may be made by or for a teacher, as long as they do not exceed one copy per student, include a notice of copyright, and as long as they meet specific requirements for brevity, spontaneity, and cumulative effect.

The brevity requirements limit the number or percentage of words and graphics (such as charts or graphs) copied from a single work. The spontaneity factor requires that the copying be initiated by the teacher and that the decision to use the work be made so close in time to the moment it will be used as to make it unreasonable to expect to be able to request and receive copyright permission in time. The cumulative effect test states that the copying must be for use only in one course; restricts the amount of material that may be copied in one term from the same author, collective work, or periodical volume (except for current news); and limits the total amount of copying per course per term. Finally, the guidelines prohibit: copying for the purpose of replacing collective works or books; copying of "consumable" works, e.g., workbooks and exercises; repeated copying from term to term by the same teacher; and charging students more than actual cost for the copies.

What other statutory protections are available to librarians?

Remember that fair use is a defense to infringing activity. In other words, in a fair use case, the defendant has infringed the plaintiff's rights, but the defendant will not be held liable for that infringement because the defendant's conduct constituted a fair use. In comparison, the Copyright Act provides several specific exemptions to a copyright owner's rights. Activities that fall into these exempted categories are not infringing activities in the first place. In other words, for example, a copyright owner has the exclusive right to reproduce her work except for reproductions that fit into the activities described in Section 108 of the Copyright Act.

Section 108: library photocopying

Section 108 of the Copyright Act provides limited rights to libraries to make photocopies for purposes such as providing interlibrary loans and archiving. Section 108 is somewhat long and detailed and is reproduced in full in Source A. What follows is a brief overview of the major subsections.

Section 108(a) paves the way for interlibrary loan services. It states that a library or archives, or any employee acting within the scope of her employment, may "reproduce no more than one copy...of a work...or distribute such copy" *if* the following conditions are met: (1) the copies are not made for commercial advantage; (2) the library's collections are open to the public *or* available to persons doing research in a specialized field other than those affiliated with the institution; *and* (3) the copy or distribution includes a notice of copyright on the copy or, if no notice is found on the work, a legend stating that the work may be protected by copyright.

Sections 108(b) and (c) allow copies to be made for purposes of preservation and replacement. A library fitting the description in 108(a)(2) above may make up to three copies of an *unpublished* work for purposes of preservation or to deposit in another library or archive for research uses *if* the following conditions are met: (1) the item being copied is currently in the library's collection; *and* (2) any digital copy must not be otherwise distributed in a digital format nor made available to the public in digital format beyond the premises of the library. Up to three copies of a *published* work may be made for the purpose of replacing a copy that is damaged, deteriorating, lost, or stolen, or to replace an obsolete format, *if* (1) "the library or archives has, after a reasonable effort, determined that an unused replacement cannot be obtained at a fair price;" *and* (2) any digital copy must not be otherwise distributed in a digital format nor made available to the public in digital format beyond the premises of the library.

Sections 108(d) and (e) apply to the above rights. A library may make a copy of no more than one article from a journal issue, or no more than one "other contribution" to a copyrighted collection, or "a small part of any other copyrighted work" *if* the following conditions are met: (1) the copy becomes the property of the user; (2) the library has had no notice that the copy will be used for anything other than "private study, scholarship, or research;" *and* (3) the library prominently displays a copyright warning at the place where orders of copies are taken, according to requirements issued by the Copyright Office.

Finally, the exemptions of Section 108 apply only to the "isolated and unrelated reproduction or distribution of a single copy...of the same material on separate occasions." The exemptions do not apply when the library or an employee is aware that the copying is being done for purposes of "related or concerted reproduction or distribution of multiple copies...of the same material," whether or not the copies are made at the same time and whether or not intended for aggregate use by a group or for use by individual members of a group. Neither does Section 108 apply to instances of systematic copying or distribution of single or multiple copies or copying intended to act as a replacement for a subscription or purchase by anyone, including another library. In addition, Section 108 does not apply to copies or distribution of a musical, pictorial, graphic, or sculptural work; motion picture; or other audiovisual work other than those dealing with news, the only exceptions being copies made for archival or replacement purposes and graphics that are a part of other works.

First sale doctrine

The first sale doctrine literally allows libraries to function. Recall that one of the exclusive rights of a copyright owner is the right to publicly distribute copies of his work. Think about what libraries do: They distribute copies of works to the public for free. Yes, lending is a form of distribution. The first sale doctrine, codified in Section 109 of the Copyright Act, states that once an individual copy of a work has been sold, the owner of that particular copy may sell or otherwise dispose of that copy without the permission of the copyright owner. (*Copyright Act of 1976,* vol. 17, sec. 109(a) (1999)) Without this exemption, libraries could not loan books nor resell them in the ever-popular annual book sale. The first sale doctrine also allows the owner of a particular copy to publicly display the work and permits libraries to create displays of their materials to attract and inform users about collections. (ibid. sec. 109(c))

The first sale doctrine does not apply to the rental, lease, or lending of computer programs or sound recordings for the purpose of direct or indirect commercial advantage. (ibid. sec. 109(b)(1)(A)) Nonprofit libraries lending computer programs for nonprofit purposes must include a copyright warning on the packaging of the copy being lent. (ibid. sec. 109(b)(2)(A)) The

> **Q** What are the exceptions for libraries in copyright law?
>
> **A** As opposed to fair use, several exemptions to copyright law exist for library uses that are explicitly and clearly stated. Those include the first sale doctrine, limited photocopying by libraries, and limited copying for classroom purposes.

wording of the warning is prescribed by the Registrar of Copyrights. (See 37 C.F.R. § 201.24 for the required wording.) This subsection of the Copyright Act also specifically states that the "transfer of possession" of a computer program "by a nonprofit educational institution to another nonprofit educational institution or to faculty, staff, and students" does not constitute commercial use and thus is allowed under the first sale doctrine. (*Copyright Act of 1976, U.S. Code*, vol. 17 sec. (109(b)(1)(A) (1999)) Nonprofit libraries and nonprofit education institutions are also allowed to rent, lease, or lend copies of "phonorecords," which would include any sound recording, such as cassette tapes or CDs as well as literal records. (ibid.)

It is very important to realize that these exemptions do *not* apply to for-profit libraries or to the resale of computer programs, such as at a library book sale.

Note that under the first sale doctrine, video stores may rent videos to the public, but record stores may not rent CDs. An interesting story lies behind this difference. Obviously, the motivating factor for excepting computer programs and sound recordings from the first sale doctrine is the ease with which such items may be copied and redistributed. The software and music industries were afraid of losing sales. Given the ease with which videotapes may be copied, why would the movie industry not have supported a similar exception for videos? The movie industry, as it turns out, did fear the invention of videotapes and VCRs in their early days. As generally happens, the industry went after the big guys with deep pockets: VCR manufacturers. The claim was contributory copyright infringement, because, plaintiffs argued, VCRs were used by consumers to tape movies and TV shows from television. In the end, the Supreme Court found that consumers used taping for "time-shifting" purposes, that is, to tape a show in order to watch later, at a more convenient time. This, the Court said, was a fair use. (*Sony Corp. of Am. v. Universal City Studios, Inc.*, 464 U.S. 417 (1984))

A few interesting details about this case: First, the Court did not address the issue of "library-building," or recording movies and shows to create a

> ### One more reason why librarians must become activists
>
> "Librarians should be as aggressive in protecting the right of fair use as the publishers are in seeking to destroy it . . . . [L]ibrarians are the last line of defense against the efforts of publishers to sacrifice the right of the people to know on the altar of profit. . . . This statement is not as hyperbolic as it may seem. The conduct of the publishers indicates that their goal is to do away with free lending libraries, to transform copyright into a pay-per-use right . . . . To succeed, they must coopt librarians to be their licensing agents. Unless librarians refuse to be coopted, the publishers will succeed." Ray Patterson, American Library Association. Users' Rights in Copyright: An Interview with Ray Patterson. Available: http://Copyright.ala.org [January 2001].

personal library, although it was raised by the plaintiffs. Second, the decision was 5–4, which means we came within one Justice's vote of essentially outlawing VCRs!

So what is the bottom line?

As you now realize, defenses to copyright infringement, even for good guys like libraries, who have absolutely no interest in profiting from actions of infringement, can be extremely complicated and uncertain. As your head spins, I would like to leave you with a few very basic thoughts to keep in mind always:

- Fair use is a defense. This means that it does not even come up as an issue for discussion until a claim of copyright infringement has been made, lawyers have been notified, and a significant amount of time, energy, and, usually, money, has been expended by a number of people. That means, in turn, that it is wise to take the fair use analysis seriously.
- Fair use is decided on a case-by-case basis. There are no hard-and-fast rules. At all. This means that one can never be 100 percent certain, no matter what the circumstances, that any given situation will be excused as fair use. While we need to stand up for users' rights and against current attempts to narrow the fair use doctrine, each library will have to make its own decision about how risk-averse it is. In other words, each institution needs to find the balancing point with which it feels most comfortable in the dichotomy of (1) furthering the right of its users by pushing the limits of fair use; and (2) protecting the library or its parent entity by

not taking impractical risks. Often, this is the point where a copyright policy (see Chapter 18) and the advice of the entity's counsel should be consulted.

- In contrast, the rights in Section 108 (library photocopying and copying for preservation and replacement purposes) and in Section 109 (the first sale doctrine) are exemptions to the exclusive rights of copyright owners. They provide solid limits of what may be done: We know in advance the minimum use that may be made safely. On the other hand, it is possible that uses exceeding those described in Sections 108 and 109 would be allowed under the fair use doctrine, so keep this in mind.

So, in general, know the rules and when they apply, and follow them. Know what your institution's policy is regarding when to challenge the rules or push the boundaries. And always, always, consult your institution's legal counsel with questions. Keep a paper trail of the discussion, both for yourself and for the just-in-case.

Bibliography

American Geophysical Union v. Texaco, Inc., 60 F.3d 913 (2d Cir. 1994).
Campbell v. Acuff-Rose Music, 510 U.S. 569 (1994).
Copyright Act of 1976, U.S. Code, vol. 17 secs. 107 and 109 (1999).
Harper & Row v. Nation Enter., 471 U.S. 539 (1985).
Salinger v. Random House, Inc., 811 F.2d 90 (2d Cir. 1987).
Sony Corp. of Am. v. Universal City Studios, Inc., 464 U.S. 417 (1984).
Wright v. Warner Books, Inc., 953 F.2d 731 (2d Cir. 1991).

4

Some Internet basics

If you choose to skip over this chapter now, keep it in mind as you read through the rest of the book. If you come across something that just doesn't seem to make sense ("why would simply browsing the Web be considered making copies?"), come back and see if your question is answered here.

How does the Internet work?

Network of networks

We've all heard the Internet referred to as "a network of networks." It is important to keep in mind the implications of this quite accurate description. A network may be as small as a handful of computers or as large as hundreds or even thousands of computers. What makes a network, however, is some type of central control over the machines, software, and connections contained on it. A network at a major university, for example, may link thousands of computers in hundreds of different departments. Each department may use different types of software, depending on its needs. However, if all of those activities are controlled from a central computing center, this is a network. This is a simple example, of course; in reality, in such a large institution, each department probably connects to both a university network and its own network. The salient point is that a network has some kind of central control and administration.

Compare this to the "network of networks" description of the Internet. A web is a very appropriate analogy. Picture the three-dimensional models of molecules used in science classes, the ones that look like spheres of Tinkertoys. Each of these models is a network of computers, each interconnected with each other, but within a contained, if somewhat complicated, environment. Now picture hundreds—no, thousands—of those models all tossed together into a huge container, tangled up in miles of string. That's the Internet. If you trace a combination of string and structures long enough, you can find a connection between any two pieces. However, there is no overall organization of the pieces, and the entire glob was not planned as a whole. It just happened.

Packet-switching

Information travels across the Internet via a process called "packet-switching." Even what seems to be a small piece of information, such as a brief e-mail message, is broken into even smaller pieces and numbered accordingly before being sent across the Internet. Each "packet" is sent over the network individually and may travel a route different from that traveled by the other packets to reach the same destination, where they will be reassembled according their assigned numbers. This allows the system to take advantage of the various routes available to it at any given time. Each packet can be sent along the first available route that can handle its size. This means that the information does not have to wait for an available route large enough to handle the entirety, which could take much longer. Once the packets all reach the destination, they are reassembled so that the recipient sees the same entire e-mail or picture or Web page as did the sender.

Professor Trotter Hardy of the College of William and Mary School of Law suggests that to understand the importance of the packet-switching system, we should compare it to the traditional telephone system, which is based on "circuit switching." (Trotter, 1998) A "circuit" is the particular path of physical wires over which a phone conversation will be carried. Typically, several physical wires run between locations. These wires meet at various switching stations across the country. When a phone call is made, it goes to a nearby switching station, where the switch determines on which outgoing wire the call should be routed. That outgoing wire may then go to another switching station, which again must find an available outgoing wire, and so on. The various wires chosen by the switching stations form an end-to-end path called a "circuit." That path remains constant for the duration of the phone call, regardless of whether anyone is actually speaking.

The disadvantage of this mechanism, compared to the Internet's "packet-switching" process, is that it "wastes" the resources of the circuit when there are pauses in the conversation, because the wires are not being used at that point, yet the call in process prevents anyone else from using them. Although the packet-switching process was originally developed when the Internet was part of the Department of Defense network to allow information transmission to continue in the face of protracted missile attacks, it now serves a different valuable purpose. The capacity of the physical connections used by the Internet has not kept up with the continuing exponential growth in Internet use. The packet-switching process allows that somewhat limited system to be used to its greatest advantage in transferring information as rapidly as possible.

Arrival

Like the circuit system, each packet may travel across several lines and through several computers before reaching its destination. Thus, one piece of information—an e-mail message or a graphic from a Web page—will be broken into several pieces, each of which may travel a different route in its journey. Along the journey, each packet goes through several computers, called "routers," each of which makes the decision of how to most efficiently send the packet on the next leg of its journey. If one route fails, the router will send a copy of that packet through an alternative route. Finally, all of the packets arrive at their destination.

Upon arrival, the packets are reassembled in the end-user's RAM, hard drive, or other storage device, depending in part upon whether the end-user has requested that the information be downloaded, or "saved." When you are simply browsing the Web, your computer, in effect, asks the computer hosting a Web site to send copies of all the files associated with the page you are viewing to your computer. A simple page without minimal graphics may exist in only one file. A page with lots of graphics may include a separate file for each graphic. Each file will be broken into packets, each of which is numbered, and sent out on its particular journey across the Internet. The packets will arrive at your computer, which will reassemble them and hold them in its RAM so that you can view the page.

Storage: What exactly is RAM, and how is it different from my hard drive?

RAM stands for "random-access memory." It physically exists separately from your hard drive, on its own chip. RAM is used as temporary storage and allows you to work more rapidly, because it stores what you are currently working on so that you may access it immediately rather than having to continually access it from your hard drive. For example, as I write this page, the sentences I am typing exist in RAM. I am viewing the copy that exists in my computer's RAM. When I click on "save," the page is saved to my hard drive. At that point, there are two copies—one on my hard drive and one in my RAM. When you browse the Web, a copy of each page that you access is made in your RAM. When you view that Web page, you are actually viewing the copy that exists in your RAM.

When you turn off your computer, or close an application, the information you have been using is erased from RAM. If you have not saved it to a long-term storage device, such as a hard drive or CD-ROM, it is gone for good, as most of us know from personal experience.

What are the implications for copyright law?

Why is the above discussion important for copyright purposes? Because it means that, potentially, several copies of each and every piece of information travelling across the Internet are made during the transfer of the information. Copies may also be made upon arrival at the end-user's computer. The end-user himself may then cause additional copies to be made. Because the copyright owner of each piece of information accessed on the Web is the only person who has the legal right to make copies of that information, this process has some very important implications for copyright law.

En route

The packet-switching process used by the Internet means that at least one copy of the information being transferred is made simply so that it can make the journey. More than one copy may be made; for example, if a packet "gets lost" during the journey, another copy of it will be made and sent through a different, hopefully more successful, route.

"But do these packets really count as 'copies?'" you ask. You're right—it does sound like a stretch, for a few reasons. First, because the information is broken into pieces, no one copy of the entire page or e-mail message or graphic exists at any given time during the journey. Each packet is only one small portion of the data. But remember: An entire work does not have to be copied to constitute infringement. Indeed, a very small portion of the work may be considered infringing if it is found to encompass "the heart" of the work.

"Nonetheless," you say, "implying that these packets might infringe copyright seems ridiculous." Again, you're right. Perhaps the best place to find support for this argument is in the definition of "copies" in the Copyright Act. A copy is a "material object . . . in which a work is fixed . . . and from which the work can be perceived, reproduced, or otherwise communicated, either directly or with the aide of a machine or device." (*Copyright Act of 1976, U.S. Code* vol. 17 sec. 101 (1999)) Is a packet "fixed" in a "material object"? A work is "fixed" when "its embodiment . . . is sufficiently permanent or stable to permit it to be perceived, reproduced, or otherwise communicated for a period of more than transitory duration." (ibid.) As discussed above, each packet exists for only fractions of a second, sometimes slightly longer, which is probably not enough to meet the definition of "fixed." However, the physical wires containing it and along which it travels may be considered a "material object." Can each packet be "perceived, reproduced, or otherwise communicated"? One might have to work hard at it, but it might be possible. Even though each packet is only a jumble of ones and zeroes, those jumbles can be copyrighted as software, even though the software may not be "perceived" as we traditionally think of viewing or reading something.

"OK, even if you could say a packet is technically a copy," you insist, "you can't say that simply using the Internet constitutes copyright infringement!" If only it were that simple. That it is not is, in a nutshell, the very reason you are reading this book. As we will discuss in following chapters, some courts have implied that some of the most basic functions of using the Internet may, by their very nature, constitute copyright infringement. These are the issues with which we are now struggling.

Copies made by end-users

You might expect that the issue of copies made by the end-user is more clear. You're probably catching on by now that very little discussed in this book is clear. Which is why we need to have the discussion in the first place.

Simply put, the end-user can make two different types of copies: RAM copies and longer-term storage copies. While there is little debate that copies on a hard drive or CD-ROM are considered copies as defined in copyright law, there is some reason for debate about whether RAM copies are so considered. Let's review the components of a copy:

1. "material objects in which a work is fixed"—RAM is a material object, a small card or chip in your computer
2. "from which the work can be perceived, reproduced, or otherwise communicated"—as explained above, RAM is what allows you to perceive a Web page
3. "embodiment . . . sufficiently permanent . . . to permit it to be perceived, reproduced, or otherwise communicated for a period of more than transitory duration"—aha! What, you ask, is "a period of more than transitory duration?" And an excellent question it is. It will be discussed in more detail in Chapter 7. For now, suffice to say that at least one court has held RAM copies in one situation to be infringing of copyright.

Briefly consider the implications should this be true generally for the Web: If you make a copy without permission, you have infringed. If you make a copy of an illegal (thus already infringing) copy, you have infringed. But you can't know what is on a Web page, and whether the information it contains is copyrighted or infringing, or whether you have permission to copy it, until you see the page. And you can't see the page until a copy is made in your RAM. But that might be illegal in certain circumstances. Yes, you're right: Something's rotten in the state of the Internet, should this be our law.

Making the Internet more friendly—caching

Copies are also made and used on the Internet via "caching." Caching is basically the use of temporary copies to increase speed and efficiency. Copies made in your RAM are cache copies. Not only do you view the Internet via copies in your RAM, but those copies may also be called up later during the same session. For example, if you go back to a page you viewed five minutes before, your browser is likely to call up the RAM copy that already exists in your RAM, rather than make a new connection to the server hosting the page and make a new copy in your RAM. This saves time and also avoids using limited network capacity when it's not necessary.

Caching is also used as a more intentional method of saving time and space. Some online services, such as Google, cache copies of Web pages frequently accessed by their users. This means that they store copies of those pages on their own server. When a user calls up that page, instead of going to the host server, the browser gets that page from Google's server. This results in quicker access for the user and lessened demand on the server's capacity. An increasing number of services are doing this, including some libraries.

You may have already guessed some of the problems inherent in this practice, including timeliness of the information contained on the cached pages. Caching is discussed further in Chapter 7.

What are the issues specifically related to the Web?

Linking

Anyone who has used the Web knows that hyperlinks are its heart. You may not realize, however, that there are two different types of links, inline links and out links. An out link is one that simply takes the user to another site on the Web. An inline link, in contrast, connects to an image, document, or other file at another site on the Web and pulls it into the page currently being viewed. In both cases, copies are made in RAM when the identified information is viewed.

Inline links bring up an additional implication: derivative works. The copyright owner has the exclusive right to make derivative works of his copyrighted work. A derivative work is defined as "a work based upon one or more preexisting works." (ibid.) This may include translations, sequels, versions in different media—such as making a movie from a book—and much more. When my copyrighted image, which I have placed on my Web page, is brought into a different context on your Web page, is that a derivative work? Quite possibly.

> ### One more reason why librarians must become activists
>
> We all know intelligent, well-educated computer-phobes . . . in deci-
> sion-making positions. Unfortunately, some of them are in Congress.
> If no one's educated them yet as to how their ignorance effects the
> rights of all Americans to access and use information, who will?

Framing

A specific form of this issue is framing. Frames basically allow more than
one Web page to be viewed in the same browser "window." Sometimes it is
obvious to the viewer when this happens, such as when a frame is delineated
by lines or scroll bars, but sometimes it is not as clear. While an in-link may
bring in only part of another page, such as a specific image, framing brings
in the entire other page.

When my page, with the URL www.gretchen.com, brings your page, with
the URL www.yourpage.com, into a frame on mine, a few things happen that
might bother you. First, I control how your page is viewed within mine, including what surrounds it and the size at which it is viewed. Second, my URL
continues to be displayed in the URL box on a user's browser, so the user
might think that your page is actually part of mine, or that I created it.

As you can begin to see, framing creates its own set of copyright issues.
These will be discussed further in Chapter 6.

Pulling it all together

Not only are several copies of Web pages made during the simple process of
using the Web, but the Internet has suddenly made a reality out of the potential for mass distribution of publications by everyone with access to a computer. Ten years ago, Ann probably wouldn't have photocopied fifty copies
of a new short story she just read to send to fifty of her best friends. At seven
cents a page, plus postage and envelopes, Ann would end up spending quite
a bit of time and money to copy and distribute that short story. But if Ann
reads that story on the Web, it takes her five minutes max, and no expense
to speak of, to copy it, attach it to e-mails, and send it to fifty friends. Once
again, the very nature of the Internet leads to some serious copyright issues.

Bibliography

Copyright Act of 1976, U.S. Code, vol. 17 sec. 101 (1999).

Hardy, I. Trotter. *Project Looking Forward: Sketching the Future of Copyright in a
Networked World*. U.S. Copyright Office. 1998.

5

Recent copyright legislation

Three pieces of legislation affecting copyright have been enacted in recent years, all of which have received a great deal of attention in the library community: the Technology, Education, and Copyright Harmonization Act of 2002 (the "TEACH Act"), the Digital Millennium Copyright Act of 1998 ("DMCA"), and the Sony Bono Copyright Term Extension Act of 1998. Each of these will be discussed in this chapter; in addition, the TEACH Act is discussed in detail in Chapter 16, in the context of distance education, and the DMCA is discussed further in Chapter 9. Chapter 5 touches on various pieces of legislation proposed in the last few Congresses that have not yet been passed. Some are still before Congress, while others have been abandoned by Congress but taken up by some state legislatures or, in one case, regulations adopted by the Federal Communication Commission.

What do these pieces of legislation mean for libraries and library users? The Sony Bono Act is fairly simple, and, for the most part, the library community is not happy about it. In fact, ALA joined other library associations and consumer rights entities in supporting a constitutional challenge to the Sonny Bono Act, which was ultimately denied by the U.S. Supreme Court in 2003. The DMCA is not at all simple, but I will try to hit the highlights here well enough to make the major issues clear. The TEACH Act falls somewhere in between the others in complexity.

Isn't the Sonny Bono Copyright Term Extension Act all about protecting Mickey Mouse?

Keep in mind, as you read this section, that the Constitution refers to the exclusive rights to be given to authors and inventors "for limited times," for the purpose of encouraging the creation of new works. The bottom line question for term limitation, then, should be: "How long a term of protection is necessary to encourage authors to create new works?"

The duration of copyright protection has been lengthening progressively, and ever more rapidly, during the last one hundred years. The original copyright act, of 1789, gave copyright owners a 14-year term, renewable for another 14 years at the end of the term if the author was still alive. The 1909

Act increased that to two 28-year terms. Under the 1976 Act, the copyright term was expressly expanded beyond the lifetime of the author for the first time, creating one term for the life of the author plus fifty years. For corporate, anonymous, or pseudonymous works or works for hire, the term was for 75 years from publication or one hundred years from creation, whichever occurred first. In 1998, Congress passed the Sonny Bono Copyright Term Extension Act, which added another 20 years to the term, for a total of life plus 70 years, or for corporate, anonymous, or pseudonymous works or works for hire, 95 years from publication or 120 years from creation.

Why this continual increase in term duration? What does this mean for libraries? Many commentators argue that when we get to the point of awarding protection long after the life of the author has ended, we move away from the original purpose of copyright law, which is to act as an incentive in encouraging the creation of works. This is especially applicable when we increase the duration of the term after death. After all, if you are not motivated to create a work by knowing that your rights in it will be protected not only throughout your lifetime, but also for two generations after your death, would adding another 20 years to that postmortem protection change your mind?

So who, then, is arguing for these extensions? Think about who benefits: obviously not the dead author. Arguably, the dead author's family, though the vast majority of works will not be wildly popular 70 years after the death of the author. More likely, the main beneficiaries are corporate copyright owners. First, a corporation is much more likely to live for one hundred or more years after a work has been published than is a human. Second, a corporate work, such as a movie, is more likely to be in demand 70 years after publication than is any given book. More specifically, the Sonny Bono Act was motivated by the impending expiration of the copyright in the Mickey Mouse character. "Ah, now the light bulb clicks on," you say; "we're doing this to support the entertainment and publishing industries, not to motivate individual authors." That is certainly what many believe.

Perhaps more clear is how this hurts libraries and other education—and information-based industries, including for-profit information businesses. It now takes 20 years longer for a work to fall into the public domain. A copyright owner now has an additional 20 years to control and charge for use of his work. During the debate over the Sonny Bono Act, representatives of the library community argued that the vast majority of works are no longer commercially exploited nor easy to find long before the proposed life-plus-seventy term would expire, thus there was no need for the extension. On the other hand, scholars and educators are much more likely to need use of those works, and the extension would only hurt this, the most likely, use. In an attempt to satisfy the library lobby, a provision was included in the Act that allows a library, archives, or nonprofit educational institution "to reproduce, distribute, display, or perform in facsimile or digital form a copy…for purposes of preservation, scholarship, or research, if such library or archives has first determined, on the basis of a reasonable investigation," that the work is no longer "subject to normal commercial exploitation" (which is nowhere defined), cannot be obtained at a "reasonable price," or if the copyright owner provides notice that either of these conditions applies. (*Copyright Act of 1976, U.S. Code*, vol. 17, sec. 109 (1999)) In other words, libraries, but not individual users, are exempted from some of the repercussions of the Sonny Bono Act. Nonetheless, the general movement toward extending copyright duration further and further into the future[1] should and does alarm many librarians and educators. It threatens the balance of copyright law, and, arguably, does nothing to "promote the progress of science and the useful arts."

Only months after the Sonny Bono Act was passed, a group of individuals and entities who earned their livelihoods by making public domain works available on the Internet filed a lawsuit, alleging that the Act was unconstitutional. Specifically, the claim was that the retroactive application of the Act was unconstitutional in that it violated the "limited terms" provision of the Copyright Clause and did not further the stated purpose of copyright law; and that passing the Act was beyond the powers granted to Congress in the Constitution. Note that the lawsuit focused on the extension of copyright protection for already existing works, including those in the public domain at the time.

The suit made its way to the Supreme Court, where many commentators expected the Act to be struck down. However, the Supreme Court upheld the Act. In a nutshell, the Court's decision was based primarily on the history of copyright term extensions; the compatibility of the Act with a European Directive extending copyright protection to life-plus-seventy; the Court's traditional deference to Congress regarding this arena of legislation; and the previously mentioned special exclusions for libraries and archives contained in the Copyright Act. Addressing the history of copyright term extensions, the Court pointed out that such extensions had always been applied to both existing and future works. It noted that a key factor considered by Congress in passing the Act was the 1993 European Union Directive; under the Berne Convention, if the term of U.S. copyright protection remained less than that in the E.U., American authors would have less protection in the E.U. than European authors. In response to the plaintiff's First Amendment argument, the Court stated that the fact that the Copyright Clause in the Constitution and the First Amendment were adopted in roughly the same time period indicated that the Framers considered copyright protection to be compatible with free speech. The Court went on to point out that the Act supplemented First Amendment protection by allowing libraries and archives to reproduce, distribute, display, and perform copies of certain works under certain conditions during the last 20 years of their copyright protection. Finally, the Court opined that "it is generally for Congress, not the courts, to decide how best to pursue the Copyright Clauses' objectives."

Interestingly, at various points in the opinion, the Court indicated that it was not entirely pleased with the effects of the Act, despite upholding it. For example, the Court ended its opinion by clarifying that although the plaintiffs "forcibly urged that Congress pursue very bad policy in prescribing the CTEA's long terms,...the wisdom of Congress' action...is not within our province to second guess."(*Eldred v. Ashcroft*, 537 U.S. 186, 222 (2003))

What is the Digital Millennium Copyright Act?

Doubtless you have heard many references to the Digital Millennium Copyright Act. You may not realize that the DMCA is not simply an amendment to one part of the Copyright Act; rather, it includes several provisions on a range of topics within copyright. Some of those provisions are discussed throughout this book as they apply to those specific areas of copyright. Here, I will hit only the highlights.

Creating the DMCA was a long and arduous job, because many constituencies had very specific concerns, and those concerns often conflicted. It is worthwhile to note that some earlier versions of the DMCA were much more unfriendly to libraries and library and information users than was the version that passed. Through the hard work, over a long period of time, of hundreds of librarians, library supporters, and library organizations, many issues of concern to libraries were addressed. The library community is not completely happy with the DMCA, and rightly so (see Chapter 9). But some sections of it provide examples of success stories of the library lobby, in which all librarians should play a role.

Limited liability of online service providers

This topic is discussed in greater depth in Chapter 11. The basic issue is whether libraries act as online service providers (OSP) when they provide Internet access to their users, and, if so, whether they may be held liable for what those users do or access while online. This portion of the DMCA, now Section 512 of the Copyright Act, allows individual libraries to choose whether they want to claim protection as an OSP under the safe harbors provided in the Act. Certain responsibilities result by virtue of claiming that protection, such as registration of an agent and developing notification and termination policies. However, benefits also result from claiming OSP status, namely limitations on liability for what we might consider completely innocent acts, such as system caching, transient storage in the process of transmitting information on the Internet, and linking to infringing sites. The bottom line is that each library must make this decision for itself, and each library should indeed make a decision.

Updating section 108 to supplement preservation and replacement options

The DMCA amended Section 108, which includes exemptions for library reproductions, to allow more copies to be made for preservation and archival purposes and to allow libraries to use a variety of technologies in making such copies.

Anti-circumvention rules and copyright management information

A major concern in the cyberworld, as evidenced by the publication of this book, is the ease with which information may be stolen and misused. In response to such concerns, the DMCA prohibits circumvention of technology that prevents access to a work. In other words, if Jimmy employs a certain type of technology to control access to his Web page to prevent others from accessing his page if they have not registered with him or paid a fee, under the DMCA, it is now explicitly illegal for anyone to try to get around that preventive technology. A limited exception gives libraries a right to "browse" items to which they are considering purchasing access.

However, the DMCA also prohibits the manufacture, importation, sale, or trafficking in anti-circumvention technologies. This concerns the library community, because even though libraries and nonprofit educational institutions are given the "browsing right" mentioned above to circumvent protection technologies, the DMCA's prohibition would seem to ensure that the technologies necessary for libraries to implement this right would not be available.

The DMCA also prohibits the removal or alteration of copyright management information, or information that is intended to identify the work as protected by copyright, including the terms and conditions of that protection.

What is the Technology, Education, and Copyright Harmonization Act?

The Technology, Education, and Copyright Harmonization Act of 2002 ("TEACH" Act) amended the Copyright Act to allow certain uses in the

> ### One more reason why librarians must become activists
>
> Representative Mary Bono stated in a Congressional hearing that Sonny Bono wanted copyright to last forever and that although she had been told by her staffers that this would be unconstitutional, maybe Congress could do something about it anyway.

course of providing distance education that were not previously allowed. It is discussed in greater detail in Chapter 16. Prior to the TEACH Act, the only provisions of the Copyright Act that addressed transmissions of displays of a work—in other words, the types of uses that would be made for distance education—were very limited in scope. The Copyright Act simply did not address the needs of distance education programs.

The TEACH Act moves in that direction. It more or less allows the transmission of the types of displays that would be allowed in face-to-face teaching. However, it is still quite lacking. Not only does it not put distance education on a completely equal footing with traditional face-to-face education, but it also fails to address many important components of complete distance education programs, such as electronic reserves.

Notes

1. Representative Sonny Bono died only months before the Act was passed. His wife, Mary Bono, argued before Congress in support of the Act. In that argument she stated, "Sonny Bono wanted to see copyright last forever."

Further resources

Primer on the Digital Millennium: What the Digital Millennium Copyright Act and the Copyright Term Extension Act Mean for the Library Community, by Arnold P. Lutzker

www.ala.org/washoff/primer.html

Digital Millennium Copyright Act: Status and Analysis, by the Association of Research Libraries

www.arl.org/info/frn/copy/dmca.html

Bibliography

Copyright Act of 1976, U.S. Code, vol. 17 (1999).
Digital Millennium Copyright Act of 1998, 105th Cong., 2nd sess., 1998.
Eldred v. Ashcroft, 537 U.S. 186 (2003).
Sonny Bono Copyright Term Extension Act of 1998, 105th Cong., 2nd sess., 1998.

PART II

Applying copyright in cyberspace

6

Hyperlinks and framing

How does hyperlinking work?

Hyperlinking is the essence of the World Wide Web; it makes the Web *the Web*! Can simply linking to someone else's page be an infringement of copyright?

Usually, we think of hyperlinking as just clicking on blue text or a thumbnail image to connect us to another Web page. But there are actually a few different kinds of hyperlinking, or ways of using hyperlinks, and each of these categories raises its own copyright issues. Some are much more likely than others to be capable of infringing copyright. In addition to directly infringing, an argument can be made that an author of a Web page should be held liable for contributorily infringing copyright by connecting to a page that contains directly infringing materials.

Types of links

Hyperlinks can be divided into three broad categories. What we typically think of as a hyperlink is an "out link." When the user clicks on the linked text or image, the Web page he is currently viewing is replaced with a new page. A subcategory, if you will, of out linking is "deep linking." Deep linking refers to connecting to a specific page buried within a site, rather than the site's home page. For example, if your library home page links to Thomas, the Library of Congress page providing in-depth information on Congressional legislation and other activities, this is an out link, because you are going beyond your library site to another site. Most likely, you will link to the Thomas home page at thomas.loc.gov. Perhaps, however, your library pages include a list of Web sites providing current news, so you decide to link to Thomas' Bills in the News page at thomas.loc.gov/home/textonly.html. This would be considered a "deep link," because it bypasses the Thomas home page and goes straight to a "deeper" page at that site.

Yet another category is "inline links." Instead of taking you to an entirely new page, an inline link pulls in an item from another page to display it within your page. Framing uses inline links, but adds a little oomph as well. An example of an inline link might be if I find a lovely image I want to include on my Web page, but because its file is so large, I don't want to store it on my computer. So instead of saving it on my own machine, I simply link to it at the sight where it resides. A user will not have to click on anything to be able to see the image; to him, it appears simply to be part of my page, and he cannot tell from viewing my page where the image resides.

In comparison, framing brings in an entire other page, but within the page currently being viewed. A common use of frames is to maintain consistency within a site. For example, on its Web site, a library might want to keep a constant menu of links on one side of the screen, or at the top or bottom, even if the main information being viewed changes. This can be done by placing the same menu repeatedly on each page, or it could be done by making a "frame" out of that list and linking to other pages within the "viewing" part of the frame. Using the picture frame analogy, which is apparently the source for the term, the list of pages would be the actual frame, and it would be constant. As a patron links to new pages, they would appear in the glass part of the frame, where pictures are viewed.

Out links

An out link (excluding deep links, discussed below) is probably the type of link least likely to pose copyright problems. Logically, simply linking does not implicate any of the rights in the copyright bundle: Where's the copy? Where's the derivative? Where's the distribution? Nonetheless, plaintiffs who really want to sue someone will use any potential ammunition they can get their hands on, and suing for copyright infringement simply by linking to a Web page is one that has been tried. Luckily, the only case to make it to trial has confirmed that linking is not a copyright issue.

The plaintiff in *Hammer v. Trendl* sought temporary restraining orders to prevent the defendant from publishing unfavorable reviews of the plaintiff's books on the Internet. (The plaintiff also tried to enjoin Amazon.com from removing his book from its Web site and to force Amazon.com to remove the defendant's unfavorable reviews from its Web site.) The plaintiff alleged that the defendant had "placed two illegal links to authors'/publishers' book Web pages on Amazon.com, illegally giving himself trespass rights to alter authors'/publishers' information at will." Holding this allegation to be insufficient to demonstrate copying, the court noted that hyperlinks are "merely the modality by which Amazon.com has enabled a Web site user to move from the book review Web page to the actual Web page where the book is offered for sale." The plaintiff, the court said, had offered no evidence that the defendant actually copied the plaintiff's works. (*Hammer v. Trendl*, 2002 WL 32059751 (E.D.N.Y. 2002))

The most likely way in which problems will occur via simple linking, then, is by using protected images or text as your link. For example, if I want to create a Web page for my library providing information about current bestsellers, I could run into trouble if I link to other pages with any of the following: a copy of the copyrighted image from a book jacket; text either from the book or from a page to which I'm linking, such as a book review; or the trademarked logo of a publisher. Let's briefly consider each situation.

Copied images as links

The use of a copyrighted image as a link is most likely to cause trouble. Let's say I want to link to a page or pages about John Berendt's book *Midnight in the Garden of Good and Evil*. The photograph on the book jacket is both lovely and immediately recognizable to fans, so it would make a good image to use as my link. But wait! That photograph is copyrighted, and the right belongs to Jack Leigh. Will using it as a link on my page be a problem? If I don't have the owner's permission, it certainly could be. Simply by including the image on my page, I am making a copy (right #1). Arguably, I am distributing it to the public via the Web (right #2). By putting it within a context other than that which the copyright owner intended, I am probably making a derivative work with the photo (right #3) (see more on derivative works below). Arguably, I am also publicly displaying the work (right #4). What to do? If you decide that your use is not likely to be considered a fair use, either seek permission from the copyright owner, or don't use the image at all. Instead, use the title of the book.

Copied text as links

The possibility of infringing copyright by using text as a link is unlikely, primarily because when we use text as hyperlinks, we usually use only a few words, if that. In the example above, the obvious choice would be "Midnight in the Garden of Good and Evil." Although no quantitative minimum is required for the amount of text used to infringe a copyright, an entire work need not be copied to constitute infringement. All that is necessary is copying a "substantial and material amount of . . . protected expression." (Leaffer, 1995: 290) How much is "substantial and material" is decided on an case-by-case basis—which is always a little frightening, because that means you cannot know beforehand whether or not you are doing something wrong. The United States Supreme Court, rather unhelpfully, has held that the key is whether or not the "heart" of the work is taken. In *Harper and Row v. Nation Enterprises*, (471 U.S. 539 (1985)) the Court held that taking as few as 300 copyrighted words from a 200,000-word manuscript, which then were published in a 2,250-

word article, constituted infringement, because the excerpted words constituted "essentially the heart" of the book. This doesn't give us much of a standard to go on.

However, as a practical matter, any text you use for linking purposes will probably be slight enough that it won't be an issue. In the United States, titles per se cannot be copyrighted. The rationale behind this is that titles are usually too short to meet the originality requirement. In theory, a longer, more unique title could be copyrighted. Keep in mind, though, that the eight-word sentence "Frankly, my dear, I don't give a damn" is a lot more likely to get you into trouble that the 20-word opening sentence, "Scarlett O'Hara was not beautiful, but men seldom realized it when caught by her charm as the Tarleton twins were." (Mitchell, 1964)

Trademarked logos as links

Although this book is about copyright law, not trademark law, issues of trademark infringement do exist in regard to creating Web pages. These are briefly described in Chapter 9, but the discussion of trademarked images as hyperlinks bears repeating in this chapter.

Trademark protection and copyright protection are based on different rationales. While copyright is concerned with protecting the creator of the work, trademark is concerned with protecting the consumer of the trademarked goods; the overarching goal of trademark is to avoid consumer confusion by misleading (i.e., infringing) uses of trademarks. Thus, the standards of infringement are completely different.

"Oh," you might be thinking, "there's no way someone's going to confuse my library's Web pages with those of Nike just because I use the Nike swoosh to link to the Nike Web site, no matter how stupid they are." That seems obvious enough. Which, you will learn as you continue through this book, is a warning sign that the next sentence you read will be something along the lines of, "Nothing is as simple as it looks." One way to be held liable for trademark infringement is to use the trademark in such a way as to cause confusion as to your "affiliation, connection, or association" with the producer of the good. It has been argued that using a trademarked logo on a Web page causes dilution because it leads the user to believe that, in the example above, Nike sponsors or supports your library. So far, this argument has proved unsuccessful. Nonetheless, it is still a wide-open issue, as is most of Internet-related law. So take the simple, safe route: Either get permission, or use a textual description ("Nike, Inc.") instead of a logo. (Keep in mind that a logo may be protected by copyright as well as by trademark.)

Deep links

"Why would the level to which my page links have anything to do with whether or not I am infringing copyright in the other page?" Good question! It sounds totally illogical, yet a few suits based on this claim have been either filed or threatened by major companies like Ticketmaster (Schiesel, 1997) and Universal Pictures. (Kaplan, 1999)

So what were these cases all about? Shouldn't Ticketmaster and Universal Pictures be happy to have someone sending more business their way? There seems to be general agreement that the cases are about advertising dollars and a company seeking those dollars losing control over access to its own media products. A great deal of disagreement exists over whether it is legitimate to use copyright law to try to address this situation.

Most likely, the plaintiffs' concerns were more about financial loss due to the links' effect on advertising than anything truly related to copyright. Ticketmaster and Universal were concerned because the links on the defendants' sites allowed users to bypass the advertisements posted on their home pages and perhaps on pages in between the home pages and the destination pages as well. When users go directly to a deeper page, the home page gets fewer hits, which means advertisers are either less likely to advertise at that site in the first place, or not willing to pay as much as if all those users needed to go through the page with their ads. In one of the Ticketmaster cases, the defendant was also a direct competitor, which probably contributed to Ticketmaster's ire.

This is certainly a legitimate problem for the hosting site, and it represents one of those areas on which the Internet has put a new spin. Sure you can turn down the volume or flip channels during TV commercials, but the advertisers have no way of knowing when you do that. Software makes it very easy for Web sites to count the number of hits each page receives. Other options, such as placing ads on every single page, may not be feasible. Of course the Web host wants to control how users enter its site.

But is copyright law the appropriate mechanism for doing that? Probably not. In order to successfully claim copyright infringement, the harmed company would have to prove that one of its specific rights (reproduction, distribution, derivative works, public display/performance) had been infringed.

The first Ticketmaster case, filed in 1997, involved Microsoft's information service Seattle Sidewalk, which provides information about local events, including where and how to purchase tickets to such events. In that capacity, Seattle Sidewalk linked to Ticketmaster Web pages about specific events, rather than to Ticketmaster's home page. Ticketmaster sued for both copyright and trademark infringement. The case was settled out of court, with part of the settlement being an agreement to keep the terms of the settlement secret.

Ticketmaster did not fare well in its 2003 suit against Tickets.com. (2003 U.S. Dist. LEXIS 6484 (C.D. Ca. 2003)) Tickets.com sold tickets online to a wide range of events and also listed events to which it did not have the right to sell tickets. It collected its information by using a spider to search the Web for relevant information. The spider identified Web pages of interest; copied them into the RAM of Tickets.com computers, where the copies resided for approximately ten–fifteen seconds; extracted the factual information it needed, such as event, date, location, etc.; then discarded the rest of the information on the Web page. One of the Web sites from which the Tickets.com spider extracted information was that of Ticketmaster. Ticketmaster sued, alleging, among other things, that Tickets.com had infringed Ticketmaster's copyright by publicly displaying the "deeper" pages without authorization. The issue came before the court on summary judgment, which means that the court did not have to make a final holding on the issue, but just to decide whether "triable issues of fact" existed or whether the case should be dismissed without going to a full trial. The court held for the defendant on the deep linking issue, meaning that the court thought the plaintiff had no good argument that deep linking constitutes copyright infringement.

The situation involving Universal Pictures never resulted in a lawsuit. Universal was upset by a young movie fan's Web site, Movie Link, that linked directly to trailers of Universal movies, rather than to the Universal home page. When Universal threatened to sue, the Web author dropped his links to Universal's sites, stating that he had neither the money nor the power to go to court with such a well-funded entity.

Inline linking and framing

The problem with either inline linking or framing is the potential for creating a derivative work. Recall that the copyright owner has the exclusive right to create derivatives of his work. "Derivative work" is defined as "a work based upon one or more preexisting works, such as a translation . . . motion picture version . . . condensation . . . or any other form in which a work may be recast, transformed, or adapted . . . " (*Copyright Act of 1976, U.S. Code*, vol. 17., sec. 101 (1999)) Most courts have held that a derivative work must have some original expression of its own, though originality is usually a pretty low standard in the copyright world. So the question becomes, "does bringing another image into my own page, or bringing other pages into my frames, constitute the creation of a derivative work?"

So far, there have been few if any verdicts. However, we do have a few cases to give us a glimpse of what future decisions might hold. Total News is a Web site that provides access to news stories published online all over the world. Originally, the pages used a frame that included, among other things, the Total News URL at the top of the frame and advertising at the bottom. When a user linked to a news story at another site, that site's page would appear within the Total News frame. Several news services sued Total News for copyright infringement, complaining that

> the effect of the framing by the defendants was to display only a portion of the original screens of material from the linked sites at any given time . . . . Thus, advertisements contained on the original pages of the linked sites were reduced in size, and in some cases were totally obscured . . . . At the same time, the user was continuously exposed to the advertising contained within the Total News frame. (Hayes, 1998: 90)

The case was settled out of court, with the agreement that Total News would stop framing the plaintiff's Web pages, and instead would simply link to those pages.

Ah! Once again it's about advertising money! Perhaps. But maybe alleging copyright infringement is more appropriate in these cases than in the deep link cases discussed above. The point of the derivative works right is that the copyright owner is the only one who should be allowed to profit from a "recast, transformed, or adapted" version of his work. By framing the work, with the resulting effect of making it more difficult than the copyright owner intended for the user to view the advertising, the copyright owner may suffer financial harm. On the other hand, as mentioned above, there is usually an originality requirement for derivative works. Does framing someone else's page meet that requirement?

Consider the earlier example of Garner Public Library linking with frames to pages from the University of Houston Libraries. Certainly, the author of the U.H. pages never intended for them to be displayed with an index to another library's collections. Thus, the work created, what the user views, seems to be a recasting or transformation of the original U.H. page.

This is just one more case in which current copyright law simply does not translate to the cyberworld. As a result, those who are harmed, or maybe just upset, by what others do in cyberspace can try to twist copyright law around until it fits their purposes. In some cases, this may be perfectly appropriate. In others, it starts to feel like copyright law is being used to accomplish purposes for which it was never intended. Have I mentioned yet that this is just one more reason for librarians to become involved in the legislative process? (See Chapter 19.)

Indirect infringement

We have established that not much is established about whether various methods of linking and framing will directly infringe copyright. Just in case you're not perplexed enough yet, let's throw another wrench in the works. Aside from directly infringing copyright—that is, violating the copyright owner's rights yourself—one may also be held liable for contributory or vicarious liability. You *contributorily infringe* copyright if you knowingly and materially induce, cause, or contribute to someone else's direct infringement. If the contribution you make is providing equipment, that equipment must not have a substantial non-infringing use. Most courts have held that "knowingly" means that you must be aware of the other person's actions, but not necessarily that they are infringing. *Vicarious infringement* does not require that you know about the other person's actions. However, you must have the right and ability to control the infringing activity *and* an obvious and direct financial interest in the activity. How do contributory and vicarious infringement apply to linking and framing?

Perhaps the biggest question is, "Can I be held liable for linking to (or framing) someone else's page that includes infringing material?" You won't be surprised to hear that this issue hasn't been directly tried yet. At least one case has made the argument, which was dismissed by the court, but the situation was extreme enough that it is probably not a good general guideline. The plaintiff in *Bernstein v. J.C. Penney* (1998 U.S. Dist. LEXIS 19048 (C.D. Cal. 1998)) sued J.C. Penney for linking through a chain of links to a page that infringed Bernstein's copyrights in some photographs. Penney's pages promoted Elizabeth Arden perfume and included biographical information about Arden. The Arden page had a "for more information" link that led to (among other sites) the Internet Movie Database that led to (among other sites) the Swedish University Network, which posted infringing photographs of Elizabeth Taylor, spokeswoman for Elizabeth Arden. The court dismissed the complaint, which means that the case was thrown out of court, but did not explain its reasoning.

The important thing to keep in mind is that this was a case about linking three levels away: A → B → C (infringer). It seems unrealistic to expect or require A to investigate all of the sites to which B links. Consider how many "B-level" links there are on A's site! However, it may not be as unreasonable to expect A to investigate each "B-level" site to which it links. All sorts of

> ### One more reason why librarians must become activists
>
> Dozens of lawsuits have been filed alleging that simply linking to another Web site infringes copyright. Almost all have settled out of court—which means the defendant may very well have thrown in the towel. Thousands of Web sites include policies purporting to disallow linking to that site without first obtaining permission. Is this a world you're willing to live in?

issues are raised by this argument, of course, including "How do I know the page I'm linking to includes infringing material?" Recall, however, that contributory infringement does not require the infringer to know that the other person's activity is infringing, only to know about the other activity. By creating a Web page with links, you are inducing, contributing, or causing the user to access the pages to which you link; and you know (or at least have reason to know, which would probably count) that users are indeed linking to those pages. That's all that's required for contributory infringement, if those pages to which you link include infringing material.

"How can I possibly investigate every page to which my library links, let alone figure out whether or not they contain infringing material?!" you ask exasperatedly. Once again, we get on the "better safe than sorry" train. In reality, you simply can't. But use some common sense when you chose pages to which you link. Consider the following:

- How *likely* is it that the producers of this page would include infringing material? Of course there's no guarantee, but a media mogul page, say Time-Warner, is much more likely to be aware of and careful to comply with copyright than a cottage industry creating pages on a computer in someone's home.
- How likely is it that the material itself is infringing? Think "Napster." 'Nough said. If the source is offering only its own products, it's not nearly as likely to include infringing material as if it's offering everyone else's products as well.
- Are there copyright statements on the page? If there is a statement saying permissions have been granted, that's a good sign.

Also keep in mind that in the real world, should you link to pages with infringing material and the copyright owner becomes aware of it, what is most likely to happen is that you will receive a "cease-and-desist" letter. If you cease, they are likely to desist in coming after you, although they may also demand monetary compensation. Finally, see Chapter 13, which discusses safe harbors for libraries in some of these situations.

Bibliography

Bernstein v. J.C. Penney, 1998 U.S. Dist. LEXIS 19048 (C.D. Cal. 1998).

Copyright Act of 1976, U.S. Code, vol. 17, sec. 101 (1999).

Hammer v. Trendl, 2002 WL 32059751 (E.D.N.Y. 2002).

Harper and Row v. Nation Enterprises, 471 U.S. 539 (1985).

Hayes, David L. 1998. "Advanced Copyright Issues on the Internet." *Texas Intellectual Property Law Journal* 7:1 (Fall 1998): 1–103.

Kaplan, Carl S. 1999. "Is Linking Always Legal? The Experts Aren't Sure." *New York Times.* August 6.

Leaffer, Marshall. 1995. *Understanding Copyright Law.* New York: Matthew Bender.

Mitchell, Margaret. 1964. *Gone with the Wind.* New York: The Macmillan Company.

Schiesel, Seth. 1997. "Choosing Sides in Ticketmaster vs. Microsoft." *New York Times.* May 5.

7

Browsing and caching

Can simply browsing the Web actually infringe copyright?

Simply browsing the Web may have implications for four of the five exclusive rights of a copyright holder: reproduction, derivative works, public display, and public performance. True, it does seem ridiculous that simply *using* the Web could infringe the copyrights of the creators of Web pages. If nothing else, wouldn't that be detrimental to the intentions of those Web authors? After all, why put material up on the Web unless you want other people to access it?

Viable arguments can be made that the functions involved in browsing the Web do in fact infringe copyrights if done without permission of the copyright owner. Viable arguments can also be made for an implied license in Web browsing. One could argue, for example, that by putting information on the Web, Web authors have given their implicit permission for others at least to browse the pages. You should also keep in mind the existence of "click-wrap" and "browse-wrap" licenses as you move around the Internet.

Even if our courts decide that a license to browse is implied by making information available on the Web, just the fact that browsing could potentially infringe is disturbing. Recall that one of the most basic intentions of copyright law is to define and maintain a balance between the rights of authors and the rights of the public to have access to information. Giving control to authors over simply browsing the Web is akin to giving authors control over who reads their books. It has been referred to as creating an "exclusive right to read." Relying on defenses, such as implied license or fair use, does not take that control away from the author; rather, it says that while you have infringed, we will excuse it this time due to the circumstances. Traditionally, an author has never had such a right.

Raymond Nimmer, a professor of copyright at the University of Houston School of Law, points out that creating a "right to read" is a shift in policy, which, "even if desirable, should occur because of an express policy choice rather than because new technology technically triggers concepts originally designed for a world of photocopy machines, recorders, and the like." (Nimmer, 1996: 4–30)

In other words, browsing may be the ultimate example of the inability of copyright law to keep up with technological developments, despite the clear intention of its authors to avoid such a situation. I would also hasten to add that Professor Nimmer's statement is just one more reason that we as librarians should get involved in this discussion. We as a profession take pride in representing the needs of our users to our city councils, university presidents, and school boards. We must also improve our representation of users at higher government levels to ensure that an "exclusive right to read" is not created, even if completely unintentionally. To learn more about what you can do, see Chapter 19.

Reproduction right
Storage
RAM

Browsing the Web creates temporary copies of whatever is viewed cached either in the computer's RAM or on its hard drive. If that material is protected by copyright, and no permission has been given, such copies could infringe copyright. The key question concerning RAM copies is whether those copies meet the requirement of being fixed for long enough to allow the work to be "perceived, reproduced, or otherwise communicated for a period of more than transitory duration." This is likely to be one of those times when many people will throw up their hands exclaiming, "That's just legalese! Anyone who knows anything about the Internet knows that the whole purpose of RAM is to store information only temporarily." While that is true, it does not change the analysis of whether RAM copies might infringe copyrights.

At the time the first edition of this book was written, one court had clearly held that copies in RAM were capable of existing long enough to infringe copyright. The facts of that case, however, did not involve the Internet. In 2003, a district court held that information collected by a spider and held in RAM for ten to fifteen seconds before being discarded did not infringe copyright. In that case, Ticketmaster sued Tickets.com for copyright infringement on various counts, one of which was that the Tickets.com spider infringed by copying Ticketmaster Web pages. Tickets.com both sold tickets online to a wide range of events and also listed events to which it did not have the right to sell tickets. It collected its information by using a spider to search the Web for relevant information. The spider identified Web pages of interest; copied them into the RAM of Tickets.com computers, where the copies resided for approximately 10–15 seconds; extracted the factual information it needed, such as event, date, location, etc.; then discarded the rest of the information on the Web page. One of the Web sites from which the

Tickets.com spider extracted information was that of Ticketmaster. The court rejected the infringement claim based on copying, since the factual information copied was not subject to copyright protection and the rest of the information was retained in RAM only "momentarily (for 10 to 15 seconds) . . . and [then] immediately discarded." However, the court repeated more than once that this holding was based on the facts of the particular case: that this type of copying constituted fair use "where the purpose is to obtain nonprotected facts." (*Ticketmaster Corp. v. Tickets.com, Inc.*, 2003 U.S. Dist. LEXIS 6483 (C.D. Cal. 2003))

While unlikely that a court would find RAM copies made during the course of browsing to be infringing, the *Ticketmaster* court did leave open that possibility under different circumstances. Unfortunately, two earlier cases could lend support to such an argument.

In *MAI Systems Corporation v Peak Computer, Inc.* (991 F.2d 511 (9th Cir. 1993)), the plaintiff manufactured both computers and operating systems to run them; it also provided maintenance for its hardware and software. MAI licensed its customers to use the software only for their own internal purposes. The defendant company maintained computer software for its clients. When Peak provided maintenance for MAI software to a customer, MAI sued, claiming that Peak had violated MAI's copyright in its software. When it performed maintenance on the software, the defendant turned on the computer, which created a copy of the software in RAM. The defendant proceeded to read an error log displayed from the RAM copy. The court held that the defendant had created an illegal copy of the plaintiff's software when it loaded the software into the computer's RAM upon turning on the computer to perform maintenance. The court did not state as a matter of law that every RAM copy is necessarily "fixed" for copyright purposes. Rather, its decision was based on the fact that the use of the error log proved that the RAM copy could be "perceived, reproduced, or otherwise communicated." (ibid.)

MAI did not involve use of the Internet, and the court's decision applied only to this specific situation. The court even pointed out that the defendant had not argued that the RAM copy was not fixed, implying that it would be open to hearing such arguments.

A district court, however, later relied on *MAI* to find infringement by the simple act of browsing. *Intellectual Reserve, Inc. v. Utah Lighthouse Ministry* (75 F. Supp. 2d 1290 (D. Utah 1999)) involved alleged contributory infringement, not direct infringement. The defendants had placed portions of the plaintiff's copyrighted works on their Web site. When the plaintiff ordered the defendants to remove the works, they did so but replaced them with a notice that the work was available elsewhere on the Web; gave URLs for those sites; and posted e-mails on their page encouraging users to go to those sites to access the works. The plaintiff then sued for contributory infringement, which charges the defendant with knowingly inducing, causing, or contributing to someone else's infringement. The court awarded a preliminary injunction to the plaintiff and, relying on *MAI*, specifically stated that, in making a RAM copy while browsing, "the person who browsed infringes the copyright." (ibid. at 1294) Although end users were not parties to the action, the court set a precedent that browsing the Web may infringe the reproduction right when the user accesses pages containing infringing material.

What specifically can be done about this problem? Recall that the *MAI* court invited arguments that a RAM copy is not fixed for more than a transitory duration. "Transitory duration" is not defined in the copyright law. One could argue that, because a RAM copy disappears when the browser is closed or the computer turned off, it is only transitory. Indeed, the *Ticketmaster* court focused on the "momentary" existence of the RAM copies. On the other hand, one court has specifically stated that the fact that one can control how long a copy exists in RAM by turning off the power supports the argument that it is fixed for more than a transitory duration. It is important to keep in mind that each of these cases was decided in the context of a very specific fact scenario: *MAI* dealt with software, not the Internet; *Intellectual Reserve* dealt with contributory infringement and linking to sites containing infringing material; and *Ticketmaster* dealt with RAM copies that were made in the course of obtaining non-protectable material.

The National Research Council addressed the situation in a 2000 report issued by its Computer Science and Telecommunications Board, *The Digital Dilemma*. The Council is an agency of the National Academy of Sciences, which has a mandate requiring it to advise the federal government on scientific and technical matters. *The Digital Dilemma* presents the results of a project designed, among other things, to make policy recommendations concerning Internet use issues. The Board recognized the problem of temporary copies such as those made in RAM during browsing and suggested that attempts be made to determine when temporary copies should and should not be under the control of copyright owners and to adapt copyright law accordingly. In addition, the Board explicitly stated its concern with developing a system of piecemeal exceptions, suggesting a process that would ultimately result in "a more general-purpose and flexible rule." (Computer Science and Telecommunications Board, 2000: 228–30) Furthermore, the Board went so far as to suggest that "the notion of copy may not be an appropriate foundation for copyright law in the digital age," precisely because the making of copies is an integral part of so many computer functions. The report recommends that the Congress explore the possibility of constructing a new basis of copyright law based on the Constitutional goal of promoting the progress of science and the useful arts. Instead of asking whether a copy had been made, the key question would be whether the use at issue was consistent with the Constitutional goal. (ibid. at 230–32)

Another approach is to create legislation specifically addressing this issue. Indeed, following the *MAI* decision, the copyright law was amended to state that making a copy on a computer is not infringement when done solely for the purpose of providing maintenance. Some people are concerned, though, with the implication that new laws must continually be made to address each specific change in technology. After all, the current copyright law clearly was written with the intention that it would address future technology changes, as witnessed by the definition of copies in Section 101: "material objects . . . in which a work is fixed *by any method now known or later developed*" (emphasis added).

Caching on the hard drive

Similar questions arise in regard to caching on a computer hard drive. Depending on how your browser is set up, "temporary" copies of files you access while browsing the Web may be made on your computer's hard drive rather than in RAM. The most important difference for our purposes is that hard drive cache is stored indefinitely. Typically, much more space is allotted to hard drive caches than is available in RAM. Your hard drive usually continues to cache until it fills, then will delete files as necessary to allow space for caching new files. Unlike RAM, it is not emptied each time an application is closed. Also unlike RAM, it is simple to call up a directory of your cached files and view them on the spot. Although the issue of infringing copies cached on a hard drive has not been raised in a courtroom yet, if RAM copies can infringe copyrights, it seems even more certain that cached copies would do so. Whatever "transitory" may be, cached copies, which can potentially last for years, is certainly not it.

Downloading and printing

Downloading a file from the Web undoubtedly creates a copy of that file, as does printing. If this is done without permission of the copyright owner, it infringes the copyright. However, downloading is not inherent in simply using the Web. While we can argue that limiting a user's right to create RAM copies limits his ability to use the Internet and thus creates the "exclusive right to read," the same argument cannot be made for downloading. The only reason to download or print a file is to come back to it later for a particular use. Control over this type of activity is precisely the kind of control copyright traditionally gives authors. We can analogize by saying that giving an author control over RAM copies is equivalent to allowing the author to say, "You may have found my book on the shelf in a bookstore or library, but you can't read it unless you ask me first." Clearly, this was never an intention of copyright law. On the other hand, giving an author control over downloading and printing is equivalent to allowing the author to prevent one person from photocopying or scanning an entire book and passing the copies along to twenty friends. Control over this type of activity is unquestionably an intention of copyright law.

How do you know when you can and cannot legally download or print a page or a file? Most often, you simply do not. If you are downloading files such as software from a site that offers these files to the public, there is likely a usage policy or a license posted. Your usage may be restricted, such as to noncommercial purposes or for a limited time. Sites offering free graphics may allow unlimited use but require you to credit the copyright owner. Some pages offer a "print-friendly" display, which is a good sign that the authors are happy for you to print from their site.

However, most pages simply do not make clear what is protected by copyright and what isn't, or what the author has given the user permission to do with copyrighted material. Not only that, but it may be that some of the information on a page you're looking at is itself infringing copyright.

Consider your reason for downloading or printing a page or file. Is it just for the sake of convenience? Do you want to use a graphic on your own Web page? Do you want to share a story you've found with friends? Then consider your alternatives. If you want to use something you've found on the Web for your own publications, whether online or print, contact the author of the page. Don't assume that the author is also the copyright owner. Instead, ask where that person obtained the file you want to use. Continue to trace it until you have located the original source. Then ask for permission to use the item. If you want to share a story or article with friends, send them the URL rather than the file.

In reality, of course, it is highly unlikely that a Web page author will come after individuals for copying from his page or printing it out for their own personal use. However, it is possible that a Web page owner who does not wish to have his page or graphics copied will discontinue making his files available if he feels his rights are being encroached upon. In other words, in addition to legal concerns, common courtesy should also be considered.

Derivative works

The copyright owner in a work has the exclusive right to create derivatives of that work. A derivative work is defined in the Copyright Act as

> A work based upon one or more preexisting works, such as a translation, musical arrangement, dramatization…motion picture version…abridgment…or any other form in which a work my be recast, transformed, or adapted…[including] editorial revisions, annotations, elaborations, or other modifications, which, as a whole, represent an original work of authorship. (*Copyright Act of 1976, U.S. Code* vol. 17, sec. 101 (1999))

Obviously, under this definition, were you to download someone else's copyrighted page, modify it in some ways, and re-post it, all without his permission, you would be infringing that person's right to create derivative works. The potential also exists for less obvious, and more questionable, creation of derivative works by simply browsing the Web.

The most common such situation is the use of frames on Web pages. The basic argument is that using frames causes other people's pages to be presented in a manner and context different from that designed by the author. Does this really create a derivative work? At least two cases have claimed it does. In *Futuredontics v. AAI* (1998 U.S. Dist. LEXIS 2265 (C.D. Cal. 1998)); the court denied the defendant's motion to dismiss, thereby allowing the argument of derivative works infringement to go forward. *The Washington Post Co. v. Total News, Inc.* (No. 97 Civ. 1190 (S.D.N.Y. filed Feb. 20, 1997)) was settled out of court, so the issue was not addressed by the court. However, the defendant agreed in the settlement to discontinue the use of frames in connection with the plaintiff's pages. These cases, and copyright issues concerning framing in general, are discussed further in Chapter 6.

A fun example of creating unauthorized derivative works is Shredder (www.potatoland.org/shredder), a Web site that transforms the pages of URLs typed in by users. Shredder works like a twisted Web browser, distorting pages into what looks at times like surreal images, at other times just like garbage. Also in the game are filters of various types of advertisements on Web pages. The techniques used range from preventing pop-up windows from popping up to muting sound recordings to "decaffing" Java script. These cyber-toys raise several issues. On the one hand, they take control away from the author of how his work is being perceived. On the other hand, they do not alter the work for everyone viewing it. However, a Web page author could argue that, in a setting like a library, an individual user does not have the choice of how to view Web pages, but, rather, that it is being forced on him. This might support an argument for infringement.

Public display and performance

A copyright owner has the exclusive right to display and perform the copyrighted work publicly. To do so is defined as

(1) to perform or display [a work] at a place open to the public or at any place where a substantial number of persons outside of a normal circle of a family and its social acquaintances is gathered; or
(2) to transmit or otherwise communicate a performance or display of the work to a place specified by clause (1) or to the public…whether the members of the public capable of receiving the performance or display receive it in the same place or in separate places and at the same time or at different times. (ibid.)

An exception to this rule is allowed under the first sale doctrine: "[T]he owner of a particular copy lawfully made…is entitled…to display that copy publicly…to viewers present at the place where the copy is located." (ibid., sec. 109)

To "display" a work is defined as "to show a copy of it," including by means of various technological devices. (ibid., sec. 107) To "perform" a work is "to recite, render, play, dance, or act it…to show its images in any sequence or to make the sounds accompanying it audible." (ibid.) A library certainly seems to fit the definition of a public place. Does this mean that users viewing Web pages in a library constitute a "public display" or "public performance"? This is entirely possible. The argument can certainly be made that users are "showing" a copy of the page they view. Although showing the page to others may not be their intention, librarians are well aware that this can be the result; witness the hair-pulling and teeth-gnashing over how to deal with patrons viewing pages that other patrons find offensive. Likewise, viewing a video or listening to an audio clip on the Web seems to meet the definition of showing images in sequence or making sounds audible.

Protection

"I understand the arguments, the reasoning, the logic," you're thinking, "but are you really suggesting that anyone, either individuals or institutions, would be held liable for simply using the Web?" Of course the idea sounds ludicrous. The point is that it is theoretically possible. In real life, and especially in areas presenting new and unresolved legal challenges, the way the law works is often like this: Although it seems quite clear that Sue has wronged Anne, because there is little law established in the area, Anne's attorneys will be creating new law in their prosecution of this case; because so few straws currently exist, Anne's attorneys will have to grab at whatever straws they can to find a basis for bringing the suit in the first place. This is the way new case law is created. In theory, it works well. In reality, one of the major dangers is that what works in Sue and Anne's particular case might have unreasonable implications in the big picture for the rest of us.[1]

Thus, until the law becomes more developed, either through the courts or through legislation, we must depend on already established protections. Unfortunately, these protections are not foolproof, and you should not feel completely safe based on them, primarily for two reasons. First, they were not developed to address the cyberworld, so how well they fit into that context is questionable. Second, they are first and foremost defenses. That means that while they might protect you from losing a case, they do not prevent charges being made against you in the first place. It means that you, as the defendant, bear the burden of making the argument and of doing so successfully. Simply naming a defense is not enough; you must convince the judge that its value excedes that of the value of the plaintiff's argument. In other words, a defense of fair use or implied license may prevail in the end and keep you from paying huge statutory damages, but you may have to go through a long and expensive legal process before you even get to make that argument. This is just one more reason why the library profession and its members need to continue to work with legislators to create the legislation necessary to address these issues on the front end rather than rely on current legislation and case law to address them on the back end (see Chapter 19).

Implied license

An implied license is a license, or privilege, that is presumed to have been given based upon another's actions rather than his words. Arguing that an implied license to browse has been given means arguing that the poster of a Web page implicitly licenses users to make whatever copies are necessary to allow them simply to view the material. Keep in mind that in using this argument, we are talking about legally browsing material legally posted to the Web. We are not talking about viewing material illegally posted, or about illegally viewing material, such as hacking your way through to a protected site.

Many argue that browsing should be protected by an "implied license": Basically, because it is impossible to browse the Web without creating RAM copies, the right to make such copies should be implied by the fact that an author has placed her work on the Web. This is pretty much the reasoning used in *Hammer v. Trendl* in relation to simple hyperlinking. In that case, the plaintiff sought temporary restraining orders to prevent the defendant from publishing unfavorable reviews of the plaintiff's books on the Internet and to enjoin Amazon.com from removing the plaintiff's book from its Web site and directing Amazon.com to remove the defendant's unfavorable reviews from its Web site. The plaintiff alleged that the defendant had "placed two illegal links to authors'/publishers' book Web pages on Amazon.com, illegally giving himself trespass rights to alter authors'/publishers' information at will." Holding this allegation to be insufficient to demonstrate copying, the court noted that hyperlinks are "merely the modality by which Amazon.com has enabled a Web site user to move from the book review Web page to the actual Web page where the book is offered for sale." (*Hammer v. Trendl*, 2002 WL 32059751 (E.D.N.Y. 2002)) Clearly, RAM copies created by browsing are just as much a "mere modality" of using the Web.

Even if the implied license argument becomes widely accepted, some issues remain. First, the scope of an implied license is not clear. Has the author given permission only to make the RAM copies necessary to view a page, or also to cache a page on the user's server for future use, or also to print the page, or perhaps more? By definition, an implied license is not articulated in words. Thus, it is difficult to know what the author intended to allow be done with her pages, and it may become increasingly difficult to argue for each additional implied right.

Second, an implied license can be defeated by an express license. In other words, if a Web page author places a statement on her page saying, "Any Internet user has the right to view my page, but no one has the right to print it without my permission," we cannot then argue an implied, or unstated, license to print the page. The author has clearly stated that this license does not exist.

Fair use

Fair use is discussed more fully in Chapter 3. The fact that fair use requires a fact-specific and case-by-case analysis cannot be overemphasized. There are no guarantees! That said, the context of browsing may also allow for some of the strongest fair use arguments. Recall that effect on the market is the fair use factor generally given the most weight. Arguably, browsing has no market effect. Again, this would not apply to someone hacking his way into a sight that requires payment to enter. On the other hand, in some cases, one could argue that some users may choose to read a Web page instead of purchasing a print copy of the same material, which would create a market effect. Then again, that user could argue that by not restricting access to the page in some way, including the imposition of a fee to access it, the author implicitly allows browsing even at the expense of losing a purchase of the printed equivalent.

What are click-wrap and browse-wrap licenses?

A click-wrap license is a license that appears when you are about to enter a certain part of a site, download something from a site, or engage in other online activity that forces you to click a button saying "I agree" or something similar before proceeding. The license governs the use of the site, software, or other applicable online activity. A browse-wrap license is also a license governing the use of a Web site or materials on it, but instead of forcing you to click to accept the license, the license simply states, "By using this Web site, you hereby agree to the terms of this license."

Can that be right? Can you be held bound to terms of a license that you never "agreed" to in any way? Yes, depending on the circumstances. Settled contract law states that a contract does not require signatures to be binding; it does, however, require some act designating the parties' assent to the terms of the contract. If you had read the browse-wrap license before browsing, you would most likely be held bound to the terms of that license. But what if you never even saw the license before browsing? Several recent cases have dealt with this issue. The bottom line seems to be that if it is clear to one viewing the site at issue that a license exists, that person can be bound to the terms of the license. This is true even if the user did not actually read the license; lack of reading the terms of a contract in itself is never a defense to being bound by the terms of the contract (which is why you should always read what you sign—before signing!). However, if it is possible for a user to browse a site without even noticing that a license exists, the license will probably not be held binding.

What does this mean for libraries?

In all likelihood, there is not much threat for libraries, for several reasons. Libraries may choose to designate themselves as protected Online Service Providers under Section 512 of the Copyright Act, as discussed in Chapter 13. Even without such protection, it is unlikely, though not impossible, that a library would be the target of such a suit. The bottom line, however, is that there is very little libraries can do until the issue of browsing is further decided, either by the courts or by Congress. Libraries can, however, limit the caching they do to the very minimum necessary (as is required to qualify for Section 512 protection, anyway).

> **One more reason why librarians must become activists**
>
> Caching clearly creates copies of works that may reside on a computer indefinitely. Most users are completely unaware of what resides in their cache at any given moment in time. One can be held liable for copyright infringement without knowing that one's actions have infringed. In an atmosphere in which frightened copyright owners will try any argument that they have the slightest hope may win over a court, this yet unsettled area of law may present a great risk to entities providing significant Internet access.

Notes

1. A great example of this is the infamous holding in *MAI v. Peak Computers*, mentioned above, that a copy in RAM can infringe copyright. Although this arguably was reasonable in that particular case, carried to the extreme, it is not only ridiculous, but also simply disastrous. However, in this kind of situation, in which the area of law is so new that it is almost nonexistent, it is often difficult, if not impossible, for a judge to specify limitations on his holding. When considering judicial opinions in which the holding seems outrageous, it is important to keep in mind the greater context of the situation.

Bibliography

Copyright Act of 1976, U.S. Code vol. 17, secs. 101 and 109 (1999).

Futuredontics v. AAI, 1998 U.S. Dist. LEXIS 2265 (C.D. Cal. 1998).

Hammer v. Trendl, 2002 WL 32059751 (E.D.N.Y. 2002).

MAI Syst. Corp. v. Peak Computer, Inc., 991 F.2d 511 (9th Cir. 1993).

Nimmer, Raymond T. 1996. *Information Law*. St. Paul: West.

The Washington Post Co. v. Total News, Inc., No. 97 Civ. 1190 (S.D.N.Y. filed Feb. 20, 1997).

8

Using digital images

- If I can't tell from looking at an image on the Web whether or not it's copyrighted, how do I know whether I can download it to use for my own purposes?
- Can I make digital copies of items my library owns for our Web pages? Isn't there something about being able to make digital copies for preservation purposes?
- If I have permission to use an image on a Web page, can I "doctor it up" a little to make it more suitable for my purposes or to improve on it?

All of these questions address some of the ways in which librarians may be most likely to get themselves into trouble as they create Web pages for their libraries. As we go through each issue, keep in mind two bottom-line, basic rules:

1. Because a copyright owner is not required to display the copyright symbol on his work in order to protect it, you cannot know by looking at an item that it is not copyrighted just because it does not have the © on it.
2. Legally owning a copy of a copyrighted work (like each book your library buys) does not give you, as the owner of that copy, the right to do whatever you want with that item. Most importantly, it does not give you, as the owner, the right to make copies of the item, even for personal use.

How do I know when I can legally download or copy an image from the Web?

The lack of a requirement to identify copyrighted works as such translates to this in the cyberworld: You cannot tell by looking at a work whether or not it is copyrighted. If it has a © attached to the work (or if there is a copyright statement, such as "copyright 1999 Joe Smith"), most likely it is protected by copyright. On the other hand, the more commonly occurring lack of such a symbol or statement does not—repeat: *does not*—mean that the work is not protected.

When does this create problems for librarians using the Web? Perhaps because they are often overworked and underfunded, librarians work hard to be efficient. An oft-heard phrase is "don't reinvent the wheel." This means that if someone else has already done what you want to do, or taken steps toward it, it is wise to borrow their ideas or even actual works, or build on the foundation someone else has laid. As an instruction librarian, I constantly turned to my colleagues for examples of what they had done in certain situations, and we frequently shared instructional material with each other. Now the Web makes that so much easier. Many library instruction programs are creating digital resources and providing them on the Web, making them easy for patrons to access at any time, from any place. When she begins a new project and wants to see what others have done, all an instruction librarian has to do is surf the Web to see what kinds of materials others have created to teach users how to search a certain database or how to conduct research in a certain subject area.

All of this is great, but what happens when we find pages we like containing materials others have created that we'd like to use? What if it's not just a colleague's Web page, but cute graphics from a totally unrelated page that would make your page so much more attractive to users? Aren't a lot of those graphics that we see repeatedly on the Web clip art anyway, free for anyone to use?

As we know, the copyright owner has the sole right to make copies of his work. Only when another person's use meets the fair use exception can he legally copy that work without permission. Thus, fair use aside, copying a protected image from a Web page infringes the copyright in that image. Even before anything is done with it. Is copying an image to use on a nonprofit, possibly educational Web page, allowed under the fair use doctrine? The short answer is: Maybe, but remember that fair use offers no guarantees, despite many misconceptions that any nonprofit or educational use is OK. For a more detailed explanation, see Chapter 3, which is devoted to the fair use doctrine. In some situations, your use might be acceptable. In many, it will not. In addition, fair use is a defense, meaning that it is your response to an accusation of infringement, not a means of preventing the accusation in the first place. So before you copy that image, think through the fair use analysis. If you are not confident that the use will be considered fair (and most of these types of uses will not be), either ask for permission or use another image.

What about clip art? Many, many Web sites provide free clip art to Web users. Clip art may be images, animations, and/or sounds. Some Web sites charge for clip art. Some sites may impose limitations on use, such as for noncommercial use only, or require the user to credit the site. "But," you ask, "how are these sites different from any other? How can I know that the

Q Can I use an image I find on the Web for purposes such as putting it on our library Web site or including on printed handouts?

A Keep in mind that you may not be able to tell just by looking at something whether it is protected by copyright. Just because it does not have a copyright notice does not mean it is not protected. It is unlikely that these types of uses would be considered fair uses, given the nature of the copyrighted work (non-factual and totally creative); the fact that you have taken the entire image; and the effect on the potential market for the work (the copyright owner's ability to license use of the work would be considered under this factor). This is true despite the fact that your use would be for nonprofit educational purposes. Many clip art sites and products are available. It is safer to use these products that to just browse the Web and copy and paste whatever you find and like. That being said, consider critically the clip art sites or sources that you are using. Although you cannot know for certain that the proprietor of a clip art site has the authority to offer the images on his site, consider how likely you think that is. Are you looking at a site of twelve-year-old Joe's Favorite Pictures, or are you looking at a site that appears to be professionally done, that has terms and conditions of use, and that provides some sort of copyright statement? For example, if the site contains a copyright statement followed by a statement saying that the images are free for noncommercial uses, you have reason to believe that the copyright owner is giving you permission for the use.

clip art itself is not copyrighted?" I'm sure you can foresee my answer: You can't. The wise Web-page designer will look for a copyright statement on the site at which the clip art he wants to use is located. Many have statements along the line of, "As far as we know, our site contains only works in the public domain and does not contain any copyrighted works." Of course, this is no guarantee, but it's as close as you can get. The options for obtaining clip art are numerous. Take the time to find a site that at least seems to have made an effort to exclude infringing materials. Once again, this is no guarantee, but nothing in life is. Under no circumstances should you use clip art from "Johnny's Favorite Junk" page, on which Johnny tells you that he's twelve years old, in the sixth grade, and loves *Star Wars* and Britney Spears . . . and then provides you with pictures from the movie and of Britney in concert!

When I do legally download an image, am I limited in what I can do with it?

Let's briefly revisit the various rights of copyright owners and discuss what the implications would be for using a legally acquired image on your Web site. We are assuming that you have the right to copy the work from another source, whether a Web page or otherwise.

The public performance and display rights

A copyright owner has the exclusive right to publicly display any literary, musical, dramatic, pictorial, graphic, or sculptural works; (*Copyright Act of 1976, U.S. Code* vol. 17, sec. 106(5) (1999)) and to perform publicly any literary, musical, dramatic works, motion pictures and other audiovisual works. (ibid., sec. 106(4)) In addition, the copyright owner of a sound recording has the exclusive right to perform the work via digital audio transmission. (ibid., sec. 106(6))

So, does putting a work on the Web constitute public performance or display?

Performance

By now, you're catching on that pretty much everything is defined in the Copyright Act, no matter how obvious the meaning of the word may be to most English speakers. "To perform" a work is defined as "to recite, render, play, dance, or act it, either directly or by means of any device or process." (ibid., sec. 101) Depending on the format of the work at issue, the performance right might be implicated. If the image you've copied is an animated John Travolta dancing to "Stayin' Alive" (or, even more clearly, a movie clip of the disco king), then to show the image is to perform it.[1] Arguably, "render" might cover any type of image, whether or not sound or animation is involved.[2]

Display

The Copyright Act defines "displaying" a work as "to show a copy of it, either directly or by means of . . . any other device or process." (ibid.) Pretty clearly, then, to place a copy of an image on your Web page is to display that image.

The public

The trick comes in the qualifier: to *publicly* perform or display. The Copyright Act defines to perform or display a work publicly as

(1) to perform or display it at a place open to the public or in any place where a substantial number of persons outside of a normal circle of a family and its social acquaintances is gathered; or

(2) to transmit or otherwise communicate a performance or display of the work to a place specified by clause (1) or to the public . . . whether the members of the public . . . receive it in the same place or in separate places and at the same time or at different times. (ibid.)

Certainly, a library is a place where "a substantial number of persons outside of a normal circle" of family and friends gather, and most libraries are open to the public. Thus, transmitting a display or performance to a library would seem to meet the definition of a public display or performance.

But what about users who access your library's Web pages from home, work, a computer lab, or anywhere outside of the library? Is this a public performance or display? If the place in which the user accesses the pages is open to the public, or is a place where a substantial number of people gather, probably so. But what about accessing the Web at home? The definition says that it doesn't matter whether people receive the performance or display at the same place and time as others. But what if none of the places are "public" places? Could one argue that "place" means virtual place as well as physical? The House Report on the Copyright Act states that subscribers to cable TV would meet the definition of receiving a performance in a public place. Internet users would seem closely analogous to this example. One federal district court has held that a party who posted infringing copies of *Playboy* photographs on a Web page that was accessible only by paying subscribers violated the copyright owner's right of public display because, "[t]hough limited to subscribers, the audience consisted of 'a substantial number of persons outside of a normal circle of family and its social acquaintances (sic)." (*Playboy Enter., Inc. v. Frena*, 839 F. Supp. 1552: 1557 (M.D. Fla. 1993)) Under this reasoning, even if a library limits access to its pages—such as limiting access to currently enrolled students—placing the image in question on a library Web page would constitute public display or performance.

Exceptions

The Technology, Education, and Copyright Harmonization Act of 2002 (the "TEACH Act") attempts to address the needs of distance education programs and allows, by or in the course of a transmission, the performance of a non-dramatic literary or musical work; or the performance of "reasonable and limited portions" of any work; or the display of a work "in an amount comparable to that which is typically displayed in the course of a live classroom session," under certain restrictions.

First, the performance or display (a) must be made by, at the direction of, or under the actual supervision of, an instructor (b) as an integral part of a class session (c) offered as a regular part of the systematic mediated instructional activities of a governmental body or an accredited nonprofit institution; and it must be directly related to and of material assistance to the teaching content.

"Mediated instructional activities" are defined as activities that use a work as an integral part of a classroom experience controlled or supervised by the instructor and "analogous to the type of performance or display that would take place in a live classroom setting." It specifically does not refer to activities using copies that are typically purchased by students for their own independent use. In other words, the TEACH Act is limited to materials that an instructor herself would typically incorporate into a live lecture and does not cover supplementary materials that an instructor would require her students to read or study on their own time. Of course, these materials may be used by the students during the transmission, but the instructor may not display these materials during the transmission. This was one of the provisions agreed upon during negotiation of the Act (discussed below), in response to publisher's fears that allowing the display of such materials to be transmitted to all students taking the course would negate the students' need to purchase individual copies of the materials (which they would have done in a "traditional" classroom setting).

Second, the transmission of the performance or display must be made for the sole purpose of, and must be technologically restricted to the extent feasible to, students officially enrolled in the course or officers or employees of governmental bodies enrolled in the course as a part of their official duties or employment.

In addition, the institution making the transmission must take various proactive steps discussed further in Chapter 16 in order to be able to rely on the TEACH Act exemptions.

The distribution right

Finally, the copyright owner has the exclusive right to distribute copies of his work to the public. (ibid., sec. 106(3)) Whether placing a work on the Web constitutes public distribution is somewhat controversial. To begin with, is placing a work on the Web, where others can come to your site to view or use it, distribution? Is that work a "copy" in the first place?

"Copy" is defined in the statute as a "material object . . . in which a work

Q Does an author give up his copyright in or ability to claim con trol over a work by posting it on the Web? In other words, once he posts his work on the Web, doesn't every Web user have an implied license to use that work?

A Absolutely not! This is perhaps the greatest and most dangerous misconception about copyright in cyberspace. A copyright owner has exclusive rights in and to his work until 70 years after his death, subject to the exemptions and defenses in the Copyright Act, such as Section 108 photocopying and fair use. Making a work freely and openly available on the Web does not change this; the fact that potentially every person on the face of the planet may access his work does not in any way imply that the author has given up his rights or that all six billion of us may do whatever we wish with that work. In a nutshell: The same rules apply to every protected work, regardless of the format or the location.

is fixed by any method now know or later developed, and from which the work can be perceived, reproduced, or otherwise communicated." (ibid., sec. 101) Copies existing on servers, hard drives, CD-ROMs, floppy disks, or other tools of long-term storage rather clearly meet this definition.

So does placing a "copy" of an image on your Web page constitute a distribution to others? Compare it to sending out an e-mail. In the latter situation, you are actively distributing something. Once you create a Web page, you sit and wait for others to come to it. When they do, it is their acts of viewing the page, including any downloading or copying they might do, that create copies of the images on that page; your role at this point is quite passive. The statute says that the author has the exclusive right to distribute "by sale or other transfer of ownership, or by rental, lease or lending." Strong arguments have been made that when end-users view your site, they themselves may make copies in order to view your site, but that no "transfer of ownership" takes place, since the item you placed on your page is still there. True, the end-user may get a "copy" meeting the statutory definition, but that is *in addition to* the copy you still possess, not a *transfer of* that copy. A good analogy is making photocopies. Electrons are transferred from the original source to a blank piece of paper, which, by storing the electrons, creates a new copy. However, very few people would argue that this is a violation of the distribution right (though it could violate the reproduction right).

So, if I have the right to copy an image from another Web page, or from a print publication, do I also have the right to put it on my page?

Technically, putting an image on a Web page may very well violate the rights of public performance and display. Distribution is more questionable. Realistically, if you have been given the right to copy an image from a Web page, the owner of that image probably assumes that you are likely to use it on another Web page. This is less true when you copy something from a printed work, or from a film or audio recording. Nonetheless, assumptions are not a good thing on which to base decisions that might have serious legal implications. If you are unsure, ask. When you ask for permission directly from the copyright owner, tell him what you plan to do with the work. If a statement of permission is provided with the work, look at it closely to see what exactly it is giving permission for. If it is only to copy, contact the copyright owner and ask specifically for permission to put the work on your Web page.

OK, then, once I have the right to copy an image and to put it on my Web page, can I do whatever I want with it, like make very minor changes to make it more appropriate for my pages?

Say you come upon a page with a statement giving permission to anyone to copy the page or parts of it for her own use on her own Web pages, as long as it's not commercial and appropriate credit is given (this is not uncommon to see on educational pages). The image you really like is a little girl looking intently at a TV, but you need to replace the TV with a book. A couple of clicks and drags in Adobe Photoshop or some other digital design program, and you're done!

Let's pause a moment, though, to consider the legal implications of this action. A copyright owner owns the exclusive right to prepare derivative works. A derivative work is "a work based upon one or more preexisting works," including "a work consisting of editorial revisions, annotations, elaborations, or other modifications which, as a whole, represent an original work of authorship." (ibid.) As discussed in Chapter 2, the standard to be met to be an "original work" is rather low. One court has even held that cutting pictures out of an art book and pasting them on tiles creates a derivative work of those pictures. (*Mirage Editions., Inc. v. Albuquerque A.R.T.*, 856 F.2d 1341 (9th Cir. 1988)) Although many commentators view this as too extreme, it is a good demonstration of how little "tweaking" it takes to create a derivative work.

In our situation, then, did replacing the TV with a book constitute creation of a derivative work? Yup, almost certainly. Was this illegal, assuming you didn't have the author's permission? Yup, almost certainly; any fair use argument would be murky, at the least. "There's this adorable dancing bear, but I can't stand the music he's dancing to. Can I change it?" Without permission of the copyright owner, probably not. "What about the cute-but-innocent cartoons of a naked Adam and Eve? Can I put clothes on them, so I can use them on a page for my children's program?" Sorry. Not without permission.

Can't I make use of *anything* I find on the Web without getting in trouble?!

It is very important to keep in mind that what you "can't" do assumes that you don't have the author's permission (and that your use is not allowed under fair use or an exemption). If you find a page that gives a permission statement, read it carefully to see if it allows you to do what you want to do—copy, post on your Web page, alter in any way. Most importantly, keep in mind that you can always attempt to contact the author and get her permission to do whatever it is you want to do with the work. Just remember to get permission for exactly what you want to do, not just permission to generally "use" or to copy the work. Get permission the old-fashioned way, in print (e-mail is probably sufficient). See the discussion in Source I, about seeking permissions, for additional important information about how to get an author's permission and for some caveats and warnings to keep in mind in dealing with the cyberworld.

What about making digital copies of printed works in my collection to then put up on my page? Isn't there some sort of exception for making copies for the purpose of preservation?

An exception from infringement exists for digital copies made from print resources for the purpose of preserving or archiving the work. However, this is a very limited exception; depending on the nature of the work being digitized, various conditions must be met.

If the original work to be copied is an *unpublished* work, the copy being digitized must currently be in the library's collection, *and* the digital copy must *not* be distributed in its digital format nor made available to the public outside the premises of the library. (ibid., sec. 108(b)) If the digital copy is being made in order to replace a *published* work that has been lost, damaged, or stolen, or that is deteriorating, the library must first make a "reasonable effort" to determine that an unused replacement cannot be obtained at a fair market price, *and* the digital reproduction must *not* be made available to the public outside the premises of the library. (ibid., sec. 108(c))

We previously discussed the thorny issue of whether placing something

> **One more reason why librarians must become activists**
>
> Section 108 of the Copyright Act allows access to digitized copies of works in a library's collection only within the library. It would seem more appropriate, and still within keeping of the spirit of the law, to allow outside access so long as it is restricted to registered library users. Congress is not going to make such a change on its own!

on the Web constitutes public display or distribution. However, Section 108 more simply disallows making a digitized copy available to the public. Thus, a library should be able to place a digitized copy of a printed work within its collection, whether published or unpublished, on its own Web page that is available only within the library, but it would not be able to place the image on a page accessible outside of the library building. Unfortunately, the statute specifically states that such copies must not be "made available . . . outside the premises of the library." In the context of current technology, it would seem more in keeping with the spirit of the law to allow outside access to registered library users; however, the current law specifically says otherwise. It is also important to keep in mind that these exceptions apply to copies made for preservation and replacement purposes only, not for purposes of providing easier access to or creating copies accessible to multiple patrons at one time—in other words, not simply for the sake of convenience.

What does this mean?

As always, proceed with caution. Know the rules, be aware of your actions, and use common sense. Use your research skills to try to find the information you need and act accordingly: Is it protected by copyright? Does my use fall within fair use or one of the exemptions? Who owns the copyright? What can I do with it? Perhaps it will help to keep in mind that many of the same actions that should keep you out of trouble with the copyright police are also a matter of courtesy. Even if it's not illegal, would you want someone using your property without asking first? Once you told someone it's OK to use your things, would you want them making changes to it without asking first? Think about what you're doing, be careful, and keep written records.

Notes

1. To be specific, remember that an audio recording has two different types of rights: the right in the musical work, that is, the right of the writer of the musical piece

(in this case, Barry, Maurice, and Robin Gibb); and the right in the sound recording itself (in this case, RSO Records). This means that there are potentially two or more different copyright owners in a musical recording. The performance right applies only to the musical work (owned by the Bee Gees). However, the copyright owner in the sound recording (RSO Records) has the exclusive right "to perform the copyrighted work publicly *by means of a digital audio transmission.*" (§ 106(6) (emphasis added)). Why the limited right? Short answer: Politics are behind almost every act of Congress! Regardless, in many cases, this would include transmission of recordings via the Internet. Thus, for our purposes, performance of a recorded piece of music on the Internet would implicate rights in both the underlying musical work and the specific sound recording of the work.

2. "Render" is not defined in the Copyright Act. However, *Webster's II New College Dictionary* defines "render" as "to give or make available." (Webster's II New College Dictionary. Merriam-Webster, Inc., 2001. p. 938.)

Bibliography

Copyright Act of 1976, U.S. Code, vol. 17, secs. 101, 106, 108(b), 108(c), 110(2) (1999).

Mirage Editions, Inc. v. Albuquerque A.R.T., 856 F.2d 1341 (9th Cir. 1988).

Playboy Enter., Inc. v. Frena, 839 F. Supp. 1552 (M.D. Fla. 1993).

9

The dark side of the DMCA

What is the Digital Millennium Copyright Act?

The Digital Millennium Copyright Act of 1998 (DMCA) amended several parts of the Copyright Act. The major changes, however, were the addition of Section 512, addressing limited liability for Internet service providers; Section 1201, prohibiting the circumvention of technological measures controlling access to or copying of works in electronic formats; and Section 1202, protecting copyright management technology. Section 512 is discussed in some detail in Chapter 11. Although cumbersome, Section 512 potentially offers some benefits to libraries and has not been very controversial.

Section 1201, on the other hand, has been extremely controversial in all arenas, not just libraries. Section 1201 was passed in part to meet the requirements of the World Intellectual Property Organization (WIPO) Copyright Treaty of 1996. The WIPO treaty requires signatories to

> provide adequate legal protection and effective legal remedies against the circumvention of effective technological measures that are used by authors in connection with the exercise of their rights…and that restrict acts, in respect of their works, which are not authorized by the authors concerned or permitted by law. (World Intellectual Property Organization. WIPO Treaty, Art. 11. 1996.)

Section 1201, however, goes well beyond the WIPO requirements, indicating that it was also a response to lobbying efforts of copyright owners. Section 1201 prohibits two things: acts of circumvention and trafficking in anti-circumvention tools. Section 1201(a)(1) states, in part, that "No person shall circumvent a technological measure that effectively controls access to a work protected under this title" 17 U.S.C. 1201(a)(1)(A) Section 1201(a)(2) asserts:

> No person shall manufacture, import, offer to the public, provide, or otherwise traffic in any technology, product, service, device, component, or part thereof, that (A) is primarily designed or produced for the

purpose of circumventing a technological measure that effectively controls access to a work protected under this title; (B) has only limited commercially significant purpose or use other than to circumvent a technological measure that effectively controls access to a work protected under this title; or (C) is marketed by that person or another acting in concert with that person with that person's knowledge for use in circumventing a technological measure that effectively controls access to a work protected under this title. (17 U.S.C. 1201(a)(2))

Section 1201(b) delineates the same prohibitions as 1201(a)(2), except in regard to technological measures "that effectively protect a right of a copyright owner under this title in a work or a portion thereof," rather than controlling access to a work.

What exactly do the anti-circumvention provisions of the DMCA do?

Note that both 1201(a)(1) and 1201(a)(2) protect measures that control *access to* works—not copying, not distribution, not creating derivative works, not publicly performing or displaying a work. Let's step back for a moment and review the exclusive rights of a copyright owner: the rights to reproduce, distribute copies of, create derivatives of, and publicly perform or display her work. Nowhere did the pre-DMCA Copyright Act address the right of a copyright owner to in any way control access to her work. Does Section 1201 create a new exclusive right for copyright owners of digital or electronic works? Arguably, yes. Especially given the additional Section 1201(b) addressing the already existing exclusive rights of a copyright owner. A wide range of commentators would say so—those supporting information users and consumers, that is. So the first thing the DMCA does, in the opinion of many respected copyright experts, is create a new exclusive right.

Section 1201(a)(2) prohibits the manufacturing of or trafficking by any means in any type of device with the primary function of circumventing protective technology. This section serves almost as a backup to ensure that copyright protection technology is not circumvented: In case you decide that you don't mind risking a violation of the provision against circumventing such technology, this provision ensures that you won't have the tools necessary to do so.

Haven't I heard something about the DMCA creating privacy issues?

The DMCA includes enforcement provisions that allow a copyright owner to obtain and serve a subpoena on an Internet service provider for the purpose of obtaining the identity of a user that the copyright owner believes to be infringing her rights. The request for a subpoena must include, among other things, declarations that the copyright owner has a good-faith belief that his work has been infringed; that the purpose for which the subpoena is sought is to obtain the identity of an alleged infringer; and that such information will only be used for the purpose of protecting the copyright owner's rights under the DMCA. If these strictly procedural requirements are met, the subpoena is issued automatically; no one has to review, analyze, or judge the request. (17 U.S.C. 512(h)) The subpoena provision has been criticized by many, including ALA, as violating privacy rights.

In June 2002, the Recording Industry Association of America (RIAA) used Section 512(h) to file a subpoena on the ISP Verizon, seeking the identity of a Verizon user whom the RIAA alleged had infringed copyrights in more than six hundred songs that the user downloaded in one day. Verizon refused to comply with the subpoena, arguing that Section 512(h) did not apply to an ISP that acted only as a conduit for information and that did not store infringing information on its computers. Although the district court held in favor of the RIAA and ordered Verizon to comply with the subpoena, the Court of Appeals for the District of Columbia sided with Verizon and overturned the order. (*Recording Industry Association of America v. Verizon Internet Services, Inc.*, 351 F.3d 1229 (D.C. 2003))

During the appeal, an amicus brief was filed by multiple parties, including ALA, ARL, the American Association of Law Libraries, the Digital Future Coalition, and the Electronic Frontier Foundation. "At stake in this litigation," declared the brief, "is whether fundamental First Amendment anonymity and privacy rights can be trampled." Specifically, the brief complained that Section 512(h) allowed issuing a subpoena—thereby obtaining a range of information about the targeted individual—with no judicial oversight and even without notifying the individual named in the subpoena.

In a nutshell, the privacy concerns are that Section 512(h) provides such an easy process for a copyright owner to obtain a subpoena, with absolutely no review of the request beforehand, that it could end up being used as a tool for copyright owners to threaten members of the public and ultimately control their right to free speech. In other words, the provision could be used to discourage people from engaging in anonymous speech or "political" speech, which is not only a cornerstone of democracy, but also clearly protected by the First Amendment.

What does all of this mean for libraries?

For starters, Section 1201 places the ability to control not only use of a work, but also access to it, squarely within the hands of the copyright owner. That means squarely beyond the various limitations on a copyright owner's rights as specified in the Copyright Act as it stood prior to the DMCA.

What if your library needs to make an archival copy of a digital work whose technological protection prevents copying under the provisions of Section 108? Too bad, because you aren't allowed to circumvent the technology protecting the work, and the tools necessary to do so aren't available anyway.

What if your library wants to lend or sell, under the first sale doctrine, a lawfully owned copy of a digital work whose technological protection prevents it from being accessed on any computer other than the one in which it is originally installed? Too bad, because you aren't allowed to circumvent the technology protecting the work, and the tools necessary to do so aren't available anyway.

What if your library wants to use a digital work during distance education sessions, abiding by the provisions of the TEACH Act, whose technological protection prevents such use? Too bad, because you aren't allowed to circumvent the technology protecting the work, and the tools necessary to do so aren't available anyway.

What if your library wants to make any one of a number of fair uses of a work whose technological protection prevents such use? Too bad, because you aren't allowed to circumvent the technology protecting the work, and the tools necessary to do so aren't available anyway.

Another potential but direct effect on libraries is being targeted by the RIAA. Most likely, it would be your institution, not the library itself, but the library could be the site of the allegedly infringing actions. In its battle against file-sharing, the RIAA has moved its focus from large corporations to individuals. In doing so, it has taken advantage of the subpoena provision of Section 512, using it to obtain the names of individual file-sharers. In 2003, the RIAA obtained subpoenas directed at MIT and Boston College. Although a court ruled that the schools did not have to comply with the subpoenas, it did so purely on procedural grounds. This type of situation is as much about privacy rights as copyright but is obviously a concern for libraries under either rubric.

How can this be?! Why haven't these provisions been struck down?

Frighteningly enough, the anti-circumvention provisions have been before various courts and have so far been upheld, even against arguments that they violate the fair use provision of the Copyright Act. The anti-circumvention provisions have been heavily criticized by a range of experts and commentators, not only for their copyright implications, but also for their potential effects on First Amendment rights, scientific research, and competition in the technology industries, all of which concern libraries. In their first five years of life, the anti-circumvention provisions have formed the basis for many lawsuits against defendants other than pirates, the presumed target of the provisions. I will hit some of the highlights for you here, many of which you may have read about already.

One of the cases that garnered the most attention was that of poor Dimitry Sklyarov, a twenty-something Russian Ph.D. candidate. (*United States v. Elcomsoft*, 203 F. Supp. 2d 1111 (N.D. Ca. 2002)) Sklyarov, as an employee of a Russian company called ElcomSoft Co. Ltd., had contributed to the writing of a software program entitled Advanced eBook Processor. This software permitted owners of electronic books existing in Adobe eBook files to translate from Adobe's secure eBook format into PDF format, thereby making the books more portable. The software only worked on legitimately purchased e-books. In other words, e-books were not licensed: An individual copy of an e-book was sold to a buyer, just like a paper copy of a book.

Sklyarov was arrested at the behest of Adobe, owner of the eBooks software, when he came to Las Vegas to speak at a DEFCON convention about the software he helped author. He was kept in jail for several weeks and detained in the U.S. for five months. Sklyarov was not accused of infringing any of the exclusive rights of a copyright owner, such as reproducing copies of the e-books, but only of removing the technological controls embedded in the original eBook files, thereby violating Section 1201(a)(1). Eventually, due in large part to public outcry, the Department of Justice released Sklyarov and proceeded to prosecute his Russian employer. Eighteen months after Sklyarov was first arrested, a jury acquitted ElcomSoft of all charges. (ibid.)

A line of cases has involved the application of the anti-circumvention provisions to software created to descramble protections for DVDs. Since the mid–1990s, most DVDs have been protected with software called Content Scrambling Systems (CSS), which encrypts the content of the DVD so that it can be read only by devices with authorized "keys" to unlock that content. The DVD Copy Control Association, a trade group affiliated with the major motion picture studios, licenses the keys to DVD-player manufacturers. Thus, when an encrypted DVD is run on a player, the key residing in the player allows the DVD to perform but prevents copying of the DVD.

In 1999, a Norwegian teenager used reverse engineering to create a software program called DeCSS and began distributing it over the Internet. Loaded on a computer, DeCSS allowed encrypted DVDs to play on that computer; otherwise, they would not be playable, because the computer would not have contained the keys, controlled by the DVD Copy Control Association.

In 2000, eight major U.S. studios sued three Web site operators for posting the DeCSS program on their sites, alleging violation of the anti-circumvention provisions of Section 1201. The court for the Southern District of New York held the software to violate the prohibition on trafficking in anti-circumvention technologies, rejecting defendants' arguments that, among other things, the distribution of DeCSS should be allowed under fair use. (*Universal City Studios, Inc. v. Reimerdes*, 2000 U.S. Dist. LEXIS 554 (S.D.N.Y. 2000))

On appeal, the sole remaining defendant argued that the anti-circumvention provisions were unconstitutional in that they constitute an undue restriction on fair use and thereby violate both the First Amendment and the Copyright Clause. The Second Circuit noted that the Supreme Court has never held fair use to be a constitutional requirement but declined to consider the matter for three reasons: (1) The defendants never claimed to be making a fair use of copyrighted material; (2) the record contained insufficient evidence to determine the impact of the DMCA on those desiring to make fair use of copyrighted material contained on DVDs; and (3) the defendants had failed to provide authority for their argument that the fair use doctrine requires users to be able to make copies of works in an identical format. The court also pointed out that many traditional fair uses are not affected by the DMCA. Finally, the court pointed out that users could copy the content of a DVD by using "a camera, a camcorder, or a microphone" to record the movie, stating that fair use "has never been held to be a guarantee of access" to a work via the "preferred technique or in the format of the original." (*Universal City Studios, Inc. v. Corley*, 273 F.3d 429 (2d Cir. 2001)) Note that one possible reason for the lack of such a holding is that, prior to the DMCA, access was never a right granted by copyright law, and so fair use as applied to an access right would never have been an issue.

A California district court applied the Second Circuit's reasoning in a similar case involving software that actually allowed copying of protected DVDs, marketed as allowing users to make back-up copies of their own lawfully purchased DVDs: "It is the technology itself at issue, not the uses to which

> ### One more reason why librarians must become activists
>
> "We protect each library user's right to privacy and confidentiality with respect to information sought or received and resources consulted, borrowed, acquired or transmitted." — ALA Code of Ethics
>
> A copyright owner or a person authorized to act on the owner's behalf may request the clerk of any United States district court to issue a subpoena to a service provider for identification of an alleged infringer in accordance with this subsection . . . . [T]he clerk shall expeditiously issue and sign the proposed subpoena and return it to the requester for delivery to the service provider . . . . Upon receipt of the issued subpoena, . . . the service provider shall expeditiously disclose to the copyright owner or person authorized by the copyright owner the information required by the subpoena, notwithstanding any other provision of law . . . . — Digital Millennium Copyright Act of 1998

the copyrighted material may be put. Legal downstream use of the copyrighted material by customers is not a defense to the software manufacturer's violation of the provisions [of Section 1201]." (*321 Studios v. MGM Studios, Inc.*, 307 F. Supp. 2d 1085 (N.D. Cal. 2004))

Ironically, two months before the *321 Studios* decision was issued, a Norwegian court found the original author of DeCSS not guilty for violation of criminal copyright law.

What do we do?!

Get involved in the lawmaking process. Chapter 19 provides guidance on how to go about doing this, but the important thing is to do *something*! Librarians are on the front lines of these issues; no one knows better than librarians how the DMCA may affect fair use rights. That makes it the responsibility of librarians to educate our legislators about how the DMCA may affect fair use rights (among other issues) and to pressure legislators to do something about it. Remember the wise words of one of the greatest leaders of change in world history, Mahatma Ghandi: "You must be the change you wish to see in the world."

Bibliography

Electronic Frontier Foundation. "Unintended Consequences: Five Years under the DMCA." 2003. p. 4. Available: *www.eff.org/IP/DMCA/20030103_dmca_consequences.pdf.*

Pruitt, Scarlet. "Two Universities Win Battle Against RIAA Subpoenas," Network WorldFusion. August 11, 2003. Available: *www.nwfusion.com/news/2003/ 0811twounive.html*.

Recording Industry Association of America v. Verizon Internet Services, Inc., 351 F.3d 1229 (D.C. 2003).

321 Studios v. MGM Studios, Inc., 307 F. Supp. 2d 1085 (N.D. Cal. 2004).

United States v. Elcomsoft, 203 F. Supp. 2d 1111 (N.D. Ca. 2002).

Universal City Studios, Inc. v. Corley, 273 F.3d 429 (2d Cir. 2001).

Universal City Studios, Inc. v. Reimerdes, 2000 U.S. Dist. LEXIS 554 (S.D.N.Y. 2000).

10

File-sharing

What exactly is file-sharing?

File-sharing, also called file-swapping, has received a lot of media attention in recent years. In a nutshell, file-sharing allows computer users at different locations, and even completely unknown to each other, to trade digital files over the Internet. However, people do tend to become confused in attempting to understand the technology. There are actually two basic different types of technology used in file-sharing, and, as we will soon see, the distinction between the technologies is very important in the copyright analysis.

One type of technology provides downloadable software that users install on their computers and use to connect to a peer-to-peer (P2P) network. The software provider maintains a server that provides searchable indexing of files residing on users' computers. Thus, users may access the server, use it to search for and locate files in which they are interested that reside on other users' computers, and then obtain those files from the other users. The second type of technology operates similarly to the first, with the primary and most significant difference being that no central server is used to index or otherwise assist users in locating desired files.

What's wrong with it, and who's upset by it?

Nothing is inherently wrong with file-sharing. It has gotten a bad rap because of its application. To date, this technology has been used primarily to copy and exchange digital files of songs and movies without authorization from copyright owners. The terms "file-sharing" and "file-swapping" are actually somewhat misleading; what happens is not the "sharing" of one file between multiple individuals or the "swapping or exchanging" of the same file between individuals, but the copying of one file, usually by numerous users, thereby creating multiple copies of what was originally one work, and distribution of multiple copies. The file-sharing technologies currently available allow a user to easily and quickly identify existing digital copies of protected works residing on the computers of other individuals, copy those files, and retrieve a copy for himself.

It is easy to see, then, that copyright owners are the ones who are upset by file-sharing practices. In particular, it is the corporate owners of huge repertoires of copyrighted works who seem to be the most upset—or at least who are putting the most resources into taking very aggressive action against individuals engaged in file-sharing. The Recording Industry Association of America (RIAA) has taken on this role with great zest. To date, the RIAA has filed legal actions based on copyright infringement against three file-sharing networks, more than 2000 individuals, and some universities (since a large number of those engaged in file-sharing are college students).

Who are Aimster and Grokster, and are they any relation to Napster?

I think it's safe to say that most Americans have by now heard of Napster. Napster was the original P2P file-sharing network and therefore the first to be sued.

The Napster software, downloadable free of charge from Napster's Web site, allowed users to: make MP3 files stored on individual computers available for copying by other Napster users; search for MP3 files stored on other users' computers; and transfer copies of the contents of other users' MP3 files from one computer to the other via the Internet.

The Napster software also provided for the indexing and searching of MP3 files. The free software, once installed on a user's computer, allowed the user to access the Napster system. Upon registering with Napster, a user was given the option of making available to other Napster users the files stored on his computer hard drive through a process that ultimately uploaded copies of the user's files to the Napster servers. Users could search for and retrieve files in two different ways. The first was by searching the files stored on the Napster server and retrieving copies therefrom. The second was to essentially search the directory of files of other users currently logged on at the same time, identify a desired file, and create a copy directly from the other user's computer.

The RIAA sued Napster for copyright infringement, alleging that Napster engaged in "wholesale reproduction and distribution of copyrighted works." The court held that Napster had infringed the plaintiff's distribution rights when Napster users uploaded file names to Napster's search index for others to copy, and the plaintiff's reproduction rights when Napster users downloaded files of copyrighted music. The court's response to Napster's claim of fair use included a couple of interesting points. In analyzing the fourth factor (the effect of the use on the potential market for the work), the court considered both studies showing reduced sales of CDs to Napster users and the plaintiff's argument that Napster "raised the barriers to the plaintiff's entry into the market for digital downloading of music." Napster claimed that the uses should be allowed because they were analogous to both the time-shifting uses allowed in the *Sony* VCR case[1] and also to allow the space-shifting allowed in the manufacturer of the Rio (an MP3 player).[2] The court rejected this argument, because those cases did not involve the distribution of copyrighted material to the public.

The plaintiffs also alleged both contributory and vicarious infringement by Napster. Recall that contributory infringement incurs when one assists, induces, or materially contributes to the infringing conduct of another. The *Napster* court found that Napster clearly had knowledge of the exchanging of copyrighted sound recordings between its users and that Napster had materially contributed to its users' infringements because, without Napster's services and software, its users would not have been able to find and exchange copyrighted works as easily, since Napster provided them with the site and facilities for direct infringement. (*A&M Records, Inc. v. Napster, Inc.* 114 F. Supp. 2d 896 (N.D. Cal. 2000))

One may be liable for vicarious infringement if one has the right and ability to control the infringing activities of another and a direct financial interest in those activities. The court found that Napster had a direct financial interest in its users' infringing activities, as its future revenue depended on the size of its user base; and that Napster had the right and ability to control its users' infringing actions, since it controlled user access to the system, retained the ability to terminate user access to the system, and expressly reserved the right to refuse service to any user and to terminate any user account. Thus, Napster was held liable for the trifecta of copyright infringement: direct infringement, vicarious infringement, and contributory infringement.

As a result of the lawsuit, the original Napster shut down in 2001. In 2003, Roxio Digital Media Services Company purchased Press Play, a major provider of online music, and used it as the basis of a new online music service using the Napster brand. The new Napster provides digital music files legally, by contracting with copyright owners, and charges users a fee for downloading songs.

Aimster and Grokster were also P2P music file-sharing networks, although the technology they used was slightly different than Napster's. Nonetheless, they each got their turn as defendants in copyright infringement suits shortly after the *Napster* suit.

Like those in *Napster*, defendants in *Grokster* distributed free software that facilitated the indexing, searching, and exchanging of files between users. Unlike *Napster*, however, Grokster's servers did not store copies of users' files. Rather, the Grokster software only facilitated the P2P file-sharing among users. The court held that Grokster was not liable for contributory infringement because, even though it did have actual knowledge of infringement, it did not have that knowledge until after the acts of infringement had occurred. The court also found that Grokster had not materially assisted in its users' infringement, since it had no control over the network established by its software between users and was not in a position to stop its users' acts of infringement. In addition, the court held that Grokster was not vicariously liable—again, because it did not have the ability to supervise the infringing users' conduct. (*Metro-Goldwyn Mayer Studios, Inc. v. Grokster Ltd.* 259 F. Supp. 2d 1029 (C.D. Cal. 2003))

The *Aimster* decision came down only two months after *Grokster*. The Aimster system, however, was more similar to Napster's than Grokster's in that Aimster users downloaded software from the Aimster Web site and then relied on Aimster's servers to search for, index, and assist in the sharing of files. Because copies of its users' songs did not reside on Aimster's servers, however, Aimster was held not liable as a direct infringer. (*In re Aimster Copyright Litig.* 334 F.2d 643, 655 (7th Cir. 2003))

On the claims of vicarious and contributory liability, however, the court held that Aimster was likely to be found liable. Aimster tried to argue that it should be absolved of liability under *Sony* because its technology could be used for noninfringing purposes. The court rejected this argument, noting that it was not enough for Aimster to simply hypothesize noninfringing uses and that Aimster had not presented any evidence of such noninfringing use.

Isn't this really just a case of the bad guys going after people downloading or copying files for their own personal use?

Keep in mind that while many opinions discuss personal uses in their fair use analysis, personal use per se is not actually one of the fair use factors. More importantly, when courts have discussed personal use, they usually use the term to refer to an individual making a copy or copies of a work owned by that individual for that individual's use, such as videotaping a television show or copying songs from a purchased CD to an MP3 player. The term "personal use" is not synonymous with noncommercial use or with uses for which one is not directly paid. These three major file-sharing cases all involve, as the *Napster* court was careful to point out, not just a series of individuals *copying* files for their own future use, but the *distribution* to others of multiple unauthorized copies of protected works.

That having been said, however, there are currently multiple threats to truly personal use on the horizon. See Chapter 5 on recently proposed legislation for more detail.

Isn't the RIAA suing hundreds of thousands of individuals now?

The RIAA has used both the subpoena provision of the DMCA and "John Doe" summons to obtain lists of names from ISPs of individuals engaged in a high level of file-sharing. Although the RIAA has filed suit or threatened to file suit against many individuals, so far, these have been individuals who have downloaded outrageous numbers of protected works. According to the RIAA, the defendants in their lawsuits average at least 1,000 downloads per day.

This is all very fascinating, but what does it mean for my library?

Most directly, it means that your institution may be on the receiving end of a Section 512(h) subpoena one day. In its battle against file-sharing, the RIAA has moved its focus from large corporations to individuals. In doing so, it has taken advantage of the subpoena provision of Section 512, using it to obtain the names of individual file-sharers. In 2003, the RIAA obtained subpoenas directed at MIT and Boston College. Although a court ruled that the schools did not have to comply with the subpoenas, it did so purely on procedural grounds. In this scenario, then, file-sharing could lead to privacy issues for libraries. What if the sharing occurred on library computers? Consider the implications of receiving a subpoena requiring you to reveal the name of all individuals using library computers in a certain situation (such as on a given day or accessing a certain Web site). Protecting our users' privacy is one of the primary ethics of librarianship. Point III of the ALA Code of Ethics states: "We protect each library user's right to privacy and confidential-

---

One more reason why librarians must become activists

A bill introduced in 2002 by Rep. Berman would have amended the Copyright Act to create a new safe harbor for a copyright owner when he or she engages in self-help by "disabling, interfering with, blocking, diverting, or otherwise impairing" the unauthorized "distribution, display, performance, or reproduction . . . on a publicly accessible peer-to-peer file trading network" of his or her copyrighted work. The bill would have allowed the copyright owner to impair files traded on a peer-to-peer network not containing any of the owner's work if such impairment is "reasonably necessary" to prevent the unauthorized use of his own work and would have allowed a cause of action against wronged victims only if more than $250 worth of damage was done to their hardware or files.

ity with respect to information sought or received and resources consulted, borrowed, acquired or transmitted."

Point IV of the ALA Code of Ethics states: "We recognize and respect intellectual property rights." Librarians are also models for all of their users regarding behavior in the information arena. Turning a blind eye to obvious acts of infringement gives the message that, as information professionals, we are not concerned about copyright infringement. It may also mean that you are not following your own copyright policy.

I do not by any stretch of the imagination mean to imply that librarians should become "copyright police." I mean only that when you are aware of a clear act of infringement, you should not let it go—for both practical and ethical reasons.

Notes

1. This case was discussed briefly in Chapter 3. In *Sony Corp. of Am. v. Universal City Studios, Inc.* (464 U.S. 417 (1984)), the Supreme Court held that individuals taping television shows for "time-shifting" purposes, i.e., to watch later at their convenience, constituted fair use.
2. In *Recording Industry Association of America v. Diamond Multimedia Systems, Inc.*, the Ninth Circuit held that the Rio MP3 player was not a digital audio recording device subject to the restrictions of the Audio Home Recording Act of 1992. Although the court compared the situation to that in *Sony*, noting that the Rio allows "space-shifting," it did not actually conduct a fair use analysis.

Bibliography

A&M Records, Inc. v. Napster, Inc. 114 F. Supp. 2d 896 (N.D. Cal. 2000).

In re Aimster Copyright Litig., 334 F.2d 643, 655 (7th Cir. 2003).

American Library Association, Code of Ethics of the American Library Association (1995).

Metro-Goldwyn Mayer Studios, Inc. v. Grokster Ltd. 259 F. Supp. 2d 1029 (C.D. Cal. 2003).

11

Non-copyright issues

Copyright, of course, is not the only law that applies to the Internet, nor is it the only law concerning use of the Internet of which librarians should be knowledgeable. Some—certainly not all—other areas include censorship; filtering; privacy; defamation; and licensing issues. You have doubtless heard about laws that have attempted to address these areas, such as the Communications Decency Act (CDA), a portion of which was invalidated by the Supreme Court as being too broad; the Child Online Privacy Protection Act (COPPA); and the Uniform Computer Information Transactions Act (UCITA), a proposal put forth by the National Council of Commissioners on Uniform State Laws addressing online contracts, which some states have adopted as state law.

Another area of law that has implications for the Internet and that, for our purposes, is actually closely related to copyright, is trademark law. For that reason, I think it is important to discuss it here. It is important to note that, unlike copyright, trademark is governed by both federal statutes and state laws. Here we will discuss only federal statues, which should be sufficient for this context.

How does trademark law differ from copyright law?

The rationale behind copyright law is to encourage the production and distribution of works of art and sciences by protecting the rights of authors. In comparison, the purpose of trademark law is to protect consumers from being misled by providing them a means for identifying the source of a good or service. For example, when you pick up a bag of Nutter Butter peanut-butter cookies, you know not only that they will be of the same quality as the last bag of Nutter Butters, but also that, because they are produced by Nabisco, they will be of the quality that you associate with Nabisco. An obvious fringe benefit arises for the producers of goods and services when consumers continue to buy their products because of the knowledge about that product associated with the trademark.

A trademark is any word, name, symbol, device, or combination thereof that is used to identify the source of the good or service and to distinguish that good or service from one produced or sold by others. Limitations apply to the types of words that may be used as trademarks and to the manner in which they are used. Unlike copyright law, an individual word or brief phrase can be protected by trademark law, since it is capable of distinguishing a particular good or service.

Generic terms, such as "car," "restaurant," or "toy" cannot alone be trademarked to describe that good. The rationale for this is that one company should not be able to control the use of the simple English word that describes the product that he and one hundred other companies make. What would happen if Nabisco trademarked the word "cookie," so that no one else could use it in a commercial context to refer to, well, cookies? It would, for all practical purposes, take the word out of the daily English language. Note, however, that a word that might be generic if used on one product would not be on other products. One could not claim trademark protection in the word "apple" for use on the round red fruit from Washington, but the word can be—and is—protectable as a trademark for computers and sound recordings.

Descriptive terms, such as "raisin bran," can be trademarked only after they have achieved "secondary meaning," meaning that consumers have come to associate the term with a particular producer of the product so that, in the minds of consumers, it is distinguished from other types of raisin and bran cereals. A similar rationale applies to descriptive terms as to generic.

Trademarks must be used; one cannot "reserve" trademarks indefinitely without using them in order to prevent others from using them. Keep in mind that a trademark is associated only with the type of good or service with which it is used. For example, Nabisco owns the trademark "Nutter Butter" for use with peanut-butter sandwich cookies; if Ford decides it wants to create a new model car and name it the Nutter Butter, it can do so. Trademarks are also limited to geographic areas. Thus, there may be a Joe's Pizza Shack in Houston, one in Seattle, and one in New York City, with no association between them. Both of these limitations make sense when you consider the purpose of trademark law: to avoid consumer confusion. No one is likely to assume that a car called the Nutter Butter has been made by Nabisco, and very few people will frequent Houston, Seattle, and New York City enough to assume that the Joe's Pizza Shacks are owned by the same Joe.

This explanation is a great simplification; there are exceptions, such as the geographic limitation incorporates areas in which the producer is likely to expand. If, for example, a Joe's Pizza Shack already exists in New York City, it would be more difficult for someone to open a Joe's Pizza Shack on Long Island than in Seattle. Again, consumers are more likely to be confused by the existence of the same good 30 miles apart than three thousand miles apart. Once a trademark has been federally registered, however, the owner has rights to use it nationwide, except in locations in which it has already been used by others.

What does this mean for me, a librarian creating Web pages?

Trademarks may be violated in two ways: (1) infringement and (2) dilution. A trademark owner has the exclusive right to use his mark on his own goods and to prevent others from using the mark in a way that might confuse consumers. A trademark is infringed when the mark is used in connection with the sale, offering for sale, distribution, or advertising of any good or service in a context that is likely to cause confusion. (15 U.S.C. 1114(1) (1999)) Dilution occurs when a mark is widely enough known that even when used on a dissimilar good or service, the uniqueness of the mark, and thus its value, is lessened, despite the unlikelihood of confusion. The diluting use must be a commercial use made in commerce. (ibid., sec. 1125(a)(1))

A trademark may be used in many ways that confuse consumers other than stamping it on "bootleg" products. In the cyberworld, two common uses of marks are in URLs and in images used to link to the pages of the trademark owner.

URLs

The limitations of trademark law, as well as the global nature of the Internet, have opened a huge can of worms concerning trademarked names in URLs. Remember the three different Joe's Pizza Shacks? There can only be one www.joespizzashack.com. Who gets it? Who gets www.nutterbutter.com—Nabisco or Ford? On a global scale, what about the Scottish hometown burger joint called McDonald's? As I said, this is a huge can of worms, and we won't go into it very deeply here, but it is good to be aware of some of the issues and how the Internet, once again, confuses our nice, neat legal systems. The short answer is that these problems are being addressed at several levels, by various organizations and agencies, many of them international in scope.

As far as URLs go, let's stick with the basics. You are most likely to want to use a trademarked word or phrase in a deeper level of a URL, such as www.library.edu/companyinfo/nike. The courts dealing with this issue so far have held that in such a case, the word is being used only as part of an address, not to identify a good or service; in other words, it is not being used as a trademark. (*Data Concepts, Inc. v. Digital Consulting, Inc.*, 150 F.3d 620 (6th Cir. 1998))

However, using a trademark in the actual domain name of a page could cause you trouble. Recall the two ways in which you can violate a trademark: infringement and dilution. If your use of the mark is in connection with distribution of services, which is likely to be true for library Web pages, and your use of the mark is likely to cause confusion, you may be infringing. What if your library in the state of Washington has the largest collection of historical legal papers in the country related to the settlement of the West: Can you use the URL www.westlawlibrary.edu? It is possible you might get by with that, under fair use or some similar argument, but, at the very least, you are ripe for a charge of infringement. What if your library was founded one hundred years ago by, and named after, the local philanthropist, Robert Lexis? Can you use the URL www.lexislibrary.com? Probably so. A use that is purely descriptive or geographically descriptive of the user's own goods or services is likely to get by as a "fair use."[1] But remember our fair use mantra: there are no guarantees!

The bottom line: Use for your domain name only words that logically identify you in the first place, but don't be afraid to use trademarked words that logically identify a path in your URL.

Metatags

You'll recall from our earlier overview of the Web that metatags are words that are placed in the HTML code of a Web page but that the user does not see. Used well, metatags can be a valuable tool in describing pages so that the user can more easily identify relevant pages when he searches for them with a search engine. Not surprisingly, some people abuse this tool. My favorite story is that of a pornographic Web page that, around tax time, repeated "IRS" and "internal revenue service" many times in its metatags; when someone searched for the IRS page—a popular search at that time of the year—she often retrieved the porn site instead. What if you offer a variety of company information on your Web pages? Can you use the trademarked company names, or perhaps other trademarks belonging to the company (say, "swoosh" for your page about Nike) in your metatags to help users more easily locate your page?

The analysis is similar to that of using trademarks in URLs. If you use trademarked terms as metatags in order to describe your own services, that's fair.[2] If you use a descriptive term to describe the content of your page, that's fair.[3] But let's say your library, Metropolis State College Library, is engaged in a raging battle with the other academic library in town, University of Gotham Library, to attract the largest number of users and thereby guarantee its place as primary beneficiary in Mr. Potter's will. If you use the trademarked mascot of UG, "Gotham Bats," as a metatag, well, you're in trouble.

One more reason why librarians must become activists

"I really didn't realize the librarians were, you know, such a dangerous group. . . . You think they're just sitting at the desk, all quiet and everything. They're like plotting the revolution, man. I wouldn't mess with them. You know, they've had their budgets cut. They're paid nothing. Books are falling apart. The libraries are just like the ass end of everything, right?" — Michael Moore

---

The bottom line: Be honest; use for metatags only words that honestly describe the content of your page.

Words or logos as links

Using a trademarked logo as a hyperlink is the least litigated area so far of trademark infringement in cyberspace, so we don't have much on which to base our analysis. We do a have a handful of cases, however. Arguably, using logos as hyperlinks goes beyond the "fair use" of a trademarked word or phrase as part of a descriptive pathway in a URL. Seldom, if ever, would it be more efficient to use an image of the Nike swoosh as a hyperlink rather than the word Nike, in the same way that it is more efficient to use the word "nike" in your URL path instead of "that-national-athletic-shoe-store-that-starts-with-an-N-and-shows-inspiring-TV-commercials-of-athletes-overcoming-great-obstacles." That's a long URL!

Why would a trademark owner care if you use his logo rather than his company or product name? Because he wants to protect the value in that logo. Companies use symbolic images to identify their goods because this can be much more effective than simply using the company name; consumers remember and react to images differently than to textual names. This is where dilution comes in. The argument is that your use of a trademarked logo may diminish the distinctiveness and value of that logo. Let's say that Larry Flynt, infamous publisher of *Hustler* magazine, takes up an interest in fashion. He designs a Web page commenting on haute courture and uses the logos of designers like Chanel, Ann Taylor, and Ralph Lauren as links to their Web pages. Why might these fashion houses be upset? They might be afraid that people viewing Flynt's page will assume a connection between his product and theirs. Which would imply, even if subtly, a more likely connection to you: a printed word, or a familiar logo that you often see on advertisements. Might you assume that the logo owner is advertising on the Web page? Wouldn't you be less likely to assume so if the name of the owner or his product is simply listed on the page? This is the type of concern and reasoning associated with dilution.

The bottom line: Don't use a logo as a hyperlink without permission if you can get by with using a word or phrase.

Notes

1. See 15 U.S.C. sec. 1115(b)(4) (stating that the following constitutes a defense to trademark infringement: "the use of the name, term, or device charged to be an infringement is a use, otherwise than as a mark, of the party's individual name in his own business, or of the individual name of anyone in privity with such party, or of a term or device which is descriptive of and used fairly and in good faith only to describe the goods or services of such party, or their geographic origin").
2. See *Playboy Enterprises, Inc. v. Welles*, 47 U.S.P.Q.2d 1186 (S.D. Cal. 1998) (holding that the defendant, a former Playboy Playmate of the Year was entitled to use the trademarked phrase "Playboy Playmate of the Year" as a metatag).
3. See *Brookfield Communications, Inc. v. West Coast Entertainment Corp.*, 174 F.3d. 1036 (9th Cir. 1999) (holding that use of the phrase "movie buff" as a metatag to describe a film enthusiast did not infringe the trademark "MovieBuff," whereas use of the word "MovieBuff" did infringe).

Bibliography

Brookfield Communications, Inc. v. West Coast Entertainment Corp., 174 F.3d. 1036 (9th Cir. 1999).

Data Concepts, Inc. v. Digital Consulting, Inc., 150 F.3d 620 (6th Cir. 1998).

Playboy Enterprises, Inc. v. Welles, 47 U.S.P.Q.2d 1186 (S.D. Cal. 1998).

Trademark Act of 1946, U.S. Code, vol. 15, secs. 1114(1), 1115(b)(4), 1125(a)(1) (1999).

12

I'm the good guy: what can they do to me?

Most likely, if a copyright owner decided that a library was infringing her copyright, by posting something on the Web without permission, for example, her lawyer would contact the library or its governing institution with a threatening letter. The cease-and-desist letter would identify the alleged infringing action, provide support for the author's claim of copyright ownership, insist that the library cease and desist use of the work immediately, and explain that failure to uphold these conditions would require the copyright owner to file an infringement action against the library.

What do you do in this case? You immediately go to your institution's legal counsel[1] with the letter, *whether or not* you decide to remove the allegedly infringing work, and explain your side of the story. Maybe you were just unaware that you did something wrong; maybe you are uncertain if you've done something wrong; or maybe you are certain that you have not done something wrong. Whatever the case, you should consult legal counsel immediately for three reasons: (1) to get her opinion on the legitimacy of your actions; (2) so that in case of any further developments, your legal counsel will be knowledgeable from the beginning; (3) so that the parent organization can help in making the decision about removal. You should make the decision about what to do together with your legal counsel. Your legal counsel should take the responsibility for replying. Nonetheless, it's always a good idea for you, as the most directly responsible person, to keep copies of all the communication concerning the issue.

In most cases, you will determine that your actions are not infringing and convey this to the copyright owner; or you will cease and desist in your actions; or you will come to an arrangement of some sort with the copyright owner. Let's say that, for whatever reason, this does not work out so well, and the copyright owner decides he wants to pursue the problem in court. What are the remedies to which you or your institution would be subject?

First, a court may issue an injunction, which is basically a court order to cease and desist use. (17 U.S.C. 502 (1999)) An injunction may be either

Q What do I do when my boss tells me to do something I think might violate copyright law?

A This is a position no one wants to be in, though I have heard enough horror stories from librarians to realize it happens with some regularity. Obviously, you have a very fine line to walk, and it is up to each individual to determine how to address the situation. Do keep in mind, however, that, even if you are "following orders," if you engage in an infringing activity, you are liable for infringement. Thus, you might couch your objection in those terms and inform your boss that, according to your understanding of copyright law, the action she is requesting is not legal; that you are therefore uncomfortable engaging in the act; and that you would like your boss to consult your institution's legal counsel to determine whether the act is permissible. Keep in mind that you are protecting yourself, your boss, *and* your institution by refusing to engage in illegal activity. You might also point out that willful infringement is punishable by fines of up to $150,000.

permanent, in which case you are ordered to refrain from use forever or take permanent corrective action; or temporary, in which case the court orders you to refrain from the action until the case is determined. Second, a court may order the impounding of allegedly infringing copies or the materials used in their creation or distribution. (ibid., sec. 503) Although courts have impounded computers, it is usually in cases involving issues such as child pornography, viruses, or fraud. Very seldom have computers been impounded in cases of copyright infringement.

Finally, the ugly stuff. An infringing person may be held liable for actual damages suffered and any profits gained by the infringer as well as statutory damages if the copyright in the work was registered at the time the infringement occurred. (ibid., sec. 504(a)) The copyright owner may choose to recover statutory damages in lieu of actual damages. Statutory damages per work range from $750 to $30,000, the precise amount to be determined at the court's discretion. (ibid., sec. 504(c)(1)) Should the court find that the infringement was "willful"—that is, knowing, purposeful, intentional—the court may award statutory damages of up to $150,000. (ibid., sec. 504(c)(2)) In addition, a willful infringer may be subject to criminal charges. (ibid., sec. 506) On the other hand, if the court finds that the infringement was innocent, it may reduce the damages to $200. (ibid., sec. 504(c)(2))

> Having a copyright policy in place helps both employees and employers deal with this kind of awkward situation. Copyright policies will be the subject of the next and final installment in this series of articles. That article will also include resources for further information about copyright law as it affects librarians.

"But, we really are the good guys," you're thinking. "Being fined at all just doesn't seem right." Congress agreed. The court must remit statutory damages to zero if the infringer believed and had reasonable grounds in believing that the use was a fair use *if* the infringer was an employee of a nonprofit educational institution, library, or archives acting in the scope of employment. (ibid.)

Is copyright infringement ever a crime?

Section 506 of the Copyright Act provides for criminal prosecution of certain infringing acts. It was intended to help fight copyright piracy. Section 506 states that one who willfully infringes another's copyright either for purposes of commercial advantage or private financial gain; or by the reproduction or distribution, including by electronic means, during any 180-day period, of unauthorized copies of protected works with a total retail value of over $1,000, shall be prosecuted for a crime. Note that the first requirement is that the infringement be willful. Regarding the commercial advantage or financial gain factor, it is not necessary that the defendant actually realized such an advantage or gain if the infringing activity was intended for such a purpose. Because criminal provisions of the law are strictly construed against the prosecution and favor the defendant, what constitutes commercial advantage or private financial gain for criminal purposes is applied more narrowly than for civil purposes. In other words, it will be more difficult to show a commercial advantage under the criminal provision than to show commercial use under the fair use analysis. In general, this provision will not affect most libraries, then, as acts by nonprofit entities are highly unlikely to meet the burden of the criminal provision.

Section 506 also provides for forfeiture and destruction of all infringing copies and all equipment used to create such infringing copies when the infringer is convicted of an act of criminal infringement. Section 506 also provides for fines for placing fraudulent copyright notices on a work, fraudulently removing a copyright notice from a work, and knowingly making a false representation on an application for copyright registration.

Q As we become aware of potential copyright problems, what is our library's duty to go through existing materials, both electronic and print, to identify and correct potential copyright violations?

A If your institution has reason to believe that it has infringed the rights of a copyright owner by using one of her works without authorization, and you continue to use that work, you are setting your institution up to be vulnerable to a claim of willful infringement. The damages under the Copyright Act for each willful infringement of work can be as great as $150,000. It is one thing to reasonably believe that you are not infringing a copyright owner's rights and then be found wrong; it is an entirely different issue to reasonably believe that you are infringing and continue to do so. The former may be considered "innocent infringement" and therefore subject in court to damages as low as $200, while the latter is likely to be willful infringement and subject to damages of up to $150,000. This being said, you should critically consider and analyze the situation: What is it that makes you concerned that you are infringing a work and how likely is it that that is the case? It cannot be emphasized enough that anytime you feel there's any possibility that you, your institution, or someone on your staff is infringing a copyright, the first thing you should do is talk to your entity's legal counsel.

Don't state entities have immunity from most lawsuits?

Some of you clever employees of state institutions are thinking that this really does not apply to you or your institution, because state institutions and employees are immune to suit. This is an uncertain area at the time of this writing. Section 511 of the Copyright Act specifically states that states, their officers, and employees are not immune to suit under the Copyright Act, despite the Eleventh Amendment of the Constitution. (ibid., sec. 511) (see Source A) However, recent cases seem to be in the process of undoing Section 511. In 1999, in *Florida Prepaid Postsecondary Education Expense Board v. College Savings Bank* (527 U.S. 627 (1999)), the United States Supreme Court heard a case concerning alleged patent infringement by a state agency. The patent statutes include provisions similar to Section 511 of the Copyright Act. Congress has the power to pass laws only as granted in the Constitution. When a federal law is challenged, it may be both challenged and defended based on various specific parts of the Constitution, depending on the situation. For example, we know that Congress' right to pass laws con-

One more reason why librarians must become activists

In 2003, the RIAA obtained subpoenas directed at MIT and Boston College in response to file-sharing activities by students of those activities. Although a court ruled that the schools did not have to comply with the subpoenas, it did so purely on procedural grounds. The entertainment industry has made clear that it has no qualms in going over educational institutions — why would libraries be any different?

cerning copyright derives from Article 1, Section 8, Clause 8 of the Constitution. In *Florida Prepaid*, the Court held that Congress did not have the necessary authority under the Patent Clause (Art 1, sec. 8, cl. 8), the Commerce Clause (Art. 1, § 8, cl. 3), or the Fourteenth Amendment (forbidding states from depriving persons of life, liberty, or property without due process of law) to abolish state sovereign immunity in the Patent Act.

Does this holding have any significance for copyright infringement? In 2000, the Fifth Circuit Court of Appeals, in part relying on the ruling in *Florida Prepaid*, held that Congress did not have the power under the Fourteenth Amendment to abolish state sovereign immunity for the purposes of the Copyright and Trademark Acts. (*Chavez v. Arte Publico Press*, 204 F.3d 601 (5th Cir. 2000))

So far, then, the Supreme Court has not specifically ruled on the Constitutionality of the abrogation of sovereign immunity in Section 511 of the Copyright Act, but given the recent line of cases, many experts believe that the Court will eventually strike down Section 511. Should this happen, it would mean that state agencies again would enjoy sovereign immunity from charges of copyright infringement.

So how worried do you really have to be? The likelihood that you or your institution actually will be sued in court is very slight. Chances are strong that the matter would be settled long before that point is reached, either because the use is excused or because you remove the allegedly infringing work from your Web pages, or by some more sophisticated negotiations. So why worry about the whole thing? Because getting to the latter point can be extremely time consuming, expensive, and frightening. Because knowing what is legal and what is not, and knowing the defenses and exceptions that apply to you, give you more power to deal with potential problems. Because nothing in copyright is certain. And because in educational institutions, we have some responsibility to serve as role models for our students.

Note

1. Note that almost every institution governing a library will have legal counsel: the city, the university, the school district, the corporation. It's not a bad idea to find out who that person is, how to contact her, just for general knowledge.

Bibliography

Chavez v. Arte Publico Press, 204 F.3d 601 (5th Cir. 2000).

Copyright Act of 1976, U.S. Code, vol. 17, secs. 502, 504, 511 (2000).

Florida Prepaid Postsecondary Education Expense Board v. College Savings Bank (527 U.S. 627 (1999).

U.S. Constitution, art. I, sec. 8, cl. 3, 8.

PART III

Specific library applications

13

Liability for content provided on the Internet and as Internet access provider

Why is it important to understand the various types of infringement?

Infringing someone's copyright is extremely easy to do. So easy, in fact, that you can do it absolutely unknowingly. The variety of rights owned by a copyright owner, which were the basis of our discussion in Part II, is one reason infringement is easily achieved. Another reason is that copyright may be infringed indirectly as well as directly.

"So you're telling me," you ask, "that not only can I infringe a copyright without knowing it, but I can also infringe without even directly violating one of the owner's rights myself?!" Yes, that is what I'm telling you. "That doesn't seem fair," you respond. Which is exactly why it behooves you to be familiar with the various rights that are part of the "bundle" of copyrights as well as the various ways in which you may infringe those rights, whether or not you are aware of your infringement and regardless of the amount of control you retain over the infringing activities.

How many different ways can you infringe a copyright?

What is most commonly thought of as copyright infringement is considered to be "direct infringement": a volitional act that infringes one or more of the various rights of a copyright owner. It is important to note, as already stressed, that simply committing an act that violates one of the bundle of copyrights is, in itself, enough to infringe those rights and thus to be subject to the various remedies associated with infringement (discussed in Chapter 12). Copyright is a "strict liability" law, meaning that "ignorance is no excuse."

A person commits "contributory infringement" when she (1) "induces, causes or materially contributes to the [directly] infringing activity of another," (*Gershwin Publ'g Corp. v. Columbia Artist Management, Inc.*, 443 F.2d 1159, 1162 (2d Cir. 1971)) *and* (2) knows or has reason to know about the infringing actions. (*Cable/Home Communications Corp. v. Network Prods., Inc.*, 902 F.2d 829, 845 (11th Cir. 1990))

Finally, one can commit "vicarious infringement" without any knowledge of the infringing activity if one "(1) has the right and ability to control the infringer's acts *and* (2) receives a direct financial benefit from the infringement." (*Religious Tech. Ctr. v. Netcom On-Line Communication Serv., Inc.*, 907 F. Supp. 1361, 1375 (N.D. Cal. 1995)) Thus, under the right circumstances, one can commit copyright infringement whether or not one knows that the act being committed infringes copyright or even whether or not one knows that the act is being committed.

How do these different types of infringement apply to library activities?

Generally speaking, libraries provide two different types of services via the Internet. First, they provide their patrons with access to the Internet, which means giving patrons the ability to use library equipment to access materials beyond the control of the library. Second, they provide content to their patrons when they create their own Web pages. For purposes of liability, this difference is important. The latter is the subject of most of Part II of this book. This chapter will discuss liability issues for libraries in their role as access provider, rather than as content provider. In this role, libraries also provide their staff with e-mail and Internet services.

What are the liability implications for libraries as Internet access providers?

The Digital Millennium Copyright Act added Section 512 to the Copyright Act, which limits the liability of online service providers (OSPs) (see Source 13). Do libraries qualify as OSPs under the Act? Usually they do. However, strict regulations must be followed to take advantage of Section 512, both before and in response to allegations of infringement. In other words, although most libraries would qualify as OSPs, protection is not automatically granted. The Copyright Act does not protect a library (a) unless and until it takes specified action to indicate its desire to be protected by Section 512, which includes registering an agent (someone who will receive complaints) with the U.S. Copyright Office; and (b) when accused of infringement, follows specific regulations in responding to the accusation. Because the latter could become quite burdensome, each library should consider seriously the trade-offs between complying with the Act and not doing so. The same answer may not be appropriate for every institution. If a library does not comply with the regulations, Section 512 does not apply.

Section 512 is lengthy and complex. It can be found in its entirety in Source A. What follows is a relatively brief summary of the points that probably most interest librarians.

What is a "service provider"?
"Service provider" is defined as "a provider of online services or network access, or the operator of facilities therefor," including "an entity offering the transmission, routing, or providing of connections for digital online communications, between or among points specified by a user, or material of the user's choosing, without modification to the content of the material as sent or received." (*Copyright Act of 1976, U.S. Code*, vol. 17, sec. 512(k) (1999)) Note that the definition seems to emphasize the passive role of an OSP: The *user* must choose where he is going and the material he wishes to send or receive. The OSP simply provides the mechanism for the user to do this, and the OSP cannot modify the content of the material sent or received nor receive any benefit from doing so. Thus, a library fits this description to the extent that it provides the means for users to surf the Net. Section 512 would not apply to a library's creation of Web pages, posting content on the Internet, intercepting and modifying information (including moderating listservs), or controlling the user's actions. Keep in mind, however, that Section 512 was written with commercial OSPs in mind; therefore, some of the provisions will not apply to libraries, and some will sound a little awkward in regard to libraries.

Exactly what kind of actions are covered?
Section 512 covers four types of Internet functions, for which a qualifying OSP under Section 512 will not be held liable:

1. Transmitting, routing, or providing connections for transmitting or routing material through a system controlled by the OSP, including the intermediate and transient storage of the material as part of the transmission, routing, or provision of connections *if:*
   - the OSP does not initiate the transmission;
   - the transmission occurs through an automatic technical process without the OSP selecting material;
   - the OSP does not modify the content of the material transmitted; *and*
   - no copy of the material made by the OSP is maintained in such as way as to make it available to anyone other than the original user and is not kept for longer than is "reasonably necessary" to transmit the material.
2. System caching of material made available by someone other than the OSP,

as long as the OSP abides by generally accepted industry standards concerning refreshing, reloading, or other updating.

3. Placing infringing information on a system or network at the direction of a user *if* the OSP:
   - does not have actual knowledge that the material is infringing or of facts that should make the infringement obvious;
   - does not receive a financial benefit directly attributable to the infringement; *and*
   - designates an agent to receive notifications of claims of infringement.

4. Linking to sites containing infringing material or using "information location tools," defined as including "a directory, index, reference, pointer, or hypertext link," *if* the OSP:
   - does not have actual knowledge that the material is infringing or of facts that should make the infringement obvious; *and*
   - does not receive a financial benefit directly attributable to the infringement.

Is there anything else my library must do to qualify for protection from liability?

In addition to the above, to qualify for any protection under Section 512, an OSP must accommodate and not interfere with technological measures used by copyright owners to protect their works, such as digital watermarks; and must adopt and "reasonably implement" a policy providing for termination of subscribers and account holders who are repeat infringers. The latter is one of those sections that sounds a little awkward when applied to libraries; it seems intended for OSPs who provide, for example, server space on which subscribers may post materials. Nonetheless, in some situations, this may apply to libraries as well. An "account holder" could be, for example, a member of the library staff who maintains pages on the library server.

To qualify for the protection from caching and posting infringing information at a user's request, an OSP must "expeditiously" remove material or disable access to it when a claim of infringement is made. The requirement that an OSP respond to such a claim without judicial oversight has raised concerns that this process may be abused by individuals other than wronged copyright owners. Section 512 makes an attempt at protecting OSPs from false claims of infringement: A detailed process must be followed by the person making the infringement claim, and anyone who knowingly makes a false claim is liable for any costs to the OSP as a result of that claim. Protection is also provided to OSPs who act in good faith to remove or disable access to material that is the subject of a claim of infringement *if* the OSP takes reasonable steps to notify a "subscriber" when material has been removed

> **One more reason why librarians must become activists**
>
> "Librarians are the secret masters of the world. They control information. Don't ever piss one off." — Spider Robinson

from the subscriber's page and, should that person provide a statement to the OSP that the material was removed as a result of mistaken identification, the OSP replaces the material.

Isn't there anything specific to libraries?

Sort of. Section 512 includes a provision for limitation on liability of non-profit educational institutions. This is a very narrow exception, however. The gist of this section is that faculty and graduate students who are employed by the institution to teach or to research are not considered to be "the institution." In other words, the institution is not liable for the actions of those persons. This provision would apply to academic libraries in which librarians are considered members of the faculty. Three requirements must be met: (1) The person's actions must not involve the provision of online access to infringing materials that were "required or recommended" for a course taught by that person; (2) The institution must not have received more than two notices within a three-year period of infringement by the person; *and* (3) the institution must provide to all users of its network or system information describing and promoting compliance with U.S. copyright law.

OK, so give me the bottom line: What do I have to do to be covered by the entire Section 512?

Because there are so many specific requirements for each activity covered, you should read through the entire section to be sure you conform with each requirement. Especially because Section 512 prescribes specific requirements that must be met to qualify for benefiting from the provision, unlike what has been discussed elsewhere in this book, you should work with your institution's legal counsel to ensure that your library meets the requirements for qualification and to verify that your policies and actions are in concert with those of the institution as a whole. Another reason to talk with your institution's legal counsel is that, should a claim of infringement be made against your library, it is that legal counsel who will be dealing with it. In addition, the institution must register an agent to receive complaints and publish the e-mail address of that person on the institution's Web site. It will also be published on the U.S. Copyright Office Web site.

Bibliography

Copyright Act of 1976, U.S. Code, vol. 17, sec. 512 (1999).

14

Interlibrary loan and resource sharing

One of the most valuable benefits the Internet provides is the ability to share information so easily, quickly, and cheaply. Certainly, electronic resources in general have been a great boon for resource-sharing projects. While it is pretty difficult for libraries hundreds of miles apart to share a subscription to a printed index, the Internet allows libraries to share electronic databases quite easily, which results in tremendous savings for various types of consortiums and resource-sharing groups. Obviously, the Internet also makes it easy (and cheap) to send electronic copies of documents to people. So what a blessing to interlibrary loan operations, which can now make digital copies of articles from print journals and send those copies to whomever requests them, right? Well, sort of. Like everything else in copyright, there are limits. "But even if I have to stick to the traditional limitations on the number of articles I can copy from one journal, at least I can take advantage of the fact that I can easily save a copy to send again, right?" Well, not exactly.

What does the copyright act say about interlibrary loan?
At least two exclusive rights of copyright owners are implicated by interlibrary loan: copying and distribution. Of course, not all interlibrary loan involves copying. The distribution right, however, stands on its own; one need not distribute copies of a work to violate the distribution right. Lending of books is allowable only because of the first sale doctrine, delineated in Section 109 of the Copyright Act (see Source A). In a nutshell, the first sale doctrine says that once you purchase a copyrighted work, you have the right to redistribute that one copy that you own however you want, including selling it. The first sale doctrine is discussed further in Chapter 3.

Many interlibrary loans, however, involve copying a work, such as a journal article, and passing along that reproduction. This is a potential violation of both copying and distribution rights. Fortunately, Section 108 saves the day. Section 108(a) states that a library or archives, or any employee acting within the scope of her employment, may "reproduce no more than one copy...of a work...or distribute such copy" if the following conditions are

> Q Can a librarian copy an entire book to transmit via interlibrary loan?
>
> A No. The right to reproduce, or copy, a protected work is the exclusive right of the copyright owner. Section 108 of the Copyright Act provides exceptions specifically for Interlibrary Loan purposes. However, those exceptions are limited to making copies of "no more than one article or other contribution to a copyrighted collection or periodical issue, or to a copy or phonorecord of a small part of any other copyrighted work." An exception might arguably exist if the "entire book" is extremely short.

met: (1) The copies are not made for commercial advantage; (2) the library's collections are open to the public *or* available to persons doing research in a specialized field other than those affiliated with the institution; and (3) the copy or distribution includes a notice of copyright on the copy or, if no notice is found on the work, a legend stating that the work may be protected by copyright.

Sections 108(d) and (e) limit this right further:

- A library may make a copy of no more than one article from a journal issue, or no more than one "other contribution" to a copyrighted collection, or "a small part of any other copyrighted work."
- The copy must become the property of the user.
- The library must have had no notice that the copy will be used for anything other than "private study, scholarship, or research."
- The library must prominently display a copyright warning according to requirements issued by the Copyright Office at the place where orders of copies are taken.

Finally, the allowances of Section 108 apply only to the "isolated and unrelated reproduction or distribution of a single copy...of the same material on separate occasions." The allowances do not apply when the library or an employee is aware the copying is being done for purposes of "related or concerted reproduction or distribution of multiple copies...of the same material," whether or not the copies are made at the same time and whether or not intended for aggregate use by a group or for use by individual members of a group. Neither does Section 108 apply to instances of systematic copying or distribution of single or multiple copies or copying intended to act as a re-

Q Can a librarian scan an entire book to transmit digitally via interlibrary loan?

A No. Although the Copyright Act does not specifically address this type of technology, Internet-related issues should be analogized to print situations. The law does not allow copying an entire book for interlibrary loan purposes; it does not matter whether the copy made is paper or digital or whether it would be mailed or transmitted digitally.

placement for a subscription or purchase by anyone, including another library. In addition, Section 108 does not apply to copies or distribution of a musical, pictorial, graphic, or sculptural work; motion picture; or other audiovisual work other than those dealing with news; the only exceptions being copies made for archival or replacement purposes, and graphics that are a part of other works.

What about guidelines?

In response to the 1976 Copyright Act, which did not provide explicit, quantitative guidelines for interlibrary loan, the National Commission on Technological Uses of Copyrighted Works (CONTU) developed guidelines to assist librarians in determining what is and is not allowable under the new law. The Commission gathered together representatives of various interested groups as they created the guidelines, so it is no surprise that the guidelines were and still are generally accepted by organizations representing librarians, publishers, and authors.

The guidelines apply to the copying of articles from periodicals published within the previous five years. The guidelines suggest that "such aggregate quantities as to substitute for a subscription to or purchase of such work," prohibited by Section 108(g)(2), will not be met if a library limits its interlibrary-loan copying to:

- For any given periodical as a whole, as opposed to a specific issue:
  - Within any given calendar year,
  - No more than five copies of an article or articles published within the previous five years.
- For any other work:
  - No more than five copies per year
  - During the entire period for which the work is covered by copyright.

Q Can my interlibrary loan department store digitized copies of works we have transmitted via the Internet for easier and cheaper access the next time they are requested?

A No. Again, the Copyright Act does not address this specific technological situation. However, it does state that the copy made for interlibrary loan purposes must become the property of the user who requested it. Analogizing to the digital world, even though the user may receive the only print copy made, a digital copy retained by the library would constitute an additional copy, which is clearly not allowed under copyright law. Thus, all digital copies made during the process of transmitting interlibrary loan materials should be destroyed.

In addition, requests must be accompanied by a statement that the borrowing library is complying with the CONTU guidelines; otherwise, the lending library is instructed not to fulfill the request. Finally, the borrowing library must keep records of its activities for three years.

How does this apply to the Internet?

The Conference on Fair Use (CONFU) included a working group on interlibrary loan and document delivery issues in the digital arena. After extensive discussion, the working group was unable to agree on guidelines for digital delivery of interlibrary loans. Thus, no guidelines have been issued specifically addressing interlibrary loan in the cyberworld. We must rely instead on the Copyright Act and on the CONTU guidelines, both of which were written pre-Internet, and apply them as best we can to the digital environment.

Number of copies

The issue of what constitutes a copy in cyberspace is discussed in Chapter 7. Certainly this tricky issue raises its ugly head again in the ILL context. Would multiple distribution of one scanned copy create multiple copies? Or would it be considered repeated distribution of the same copy, comparable to repeated lending of the same book?

Under Section 108(g), a library may make a single copy of a work on more than one occasion. Under the CONTU guidelines, a library may borrow copies of the same item up to five times in five years. So why not save a copy once it's been made?

Copy must become property of the user

Another very important issue for digital copies is the requirement that the copy become the property of the individual user. Depending on the technology being used, the one and only digital copy of an item may not be transferred. Consider what happens when you e-mail an attachment. You do not actually send the only copy of your file; rather, an additional copy is made and sent, and you still retain a copy on your computer. The requirement that the copy become the property of the owner technically cannot be met in some technological situations.

"Does this mean ILL activities should not use these technologies?" you ask. Keeping in mind that no law or guidelines supply the answer to this question, it would seem in spirit with the law and the CONTU guidelines to destroy any copies made during filling a request that remain with the library. Quite clearly, a library may not keep "on file" a digital copy of an article it expects to distribute via ILL at a later time.

"How about, instead of e-mailing a requested item to a patron, providing a site on which the library would post digital images of requests, which patrons could then download?" you suggest. "We would restrict access, of course, to the individual who requested that piece." This, again, runs into the problem of the copy becoming the property of the individual requestor. Theoretically, the library could leave an item online for a limited period of time and then destroy that copy. Tom could be sent a notice stating that his request is available at www.illrequests.edu for ten days only, at which point it will be deleted, and giving him his password of ilovelibraries that he will need to access the article he requested. In this scenario, Tom would be making his own copy if he chose to download a copy of the article. He might decide simply to read it online. Regardless, the library remains in possession of a copy, which clearly violates Section 108. Instead of destroying its copy as soon as another copy is sent out to the user, as in the e-mail scenario, the library holds on to its copy for a specific period of time. This seems further removed from keeping in spirit of the law, especially given that other options are available. However, given the specified and limited time in the original scenario, you would probably have a decent argument that this type of use should be allowed, assuming the copy is destroyed once the specified period expires.

It is possible that the analysis would change should one important aspect of this scenario change—the amount of time for which the item is kept online. Libraries commonly make photocopies of a work and then use the photocopy to fax to an ILL borrower. In these cases, obviously, the user receives one copy that becomes his property, but an additional copy is made in the

> Q I work for a university library that has several satellite librar-
> ies on the main campus. In addition, we have other campuses,
> both in the same city as the main campus and also in other cities.
> Are all these libraries considered one entity for the purpose of shar-
> ing our resources?
>
> A For resources that any one of the libraries has purchased, of
> course, the first sale doctrine will apply. This means that the li-
> braries are free to share those resources among themselves—as they
> are between themselves and any other library in the world. The first
> sale doctrine does not give the right to reproduce a work. Therefore,
> one library could not make a copy of a work and forward that copy
> on to another library within the institution; the fact that the librar-
> ies are all part of the same institution has no bearing on this.
>
> The bigger question is what this means for licensed works. As is
> always the case with questions about what uses may be made of li-
> censed works, you must begin by reviewing the license.

process. Clearly, the lending library would not be allowed to file the photocopy to use at a later time for the same purpose. Presumably, then, the photocopy is destroyed. Analogizing this situation to our digital scenario, one
could argue that leaving a digital copy online for a patron to access for a
much shorter time period, such as a day or two, is similar to the photocopy
made in the process of sending a fax.

What is the bottom line about using the Internet for interlibrary loan activities?

The bottom line is that there are no specific guidelines or laws to direct us
in how to legally make use of the Internet in interlibrary loans. We must follow the not-so-specific law and use guidelines written long before "Internet"
was a word. On the other hand, one of my pet peeves is people who pro-
claim that the Internet has changed *everything*, so we must start from scratch
in creating new rules for its use. Seldom do we truly have to start all over.
To some extent, applying the guidelines we already have is common sense:
If you cannot borrow more than five copies of the same article in one year
via photocopying and snail mail, then you certainly can not receive electronic
copies of the same article from more than five people in one year. The bottom line, then, is to know the rules, keep the rules in mind, and use common
sense in trying to apply them to a new environment. And when you hear that

> **One more reason why librarians must become activists**
>
> "The right of access on behalf of copyright proprietors raises significant concerns for libraries and their patrons in their efforts to access and use copyrighted works. The first sale doctrine permits libraries to lend their copies of copyrighted works to users without seeking permission or paying fees to the copyright holder. Access controls have the potential to disrupt traditional library service by converting access to materials to a pay-for-use system regardless of the purpose of the user who is accessing the work. Although libraries could fund access for all of its patrons, the reality of library budgets makes this highly unlikely. Thus, individual library users are likely to have to pay for their access or for various levels of access which will create a world of information haves and 'have nots.'" — Lolly Gassaway, The New Access Right and Its Impact on Libraries and Library Users (2002)

new discussions are beginning about writing guidelines for ILL in cyberspace, get involved and represent the needs of your users to the decision makers.

Bibliography

Copyright Act of 1976, U.S. Code, vol. 17, sec. 108 (1999).

Final Report of the National Commission on New Technological Uses of Copyright Works. 1978. Washington, D.C.: Library of Congress.

Lehman, Bruce A. 1998. *The Conference on Fair Use: Final Report to the Commissioner on the Conclusion of the Conference on Fair Use.* Washington, D.C.: Working Group on Intellectual Property Rights of the Information Infrastructure Task Force.

15

Electronic reserves and class-based Web pages

The Internet opens an entire world of possibilities for offering Reserve collections to patrons more efficiently for both them and librarians. If librarians can digitize items on reserve and offer access to them over the Internet, patrons can access them from anywhere they please, at any time. Even better, an unlimited number of patrons can access one item at any given time. We can make our patrons happier than ever and at less cost to us. So can we do this?

Similarly, many faculty and teachers have discovered the value of the Internet as a tool for disseminating works they once put on reserve, or distributed via paper copies, and so forego using the library reserve service in the first place. Likewise, instruction librarians jumped on the Internet train as a means of providing students with access to materials they previously handed out as photocopies. Are educators and librarians allowed to do this? What if a teacher or faculty member comes to you as her librarian and asks you to create or assist with creating Web pages that would contain digitized copies of items she used to photocopy and distribute in class?

The ability for libraries to provide traditional reserve services and for teachers to distribute photocopies of a work in class is based on the fair use doctrine (*Copyright Act of 1976, U.S. Code*, vol. 17, sec. 107 (1999)) and on limitations provided on certain types of performances and displays. (ibid. sec. 110) No limitations are written into the Copyright Act specifically allowing library reserves or classroom copies. However, various sources, including the American Library Association, have provided guidelines for staying within the law while providing electronic reserves and making classroom copies, which can be transposed into the Internet environment (see Source G).

How does fair use apply to reserves and classroom copying?
Let's review the four fair use criteria and briefly apply them to both traditional and electronic reserves and classroom copying. (Fair use is discussed in much greater detail in Chapter 3.) Recall the basic rules of fair use analysis: (1) there are no clear-cut standards; rather, the analysis is made on a case-by-case basis; and (2) no single factor is determinative.

Purpose and character of use

This factor asks, among other questions, whether the use is for commercial purposes. This factor usually will weigh in favor of libraries and educators, as most libraries are nonprofit entities, and most of the uses associated with reserves and classroom copying are for nonprofit purposes.

Nature of the copyrighted work

With this factor, the concern is whether the work is creative or factual and whether primarily for entertainment or scholarly purposes. Use of factual works is favored in the fair use analysis over use of purely creative works. In an academic library's reserve collection, there is likely to be a mix of creative and factual materials. Presumably, a court would weigh the fair use of these materials differently. The same is likely to be true of copies made for use in classrooms outside of the library. For library instruction uses, the concern is more likely to be with factual works, such as copying pages of research or reference materials in order to teach students how to use them. This is not to say that no use is allowed for creative and entertainment works or that every use is allowed for scholarly and factual works. Keep in mind that the nature of the work is just one of the four fair use factors, and that both CONFU and ALA Guidelines provide guidance in determining what uses and how much use is likely to be considered fair (see Sources C, D, F, and H).

Amount and substantiality of portion copied

This factor, also, probably varies greatly. Professors often ask to make available on reserve an entire book or an entire article. Remember that one article is usually considered to be a work as a whole, which makes sense if you consider that journal articles stand on their own and need not be read in the context of the journal in which they are collected. Section 108(d), however, treats one article from a journal issue as okay for interlibrary loan purposes. By analogy, one could argue for the same treatment for reserves. At other times, only a portion of a work may be used; this is often the case in library instruction. Thus, whether this factor weighs in our favor will vary greatly from situation to situation.

Effect on the potential market for the work

How this factor is measured is changing as technology changes and develops. In the print world, the question was akin to asking whether the copies being made were replacing what would otherwise be sales of an item. For example, a professor could not distribute photocopies of a textbook in order to save his students the cost of buying the book. Two changes in technology

Q Can a library digitize an article on reserve to allow students to have remote access?

A The CONFU guidelines are modeled somewhat on the ALA guidelines for traditional reserves and are rather detailed. In sum, they suggest the following:

- The total amount of material included in an electronic reserves system for a specific course should be a small portion of the total assigned.
- The system should display on an introductory screen a notice stating that making copies of the material may be subject to copyright law and cautioning against further distribution.
- Access should be limited to students registered in the course and to faculty and staff responsible for the course and the system.
- If the work is to be reused in a subsequent term for the same course taught by the same instructor, permission from the copyright owner should be obtained.

have begun to shift the focus of the question. First, with the Internet, copies can be distributed more easily, so that buying a hard copy in many cases becomes unnecessary in the first place. But that does not let us off the hook, because, second, with the establishment of collective licensing services, like the Copyright Clearance Center, librarians have a way to pay for the use of materials, whether in paper or electronic format, even when they do not buy copies of them.

Courts now are beginning to take these technologies into account in evaluating the fourth fair use factor. For example, in response to a library's arguing that its copying and distribution of several copies of a journal article to faculty members does not have an effect on the market for the journal because it could not have afforded additional subscriptions anyway, the courts are listening to the publisher's response that it lost money because the market in licensing royalties was affected. In other words, the copyright owner in such a case is asking the court to consider the market for licensing royalties, as opposed to the market for the original work, which is what this factor traditionally has examined. Concerned that the availability of licensing services will lead to the argument that any use that could have had royalties paid through such a service will by definition be unfair, courts are still trying to sort out this issue. (See *American Geophysical Union v. Texaco, Inc.,*

37 F.2d 881 (2d Cir. 1994); *Williams & Wilkins v. United States*, 487 F.2d 1345 (Ct. Cl. 1973)) Right now, then, it is possible that this factor would weigh against fair use in reserve or classroom copying situations if the copying could result in a loss of licensing fees and royalties to the copyright owners.

What limitations apply to the performance and display rights?

We have already discussed the issues concerning what, in the cyberworld, constitutes a public performance or display. The Technology, Education, and Copyright Harmonization Act of 2002 (the "TEACH Act") allows the performance of a non-dramatic literary or musical work; or the performance of "reasonable and limited portions" of any work; or the display of a work "in an amount comparable to that which is typically displayed in the course of a live classroom session" by or in the course of a transmission under certain restrictions.

First, the performance or display (a) must be made by, at the direction of, or under the actual supervision of, an instructor (b) as an integral part of a class session (c) offered as a regular part of the systematic mediated instructional activities of a governmental body or an accredited nonprofit institution; and it must be directly related to and of material assistance to the teaching content.

"Mediated instructional activities" are defined as activities that use a work as an integral part of a classroom experience controlled or supervised by the instructor and "analogous to the type of performance or display that would take place in a live classroom setting." It specifically does not refer to activities using copies that are typically purchased by students for their own independent use. In other words, the TEACH Act is limited to materials that an instructor herself would typically incorporate into a live lecture and does not cover supplementary materials that an instructor would require her students to read or study on their own time. Of course, these materials may be used by the students during the transmission, but the instructor may not display these materials during the transmission. This was one of the provisions agreed upon during negotiation of the Act (discussed below), in response to publishers' fears that allowing the display of such materials to be transmitted to all students taking the course would negate the students' need to purchase individual copies of the materials (which they would have done in a "traditional" classroom setting).

Second, the transmission of the performance or display must be made for the sole purpose of, and must be technologically restricted to the extent feasible to, students officially enrolled in the course or officers or employees of governmental bodies enrolled in the course as a part of their official duties or employment.

In addition, the institution making the transmission must take various proactive steps discussed further in Chapter 16 in order to be able to use the TEACH Act exemptions.

Are there any guidelines to help us determine what is allowed?

So where do we stand? The Copyright Act does not address electronic reserves systems. Even the TEACH Act did not address reserves. Fair use is one of the trickiest parts of the entire, 50,000-plus words of the Copyright Act. You have seen why. Several guidelines are available to help librarians make decisions and set policies concerning use of electronic reserves and providing access to class materials, whether for a library class or other, on the Internet. It is important to keep in mind that these are only guidelines, not law. Even the guidelines put forth by Congress are not part of the law. In addition, it is important to keep in mind that these guidelines are *suggested minimum* standards to help make determinations of what constitutes fair use. They are not maximum limitations. Many uses that go beyond the numbers in these guidelines will be fair uses.

House Judiciary Committee

The House Judiciary Committee included in its report to Congress on the 1976 Copyright Act an "Agreement on Guidelines for Classroom Copying in Not-For-Profit Education Institutions With Respect to Books and Periodicals" (Congress is fond of long titles). (see Source H) The stated purpose of these guidelines is to "state the minimum standards for educational fair use." Unfortunately, some courts seem to interpret the guidelines as a maximum limit instead of minimum standards. The guidelines go on to warn that things may change in the future, including how much copying will be permissible for educational purposes, as well as what types of copying may and may not be permissible. Finally, the guidelines emphasize that they are not meant to limit permissible copying; copying beyond that described in the guidelines may meet fair use.

The complete text of the guidelines is in Source H. In a nutshell, the guidelines suggest that, for research purposes, or to use in teaching or preparation for teaching, one copy may be made by or for a teacher of a book chapter; a journal article; a short story, short essay, or short poem; or a chart, diagram, drawing, cartoon, or picture from a book, periodical, or newspaper. Multiple copies for classroom use may be made by or for a teacher, as long as they do not exceed more than one copy per student, and so long as they meet specific requirements for brevity, spontaneity, and cumulative effect, and include a notice of copyright. The brevity requirements limit the number or percentage of words and graphics (such as charts or graphs) copied from a single work. The spontaneity factor requires that the copying be initiated by the teacher and that the decision to use the work be so close in time to the moment it will be used as to make it unreasonable to expect to be able to request and receive copyright permission in time. The cumulative effect test states that the copying be for use only in one course; restricts the amount of material that may be copied in one term from the same author, collective work, or periodical volume (except for current news); and limits the total amount of copying per course per term. In addition, this test says that a faculty member cannot repeat copying of the same item from term to term. Finally, the guidelines prohibit copying for the purpose of replacing collective works or books; copying of "consumable" works, e.g., workbooks and exercises; repeated copying from term to term by the same teacher; and charging students more than actual cost for the copies.

Let's apply these standards to using the Internet, either for electronic reserves or for a specific class project. The limits on how much of an item may be copied have implications on electronic reserves in that, in many cases, what a library keeps on reserve is the actual copy of a work owned by a professor—the book or journal article he wants his students to read—rather than photocopies of that article. This is allowed under the first sale doctrine; it is clearly not an infringement to place a lawfully owned work on reserve. Placing a digitized version on the Web, however, might violate the House guidelines. Digitizing means making another copy of the work. The guidelines suggest limitations on how much of one work may be copied, whether it be for purposes of making a single copy for the instructor's use or multiple copies for the students' use. If the instructor wants her students to read one chapter out of a book, no problem—digitizing the single chapter falls within the guidelines. But if she wants the whole book read, there could be a problem. Under these guidelines, one would not be able to make a copy of the whole book (i.e., digitize it) to put on the Web. Likewise, one would have to be very careful with the limitations placed on making multiple copies for classroom use.

The greater potential problems, however, come with the requirements concerning copies per student, cumulative copying, and repeated copying. The argument could be made that when a teacher or librarian digitizes a work to place it on a Web site, she is making only one copy of the work. I have argued in previous chapters that the claim that a librarian in this situation is making multiple copies each time a user accesses a page is a poor argument indeed. Nonetheless, this might be a classic example of a good time to look to the spirit of the law rather than the letter of the law. To begin with, these

---

Q Can I digitize book jackets and include them on my library Web page, for purposes such as use with a summer reading program or to highlight new additions to the collection?

A The book jacket will be considered a separate work from the book itself, regardless of whether the copyright owner in both is the same. It is possible that a fair use argument for such use would succeed, although it is not clear. The jacket will likely be a creative work, and you will be using all of it, so the second and third factors would go against your use. You would win on the first factor, since your use is noncommercial and probably educational. The fourth factor is tricky—on the one hand, the author could license such a use, and this is becoming increasingly common. So the author would lose out on those royalties (bad for you). On the other hand, it is possible that your use would lead to increased sales of the work, which would go in your favor (this argument has been used successfully in the context of a search engine displaying thumbnails of entire photographs for sale). So there is some risk. This is one of those decisions that you should make in conjunction with a review of your institution's copyright policy. It would also be wise to write a memo to your institution's legal counsel informing them of your plans and telling them that you will proceed unless you are instructed otherwise by them.

---

guidelines are not law; they are meant to serve as suggestions and examples and to provide a minimum standard, not a strict definition. Secondly, the Judiciary Committee emphasized that "the conditions determining the extent of permissible copying for educational purposes" may change over time. Certainly, the Committee did not foresee, in 1976, the Internet! The "spirit" of the per-student restriction probably is intended to prevent use outside of the very specific use the teacher has in mind for his particular class. Similarly, the cumulative effects test requires that the copying be used only in one course in one term, and repeated copying for more than one term by the same instructor is forbidden. These restrictions support the spontaneity factor, which basically states that multiple copying may be done only when there is not time to obtain copyright permission from the copyright owner.

Boiling it down, here are some specific suggestions to consider when you digitize works to place them on the Internet either for reserve purposes or to create a Web page for a class (that line blurs in this context):

- Follow the guidelines as much as possible.
- If your needs greatly exceed what is suggested in the guidelines, and if there is time to seek copyright permission to make copies, do so. Discuss with the copyright owner the manner in which you wish to use the copies, that is, that you want to make the work available on the Web.
- Follow the restrictions in the guidelines concerning what portion of a particular work you may copy.
- Limit access to the materials to the single class for which they are intended. This usually will mean using password protection.
- When the course ends, take down the materials. Do not re-post them without copyright permission.

ALA model policy concerning college and university photocopying for classroom, research and library reserve use

In 1982, the American Library Association published a Model Policy intended to assist academic librarians, faculty, administrators, and legal counsel in implementing "the rights and responsibilities" of the 1976 Copyright Act. (see Source G) The Model Policy provides guidelines for exercising fair use rights in the academic environment for classroom teaching, research activities, and library services. The Model Policy is based on an analysis of fair use rights and how they can be reflected by specific uses. It was a result of the joint efforts of ALA's legal counsel, the Copyright Subcommittee (ad hoc) of ALA's Legislation Committee, the Association of College and Research Libraries Copyright Committee, the Association of Research Libraries, and other academic librarians and copyright attorneys.

Sections of the Model Policy are available in Source G. Section III.C. addresses photocopying for library reserves purposes. This section states that, at the request of a faculty member, a library may copy and put on reserve an entire article, an entire chapter from a book, or an entire poem, if the request is to have only one copy on reserve. If the request is to provide multiple copies on reserve, the following guidelines are suggested, along with the relevant sections of the Copyright Act:

1. the amount of material should be reasonable in relation to the total amount of material assigned for one term of a course taking into account the nature of the course, its subject matter and level, 17 U.S.C. secs. 107(1) and (3);
2. the number of copies should be reasonable in light of the number of students enrolled, the difficulty and timing of assignments, and the number of other courses which may assign the same material, 17 U.S.C. secs. 107(1) and (3);

3. the material should contain a notice of copyright, see 17 U.S.C. secs. 401;
4. the effect of photocopying the material should not be detrimental to the market for the work. (In general, the library should own at least one copy of the work.) 17 U.S.C. sec.107(4). (American Library Association, 1982.)

Conference on Fair Use (CONFU) Guidelines

The Conference on Fair Use was convened by the Working Group on Intellectual Property Rights of the Information Infrastructure Task Force. The goal of CONFU was to provide a forum to discuss the interests of copyright owners and users in the fair use context and, if appropriate, to develop guidelines to be used by educators and librarians. CONFU met several times from 1994 through 1998. However, the ninety-three organizations participating were unable to reach agreement on guidelines for several types of use, including electronic reserves.[1] Library representatives generally believed that the guidelines were too narrow, while publishing representatives believed they were too broad. As a result, many library organizations did not support the resulting guidelines that were issued. Nonetheless, the guidelines are worth considering when you establish an electronic reserves policy. Just keep in mind that many uses that go beyond those delineated in the guidelines will be fair uses.

Georgia Harper, a leading expert in copyright in the higher-education arena, suggests that, if anything, the guidelines are too conservative, and that if the issue is again put to a national body, guidelines more in favor of users are likely to prevail. (Harper, 2000) Thus, while there is no guarantee, and these guidelines are not official in any capacity, they do provide some fodder for thought. They are handy to have in that they apply specifically to the electronic environment, unlike the Judiciary Committee's guidelines. In addition, they seem to follow the Committee's guidelines in many ways.

The entire CONFU Guidelines are available in Source. Some of the most pertinent statements include:

- The total number of materials included in electronic reserve systems for a specific course should be a small portion of the total assigned reading for a particular course. This is based in part on the fair use factor of amount and substantiality.
- On a preliminary or introductory screen, electronic reserve systems should display a notice stating that the making of copies of the material included may be subject to copyright law and cautioning against further electronic distribution of the material.
- Access should be limited to students registered in the course and to instructors and staff responsible for the course and the electronic system.

> ### One more reason why librarians must become activists
>
> "Whatever the cost of libraries, it is cheap compared to that of an ignorant nation." — Walter Cronkite

- Permission from the copyright holder is required if the item is to be reused in a subsequent term for the same course taught by the same instructor.

What is the Copyright Clearance Center all about?

Having been through the analysis of what might and might not be permissible uses of electronic reserves and providing class materials on Web pages, I should share the secret of the easy way to go about protecting yourself and your library: The Copyright Clearance Center will request copyright permission for materials to be used in electronic reserves systems. Of course, the Center is not able to obtain permission for everything ever published, but it is a good place to start. Because they have limitations, however, it is very important to understand the issues discussed in this chapter and to prepare a policy for how you intend to handle requests.

Note

1. For the record, organizations either endorsing or supporting the Fair Use Guidelines for Electronic Reserves Systems included the American Association of Law Libraries, Association of American University Presses, Music Library Association, and Special Libraries Association. Those opposing the Guidelines included various organizations supporting copyright-owner interests and the Association of Research Libraries.

Bibliography

American Geophysical Union v. Texaco, Inc., 37 F.2d 881 (2nd Cir. 1994).

American Library Association. 1982. *Model Policy Concerning College and University Photocopying for Classroom, Research and Library Reserve Use.* Washington, D.C.: American Library Association.

Copyright Act of 1976, U.S. Code, vol. 17, secs. 107 and 110 (1999).

Harper, Georgia. 2000. *Copyright Crash Course* [Online]. Available: www.utsystem.edu/OGC/IntellectualProperty/confu.htm (August).

House Committee on the Judiciary, *Copyright Act of 1976*, 94th Congress, 1976, H. Rept. 1476.

Lehman, Bruce A. 1998. *The Conference on Fair Use: Final Report to the Commissioner on the Conclusion of the Conference on Fair Use*. Washington, D.C.: Working Group on Intellectual Property Right of the Information Infrastructure Task Force.

Williams & Wilkins v. United States, 487 F.2d 1345 (Ct. Cl. 1973).

16

Library instruction and distance education

When I first began teaching library instruction classes, slightly over ten years ago, the only electronic tool we taught on a regular basis was the online catalog; all the other sources we taught were print based. Our library subscribed to one or two Infotrac databases and to ERIC and PsycLit, all of which were on CD-ROM. The Web at that time was completely text based; there were no graphics on the Internet. During the next two years, the Web as we now know it arrived. By the time I moved into the position of Coordinator of Library Instruction two years later, my new library relied more on electronic databases than on printed materials for many common research purposes. One of my first projects was to join a team creating that library's first Web pages. Our instruction quickly became almost entirely electronic based, and we developed an extensive program of classes specifically teaching users how to use the Web. Today, library users use databases accessed through the Web as well as material on the Web itself for research, sometimes the latter to the chagrin of librarians. Instruction librarians are concerned with use of the Web, both as a research tool and as a teaching tool.

The arena of library instruction pulls together many of the copyright issues already discussed. Library instruction may involve distributing to students printed copies of Web pages, creating Web pages for use in teaching, demonstrating Web pages in the process of teaching students how to use them, and providing distance learning. These uses potentially implicate a copyright owner's rights of reproduction, distribution, public display or performance, and even creation of derivative works.

Can I give live demonstrations in the classroom?
Demonstration of the Web or any other digital tool during teaching is potentially subject to the copyright owner's rights of public performance and display. Such uses would have a strong argument of being excused by the fair use doctrine, but one need not even worry with that analysis, because under the Copyright Act, demonstrating the use of the Web in a classroom setting for library instruction purposes is not a problem for nonprofit educational

institutions. Section 110 of the Copyright Act allows "the performance or display of a work by instructors or pupils in the course of face-to-face teaching activities of a nonprofit educational institution, in a classroom or similar place devoted to instruction." (Section 110(1))

Might the reproduction of pages cause problems? The answer to this question draws on issues already discussed in different contexts. Certainly there is a good fair use argument, especially if you stay within published guidelines. Available guidelines do not specifically address this situation, however. The two that come closest are the Conference on Fair Use (CONFU) Guidelines for Digital Images (see Source C) and the CONFU guidelines on Educational Multimedia (see Source F). The Guidelines for Digital Images are meant to address the digitization of images for the creation of "databases of individual visual images from which images intended for educational uses may be selected for display." (CONFU Guidelines for Digital Images, 1998: 1.1 n.4) The guidelines for educational multimedia are meant to address multimedia projects that include the original work of educators or students in combination with copyright works in various media formats. (CONFU Guidelines for Educational Multimedia, 1998: 1.3) The two sets of guidelines are very similar—in fact, there is some repetition between them. Neither quite meets the situation of creating straightforward electronic slide presentations of electronic databases or Web pages, but both are meant to provide guidance in determining uses that should qualify as fair uses, so one can draw on both sets of guidelines to make inferences to apply to the situation of "canned" Web presentations.

The Guidelines for Digital Images say that an educator may compile digital images and display them on the nonprofit educational institution's secure network for classroom use, among other uses. The Guidelines also note that fair use "limits the number and substantiality of the images that may be used from a single source." Unhelpfully, the Guidelines do not expand on this point. The Guidelines on Educational Multimedia give more specific limitations, depending on the format used, but based on the Agreement on Guidelines for Classroom Copying in Not-For-Profit Educational Institutions from the House Judiciary Committee Report on the 1976 copyright revisions. It is doubtful how useful these guidelines would be in the "canned" presentation situation, however. Realistically, in demonstrating databases, you will be using a very small number of the total potential Web pages included in the database. If the database contains 200,000 records, there are well over 200,000 potential Web pages that may be displayed from that database. Your use of a limited handful of pages is not likely to conflict with the amount and substantiality factor of fair use. What if you are demonstrating a particular Web site that only includes a half dozen pages? Although the numerical analysis may not help, your fair use position probably will remain strong as long as you copy no more than is truly necessary for your means. For example, if you want to show an example of Yahoo's organizational structure, you might copy four or five pages at different levels of the hierarchy, but you certainly would not attempt to copy all of Yahoo's pages within a given top-level category.

The Guidelines for Digital Images also state that credit must be given to the sources and a copyright notice displayed. This could be difficult, or at least tedious, when making electronic slides from Web pages. The Guidelines for Educational Multimedia allow the credit and copyright notice information to be combined and shown in a separate section of the presentation. Thus, the simplest option might be to include a slide containing credit and copyright notice information at the beginning or end of each section or of the presentation as a whole.

Both sets of guidelines contain time restrictions. The time restrictions in the digitized images guidelines specifically apply only to the digitization of newly acquired analog visual images, which does not include the situation with which we are concerned. (CONFU, Guidelines for Digital Images, 1998: 2.4) The multimedia guidelines, however, state that "educators may use their educational multimedia projects created for educational purposes…for teaching courses, for a period of up to two years after the first instructional use with a class. Use beyond that time period, even for educational purposes, requires permission for each copyright portion incorporated in the production." Again, the type of demonstration with which we are concerned does not meet the definition of multimedia projects contained in the guidelines. Nonetheless, it could be argued that, in the absence of guidelines specifically designed for our situation, the multimedia guidelines should apply. On the other hand, the type of material with which we are concerned changes so frequently that one is not likely to be using the same "canned" demonstration for anything close to two years.

Is there a problem with enhancing electronic presentations?

What if you want to do more than just create demonstrations involving screen captures from Web pages, such as including your own commentary or instruction within the electronic presentation, or creating a presentation that involves not just demonstrations of online materials but also print materials, or a presentation that includes information about library hours or pictures from of the library? As mentioned above, the Guidelines on Educational Multimedia apply to multimedia projects that incorporate an educator's "original material, such as course notes or commentary, together with various copyrighted media formats." (CONFU, Guidelines for Educational Multimedia, 1998: 1.3) (See Source F.) Such presentations are allowed under Section 110(1) (see Source A), and the guidelines give more specific direction, such as the limitations on proportions of the work used, time restrictions, and requirement of providing credit and copyright notice, as discussed above.

What are the copyright implications for distance learning?

The Technology, Education, and Copyright Harmonization Act of 2002 (the "TEACH Act"), signed into law on November 2, 2002, amended the Copyright Act to allow certain public performances and displays of works in the course of providing distance education. Although Section 110(1) of the Copyright Act allows the performance or display of a work in the course of face-to-face teaching activities of a nonprofit educational institution, until the TEACH Act was passed, such rights in the context of distance education were dramatically limited by Section 110(2). That section allowed the transmission of the performance only of a non-dramatic literary or musical work, or the display of a work, only for "reception in classrooms or similar places normally devoted to instruction, or reception by persons to whom the transmission is directed because their disabilities or other special circumstances prevent their attendance in classrooms or similar places normally devoted to instruction" or to officers or employees of government bodies. Thus, the Section 110 exemption did not address the typical situation of modern distance education, in which the student is unlikely to be found in a "classroom or similar place normally devoted to instruction." As distance education rapidly expanded, Congress directed the Copyright Office to prepare a report containing recommendations of changes necessary to accommodate the use of digital technologies in distance education. The Copyright Office submitted its report to Congress in 1998. The TEACH Act is based on the recommendations contained in that report and closely tracks those recommendations.

The TEACH Act replaces the current Section 110(2) and adds a new Section 112(f). The new Section 110(2) allows the performance of a non-dramatic literary or musical work; or the performance of reasonable and limited portions of any work; or the display of a work "in an amount comparable to that which is typically displayed in the course of a live classroom session" by or in the course of a transmission under the following restrictions:

- The performance or display must be made by, at the direction of, or under the actual supervision of, an instructor
  - as an integral part of a class session

- offered as a regular part of the systematic mediated instructional activities of a governmental body or an accredited nonprofit institution;
- The performance or display must be directly related and of material assistance to the teaching content; and
- The transmission must be made for the sole purpose of, and must be technologically restricted to the extent feasible to, (1) students officially enrolled in the course or (2) officers or employees of governmental bodies enrolled in the course as a part of their official duties or employment.

The body or institution making the transmission must abide by the following restrictions:

- Implement "policies on copyright";
- Provide educational material to faculty, students, and relevant staff members regarding U.S. copyright law and promoting compliance with those laws;
- Provide notice to students receiving the transmission that materials used in the course may be subject to U.S. copyright law;
- Use technological measures to ensure that recipients of the transmission cannot retain copies of a work for longer than the class session;
- Use technological measures to prevent the unauthorized dissemination of the work by the recipients of the transmission; and
- Not interfere with technological measures to protect works.
- The new exemptions do not apply if the performance or display is of a copy not lawfully made and acquired under the Copyright Act and the transmitting entity knew or had reason to believe such; nor with respect to a work "produced or marketed primarily for performance or display as part of mediated instructional activities transmitted via digital networks.

"Mediated instructional activities" are defined as activities that use a work as an integral part of a classroom experience controlled or supervised by the instructor and "analogous to the type of performance or display that would take place in a live classroom setting." It specifically does not refer to activities using copies that are typically purchased by students for their own independent use. In other words, the exemptions are limited to materials that an instructor herself would typically incorporate into a live lecture and does not cover supplementary materials that an instructor would require her students to read or study on their own time.

The new Section 112(f), which addresses ephemeral recordings, allows the making of copies of digital works, or making digital copies of analog works, to be used in transmissions authorized under Section 110(2), if:

- the copies are retained and used only by the entity that made them;
- no further copies are reproduced from them;
- the copies are used solely for transmissions authorized under Section 110(2); and
- in the case of converting analog works into digital formats, no digital version of the work is available to the institution without being subject to technological protection measures.

The TEACH Act does not address all situations encompassed by a fully developed distance education program, most notably electronic reserves used in such programs. The CONFU Guidelines on Educational Multimedia, written four years before the TEACH Act was passed, may help fill in some of the gaps. Keep in mind, however, that Guidelines are not law.

The multimedia guidelines allow performance or display of an educator's multimedia project when assigned to students for directed self-study and for remote instruction to students enrolled in curriculum-based courses, as long as the transmission is provided over the educational institution's secure electronic network in real-time (i.e., "live") or for after-class review or directed self-study. The network also must have technological limitations on access, such as password protection and must prevent the ability to make copies of copyrighted material. If the institution cannot provide the technology to prevent copies being made, the project can be provided for remote access only for a period of fifteen days after the initial real-time remote use or fifteen days after the assignment for directed self-study. (CONFU Guidelines on Educational Multimedia, 1998: 3.2) Under these guidelines, a library could provide access to a multimedia presentation on its network for an extended period of time only if it meets the following technological requirements. If it cannot do so, it can provide access only for fifteen days. However, after that time, a copy may be placed on reserve. So students could check out a diskette, for example, containing the presentation.

The Guidelines on Distance Learning apply to situations other than ours: They apply only to live transmissions that include works or uses not covered under Section 110(2) (see Source A).

Do vendor licenses play a role?

As our electronic environment becomes more advanced and omni present, librarians have become more sophisticated about licensing the use of electronic databases. Unfortunately, too many libraries still do not appreciate the importance and implications of the licenses they sign with vendors. Many libraries automatically sign the standard license provided without giving much

> **One more reason why librarians must become activists**
>
> "In the nonstop tsunami of global information, librarians provide us with floaties and teach us how to swim." — Linton Weeks

thought to the contents of the license and whether the license truly meets the need of the library. If you are sent a license that does not comport with the manner in which you intend to use a resource, talk to the vendor about it. Never sign something you have not read, and never sign a license with whose terms you know your library will not be able to comply.

That said, some vendor licenses may contain clauses addressing the use for instructional purposes of databases or information taken from databases, although this is not yet the norm. If your license addresses instructional situations, be sure to abide by the license. This may mean that you do not have to worry about the preceding analysis of what is and is not allowed, because your license will tell you explicitly what that particular vendor allows. On the other hand, if it is more restrictive than what you would like to be able to do, work with the vendor to come up with an agreement that is mutually acceptable.

17

Licensing

As I did when I wrote the first edition of this book, I posted a general question to several library discussion groups asking basically, "What do you want to know about copyright law?" The result this time was fascinating: Many people asked about specific uses and situations, but well over half of the responses asked questions about licensing. I don't recall getting a single question about licensing in 2000. Why the sudden interest and concern? Because, as librarians well know, the radical and ever-increasing shift to the use of information in digital formats is almost always based on licensing the materials, not purchasing them. If we aren't there yet, we will soon reach the point where licensing is another subject (along with copyright in general) of which most librarians must be educated. A full and thorough discussion of licensing requires its own book, and indeed, I highly recommend two specifically on this subject: *Licensing Digital Content: A Practical Guide for Librarians* and *Interpreting and Negotiating Licensing Agreements: A Guidebook for the Library, Research, and Teaching Professions* (see the Bibliography at the end of this chapter for complete information). In this chapter, I will attempt only to cover some basic principles of licensing to help librarians understand what it means, why it's important, and how to identify some potential problems.

What is licensing?!

Black's Law Dictionary defines *license* as "A personal privilege to do some particular act or series of acts on [a piece of property] without possessing any estate or interest therein, and is ordinarily revocable at will of the licensor and is not assignable." So a license is the ability to use a piece of property that belongs to someone else without obtaining any ownership rights in the property. A rental agreement is an excellent example of a license—as the licensee, you obtain the right to live in an apartment or a house, perhaps for a specified period of time, but the licensor continues to own the property. You may be allowed to paint the walls, plant a garden, or make other changes to the property, but even that does not grant you any ownership interest in the property.

One respondent to my e-mail asked if licensing is really a copyright issue. The answer is: Yes, of course! The copyright is the subject of the li-

> Q What is the difference between copyright, licenses, and terms and conditions of use?
>
> A "Copyright" is the bundle of rights conferred on the author of a work consisting of the exclusive rights to reproduce, distribute, publicly display, and publicly perform the work and to make derivatives of the work. The original author of the work may transfer her copyrights by giving them completely to someone else. Or she may allow others the right to make certain uses of the work without giving up her own rights in the work; this is a license. A rental agreement is an excellent example of a license—as the licensee, you obtain the right to live in an apartment or a house, perhaps for a specified period of time, but the licensor continues to own the property. You may be allowed to paint the walls, plant a garden, or make other changes to the property, but even that does not grant you any ownership interest in the property.

cense. The above quoted definition refers to "property." Remember that copyright is a type of intellectual property. This means that copyright owners may grant others the right to do certain things with their copyrighted works without the licensee obtaining any ownership interest in the works. Think of your license of electronic resources as renting those resources: You may be allowed to download or print items from the database, or to do various acts in regard to those databases and information, but you do not obtain any ownership of the resources.

What is the significance of licensing from a copyright perspective?

For several years, librarians have been concerned about various effects of licensing electronic works as opposed to purchasing copies of the works (whether in print or electronic format), such as the inability to control archiving the works. If you don't own a copy of the works contained in a database, you have no control over whether they will always be in that database.

From a copyright perspective, licensing has several major effects. First, the fact that you do not own a copy of the works at issue effects what you can do with those works. Remember the first sale doctrine—when you own a particular copy of a work, you can dispose of or display that work however you like. The same is not true for a work that you license, since you do not own that copy.

Second, one can always contract around the law. Think of the law as being the default of what your rights are as an information user. By default, you have the right to fair use, for one. By the same token, the copyright owner, by default, has exclusive rights in the work. But you can always agree to rights or restrictions that go beyond the law. Thus, the copyright owner can give away her exclusive rights entirely if she so desires. More importantly for you, you can give away your fair use and other rights. How does this happen? When you sign a license that says something along the lines of, "Copies may be made for personal use only" or "The contents of this database may not be transmitted to any site outside the premises of the licensing institution."

Having to deal with licenses is yet another reason for librarians to be knowledgeable about copyright law. Under copyright law, you have the rights, among others of course, to make and distribute copies for limited purposes; to display or transmit an electronic copy of a work for certain purposes; and to quote or excerpt a work if it meets fair use standards. Some licenses may prohibit the end user or library staff from doing any or all of these activities under any circumstances. One question I received from my discussion-list postings asked, "Why, if a publisher knows it is selling to a library, does its license say 'Do not lend'?!!" All this to say: Know what you're agreeing to, and be sure you have the rights you need in every license you sign or that you are willing to give up those rights.

How do I protect my users' rights?
You must follow three fundamental rules:

1. Read every license you receive before signing it! This sounds simple enough, but many librarians do not do it.
2. Understand the terms of the license. If you are uncertain of anything, ask questions. But use your critical thinking skills to decide who to ask—do you trust the vendor to give you an unbiased answer? The best possible option would be to discuss all terms of the license with your entity's legal counsel before signing anything.
3. Do not sign the license if you are not willing to agree to and abide by the terms of the license.

Many librarians assume that they have no control over the content of licenses they sign, so they don't pay attention to those terms. Even if this were

> Terms and conditions of use are basically a license for using material you find on the Web. Most sophisticated Web sites have terms of use, the terms of which are often rather general, such as "do not infringe our site," "we are not liable for anything you do with information obtained from this site," etc.

true, you need to read and understand the terms, because by signing the license, you are committing yourself and your institution to abiding by those terms. In this age of increasingly litigious copyright owners, licensees need to be especially careful that they know what they are agreeing to.

But in actuality, it is not always true that you have no control over the terms of a license. In many cases, the licensor will be willing to negotiate, because, after all, he wants your business. If you've never approached a licensor about negotiating changes in the licensing terms, you may be surprised to learn that he will be open to making certain changes. On the other hand, of course, some licensors will almost never be willing to negotiate. In those cases, you must decide whether to accept the terms of the agreement or to do without that particular product (or find another vendor). Before negotiating the terms of a license, you should take time to bone up on licensing by reviewing some of the resources listed later in this chapter. As a bare minimum, be sure you know what you want before you enter negotiations; what you're willing to give up; and how much you want to pay.

What should be addressed in a license?

A license should include provisions addressing all of your needs, and it should be clear to you what the license allows your library to do and what it prevents your library from doing. I urge you to consult a more thorough resource on licensing, such as those listed below, rather than depend on this as your sole resource for negotiating licenses. The following is a list of issues that either should be addressed in every license or commonly occur in licenses, even if not necessary:

- What material is it that is being licensed? Does the licensor have the right to remove or change the material during the term of your license? Is the licensor required to notify you if this happens?
- How will the licensed material be accessed?
- Who can access the licensed material?

Q If I'm working with a user from an institution other than my own, is it okay to send him or her articles from a database that is licensed by my institution as part of our virtual reference services?

A This totally depends on the terms of your license with that database vendor. Anytime you have a question of what you can and cannot do with material or works obtained from a database, the first place you should turn to find an answer is your license. This is true even if you are quite confident that the use you want to make would be considered a fair use or otherwise allowed under copyright law. The Copyright Act is basically a default; in the lack of any agreement with a copyright owner, the provisions of the Copyright Act apply. However, if a user enters into an agreement with a copyright owner, that agreement will prevail over the terms of the Copyright Act. In other words, it is entirely possible for you to contract away your users' rights when you enter into a license agreement. This is why you should take licensing very seriously and read all of your license agreements closely, making sure you understand and are willing to accept all of the terms in the license before signing it.

Assuming that your license does not prohibit you from sharing works in this manner, you should go through standard analysis of whether this use would be allowed by the Copyright Act: Does it fall under one of the exemptions? Would it be considered a fair use?

- What uses are authorized? What kinds of limitations are in place? Consider all possible uses, including various media or technology, remote access, categories of users, archival needs, reserve usage, ILL usage, and so on.
- Is fair use specifically addressed? If not, it is deemed to apply, to the extent that you have not agreed to not engage in activities that would otherwise constitute fair use. Ideally, a license will contain language that says nothing in the license should be deemed to limit the licensee's fair use rights. On the other hand, a licensor may ask the licensee to give up rights that are his under the fair use doctrine but without mentioning the term "fair use," so read very critically for this.
- Is the licensor required to provide all the necessary support services you will need?
- How long is the term of the license, and what are your renewal options?
- How are fees calculated and paid?

Q If my library has licensed a word-processing program that includes clip art, may we use the clip art on a poster, on our Web site, or on printed handouts?

A First, look at the provisions of your license for the program. It may tell you what you can and cannot do with the clip art. If it does not, then copyright law will apply. Would the use qualify as a fair use? This type of situation also has a good argument of implied license: The creator of the software knows that people will be using it to create items like posters, printed handouts, and Web sites, so it seems likely that the creating entity would know that the clip art included in the package would be used in the same ways. Thus, the argument would go, the creating entity has licensed such uses by implication.

- Does the licensor warrant to you, the licensee, that the licensor has the right to license the rights it purports to license? Is your library indemnified in case a third party comes out of the woodwork with a hunger to sue someone for alleged infringement?
- Is either party allowed to transfer the license?
- What termination rights does each party have? What happens to your rights if the licensor terminates the license before the term expires?

Where can I go for more thorough help with understanding and negotiating licenses?

Two books do a good job of providing practical guides for librarians:

Bielefield, Arlene, and Lawrence Cheeseman. 1999. *Interpreting and Negotiating Licensing Agreements: A Guidebook for the Library, Research, and Teaching Professions.* New York: Neal-Schuman.

Harris, Lesley Ellen. 2002. Licensing Digital Content: A Practical Guide for Librarians. Chicago: American Library Association.

In addition, various resources are, of course, available on the Web. Some of the better ones are the following:

Liblicense
www.library.yale.edu/~llicense/index.shtml
This Web site is an excellent source for detailed advice about language in

> **One more reason why librarians must become activists**
>
> "Many . . . libraries are also investigating their options, recognizing — as we all do — that the push to build an all-electronic collection can't be undertaken at the risk of: (1) weakening that collection with journals we neither need nor want, and (2) increasing our dependence on publishers who have already shown their determination to monopolize the information marketplace." Kenneth Frazier, "The Librarian's Dilemma: Contemplating the Costs of the 'Big Deal,'" *D-Lib Magazine* (March 2001)

licenses—both what to include and what to look out for or to try to avoid. It breaks down the provisions in a typical license, explaining what each means, and providing examples of language both good and bad for libraries as licensees. In addition, downloadable software is available on the site that assists you in writing your own license. An excellent resource.

Principles for Licensing Electronic Resources
www.arl.org/scomm/licensing/principles.html
This statement of principles was coauthored by six library associations, including ALA and the American Association of Law Libraries. The stated purpose is to guide libraries in negotiating license agreements for access to electronic resources and to provide licensors with a sense of the issues of importance to libraries and their user communities in such negotiations.

Licensing Electronic Resources: Strategic and Practical Considerations for Signing Electronic Information Delivery Agreements
www.arl.org/scomm/licensing/licbooklet.html
Just as the title implies, this page provides straightforward advice regarding issues to consider before beginning to negotiate a license.

18

Writing a copyright policy

What is a copyright policy?

A copyright policy acknowledges your institution's commitment to abiding by copyright law and provides guidelines to assist the members of your institution's community in doing so. It may be a very simple, brief statement, but it will be more valuable if it addresses issues specific to how your institution uses copyrighted works. A copyright policy should provide some general guidelines for how to use copyrighted works without infringing and where users may go for more information.

Note that a copyright policy may be specific for your library, or it may be intended for your institution as a whole. If you are starting from scratch in preparing a policy, the first thing you should do is determine whether your institution has already implemented a policy and whether your library needs a separate policy. If you decide not to write your own, you should ensure that the library's needs are addressed in the institution's policy and work with your administration to make this happen.

Why do you need one?

Under current law, libraries may be granted safe harbors from liability for copyright infringement resulting from certain actions only if they have copyright policies in place. The Digital Millennium Copyright Act (DMCA) provides a safe harbor for entities providing "online services or network access" or that operate facilities providing such services or access. The Technology, Education, and Copyright Harmonization Act (TEACH Act) provides a safe harbor for entities providing certain services or information as part of distance education activities. These statutes are discussed below.

Implementing a copyright policy also shows employees and employers, boards of directors, faculty, staff, students, and users that your library is serious about upholding copyright law. As all librarians well know, users at all levels have many misconceptions about what types of Internet-related activities are allowed under copyright law. A common myth is that if a work is posted on the Internet, it is, by definition, not protected by copyright law. This is simply not true. But due to this type of misconception, it is increasingly important that all information users have some basic awareness of copyright. And it is part of the professional duties of all librarians to assist in this aspect of user education. Having a well-placed, easily accessibly copyright policy can point out to users that their actions are limited by copyright law, when they might not otherwise have considered it.

Finally, implementing a copyright policy may help a library accused of infringement to show that the infringement was "innocent," thereby significantly limiting the damages to which the library would be subject.

DMCA policy requirements

As was discussed in Chapter 13, online service providers (OSPs) may potentially be liable for the infringing activities of others where the OSP provides access to the infringing work, even if the OSP has no actual knowledge of the infringement. The DMCA limits the liability of OSPs in regard to transmitting or routing activities; caching material made available by someone else; placing infringing material on a system or network at a user's direction; and linking to sites containing infringing information. Since libraries usually provide online services or network access and/or operate facilities that provide such access, they will usually be considered OSPs under the DMCA.

To be able to take advantage of the safe harbors, however, OSPs must abide by several requirements (see Chapter 13). Although the DMCA does not specifically state that an OSP must create a publicly accessible copyright policy, some of the rules it sets forth are well suited to such a policy. In addition, simply having a copyright policy in place will help meet some of the DMCA requirements.

Those rules include:

- implementing a policy to terminate subscribers or account holders who are repeat offenders
- prohibiting the selection and modification of the content of material received by users
- prohibiting the maintaining of copies of material received by users for longer than is necessary to perform normal Internet functions
- abiding by industry standards regarding refreshing, reloading, and other updating of information
- designating an agent to receive notification of infringement claims and making contact information for such agent publicly available on the pertinent Web site

- disabling links when the entity has actual knowledge that they provide access to infringing material
- taking specific steps laid out in the DMCA should your library receive notification of a claim of infringement.

The above is not a complete explanation of how to qualify for DMCA safe harbors. Please refer to the Copyright Office summary of the DMCA for more information: www.loc.gov/copyright/legislation/dmca.pdf.

TEACH Act policy requirements

As opposed to the DMCA, the TEACH Act specifically requires implementation of a "copyright policy," although it does not explain what should be included in such a policy. (See Chapter 16 for a thorough discussion of the TEACH Act.) Kenneth Crews, law professor and Director of the Copyright Management Center at Indiana University School of Law, believes that the context of the Act suggests that copyright policies should incorporate the standards that the entity requires to be followed when using protected works in distance education programs.

Who should be involved in the process of writing a copyright policy?

First and foremost, include your entity's legal counsel in the process of creating your copyright policy. Essentially, part of your policy will involve interpreting the law; even if your legal counsel is not a copyright expert, it is paramount that she be involved in the process from beginning to end.

Your entity's administrators should be involved and kept up to date. As is true for creating most policies, it is wise to involve librarians on the frontline, since librarians interact with users in different contexts; in doing so, your policy will likely address as many relevant issues and situations as possible. It might also be useful to include representative users, at least early in the process, whose understanding of what is and is not allowed under copyright law may differ from that of library staff; including users in your process may bring to light issues to be addressed in the policy that might otherwise be overlooked.

What should it say?

In drafting your library's copyright policy, it might be helpful to review those created by other similar libraries. Most such policies are posted on library Web sites. Of course, you must draft a policy that is appropriate for your own library; do not base your policy on someone else's without analyzing the appropriateness of the provisions of the policy for your library. And of course do not simply copy someone else's policy, who would infringe the copyright in that policy!

Keep in mind that your copyright policy will have several target audiences: users of all sorts, who may be as diverse as faculty, students, and staff; library employees; and non-library employees of your institution. In some cases, it might be helpful to organize your policy according to the different audiences, especially if it becomes at all detailed.

Your copyright policy should, at the minimum, include the following information:

- Generally
  - Brief review of what is covered by the Copyright Act
  - Explanation of what constitutes fair use
  - Guidelines for determining when one should obtain permission to use a work
  - Guidelines for use, i.e., what one may do without obtaining permission
  - The institution's policy for addressing claims of infringement
- Information required by the DMCA:
  - An agent designated to receive notice of alleged infringing actions
  - A statement that the institution will terminate the services of users and account holders who are repeat infringers
  - A statement that the institution will accommodate and not interfere with technological protection measures
- If your institution assists in the delivery of distance education, information suggested in the TEACH Act:
  - State your institution's policies regarding the use of copyrighted work in distance education programs (per the limitations of the TEACH Act).

Your policy should also address your institution's position regarding its rights under the work-made-for-hire doctrine. That doctrine says that the copyright in anything you create as part of your job is deemed to belong to your employer. Traditionally, however, exceptions are made for academic faculty and their works. For this reason, your copyright policy should include information about:

- Your institution's claim of ownership in works created by employees
- Your institution's claim and/or release of specific rights in works created by employees
- What the copyright notice to be displayed should look like.

> **One more reason why librarians must become activists**
>
> "My mother and my father were illiterate immigrants from Russia. When I was a child they were constantly amazed that I could go to a building and take a book on any subject. They couldn't believe this access to knowledge we have here in America. They couldn't believe that it was free." — Kirk Douglas

What should you do with your policy once you've written it?

First and foremost, abide by it! Having a policy in place and not following it can sometimes be worse, from a legal perspective, than not having a policy in the first place.

Your copyright policy is of little good if no one sees it. Distribute the policy to all employees of the institution upon completion. Anytime the policy is modified, notice should be sent to employees. Sending regular reminders of the policy and your institution's commitment to follow copyright law is also a good idea. Post the policy on Intranet and Internet sites, and consider posting it, or at least referring to it, in appropriate areas such as in computer/research labs and near photocopy machines. Include the policy in relevant manuals, such as orientation material for new employees, faculty, and students; and in manuals used in programs where works are created, such as your library instruction program or your Web design program. Refer to the policy in library instruction classes.

Finally, review your policy annually with your legal counsel to determine if any updates or other modifications may be necessary.

19

Librarians as representatives of libraries and library users

Clearly, many questions regarding copyright that are important for librarians remain unanswered: How do I know how to behave when the answers aren't so clear? Should librarians be conservative and safe, or should we push the envelope? How do librarians work in their daily jobs to stand up for their rights without being run over by publishers and other groups that are being increasingly aggressive in pushing to increase the rights of copyright owners?

What role do librarians play in making copyright law?
Various limitations on copyright, expansion of the rights of copyright owners, and concern for the rights of users engender lengthy and ardent debate. Chief among the issues are fair use; various schemes that would create what Professor Litman refers to as an "exclusive right to read," such as "pay-per-use" database licenses; and a wide range of proposed changes in technology law that would ultimately result in the elimination of users' rights under the Copyright Act.

The lengthy and ardent debates are not *among* librarians, but between librarians and members of the commercial end of the information industry, primarily publishers. At a basic level, one could say that the objectives of librarians and publishers are at opposite ends of the information-access spectrum: librarians want to ensure free access to information for everyone, and publishers make their living off of making everyone pay for access. Obviously, this is oversimplified and exaggerated. Nonetheless, it makes the point.

Recall that the entire history of modern and American copyright law has been an attempt to balance the interests of authors with those of users. Also keep in mind that American copyright is based on the Constitution, which guarantees rights to authors, but within limitations, and for the motivational purpose of promoting the development of the arts and sciences. Publishers and other copyright owners are not "bad guys" because they want to get paid for their work; and librarians are not "bad guys" because they want to give people free access to property owned by others. The problem is in finding the middle ground—that which is most fair to as many parties involved as possible, and, more importantly, that which does not damage the basic rights of either copyright owners or information users. The problem is finding that balance. And right now, the tide is clearly running in favor of copyright owners.

How do recent and currently proposed legislation threaten that balance?

Term of copyright protection

The Sonny Bono Copyright Term Extension Act is a good example; the Act and a critique of it are discussed in Chapter 5. Recall Rep. Mary Bono's statement that Sonny Bono wanted copyright to last forever: that she had been told by her staffers that this would be unconstitutional, but maybe Congress could do something about it anyway. The Sonny Bono Act is an excellent example of copyright law completely ignoring its foundation. In addition to the "limited time" restriction in the Constitution, the constitutional purpose of copyright is to motivate authors to write and to publish their works. It is highly unlikely that extending the duration of copyright protection from 50 years to 70 years *after the death of the author* would motivate an author who otherwise would not create. Note that the Supreme Court's upholding this law was based in large part on its belief that the term of copyright protection should be determined by Congress, not the courts.

The Public Domain Enhancement Act of 2003 was introduced by Rep. Zoe Lofgren to respond to the exponential shrinkage of the public domain.

The bill addresses critics' concerns with the continual increases in the term of copyright protection that most copyright owners—the Walt Disney company aside—do not benefit significantly, if at all, from the last many decades of protection in their works. The bill would require renewals of copyright every ten years, beginning fifty years after the date of first publication. The bill mandates that the burden of submitting a renewal request form must be minimal and allocates a fee of only one dollar for renewing the copyright. If the renewal request and fee are not submitted, the work would go into the public domain.

Note that the rationale, and in a general sense, the process, of the proposed renewal system are similar to those under current trademark law. Federal registrations of trademarks must be renewed every ten years. This renewal process includes showing proof that the mark is still being used. Of course, trademark protection is based on a different rationale than copyright: If a trademark ceases to be used for a significant period of time, its protection is

Copyright Reform: the Stagnation of the Public Domain

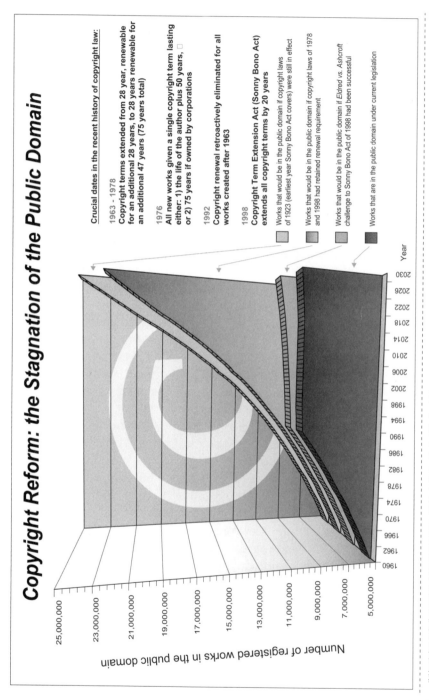

Crucial dates in the recent history of copyright law:

1963 - 1978
Copyright terms extended from 28 year, renewable for an additional 28 years, to 28 years renewable for an additional 47 years (75 years total)

1976
All new works given a single copyright term lasting either: 1) the life of the author plus 50 years, or 2) 75 years if owned by corporations

1992
Copyright renewal retroactively eliminated for all works created after 1963

1998
Copyright Term Extension Act (Sonny Bono Act) extends all copyright terms by 20 years

Works that would be in the public domain if copyright laws of 1923 (earliest year Sonny Bono Act covers) were still in effect

Works that would be in the public domain if copyright laws of 1978 and 1998 had retained renewal requirement

Works that would be in the public domain if *Eldred vs. Ashcroft* challenge to Sonny Bono Act of 1998 had been successful

Works that are in the public domain under current legislation

Year

Number of registered works in the public domain

lost. Although the rationale of trademark and copyright protections are different, in a general sense, the Lofgren bill may be getting at the same broad rationale as that behind trademark law, in that if a copyright owner is no longer benefiting from protection of his or her work, there is no legitimate reason to continue to exclude the ability of others to use that work, and it should be freely and openly available for any and all to use. Again, as of the writing of this book, this bill was sitting in committee.

Perhaps the most serious threat to the public domain has not yet become law, but multiple attempts have been made over the past several years. One of the basic tenets of American copyright law is that facts are not protectable, although the expression of facts may be. The rationale for this is based on the ultimate purpose of copyright law: to encourage the further creation of works and contributions to the body of human knowledge. Allowing anyone to control access to pure facts clearly undermines this purpose. For several years, however, various parties have lobbied Congress to amend the Copyright Act to provide protection for databases. Recall the holding in *Feist Publications, Inc. v. Rural Telephone Service Co.* that although facts are not protectable, the selection and arrangement in a compilation of facts may be protectable. Note that databases may also be protected under the No Electronic Theft Act as well as some state laws. Applied to purely factual databases, this means that the facts in the database themselves cannot be protected by copyright, although the selection and arrangement of the database as a whole could be. This protection in the compilation prevents an unauthorized person from copying the database in its entirety.

However, for several years, various parties have lobbied Congress to extend copyright-type protection databases themselves. ALA and other entities have been active and tenacious in lobbying against such a bill, and until recently have been successful in preventing such a bill from being pursued in Congress. In the 106th Congress, these entities were able to defeat attempts by Congressional representatives to bring a database protection bill, the Collections of Information Antipiracy Act, to the floor for a vote.

However, in 2003, a database protection bill titled "The Database and Collection of Information Misappropriation Act of 2003" was introduced in the House. Due to strong lobbying against the bill, it was reported out of committee unfavorably in March 2004. This bill would make it illegal to copy a "quantitatively substantial" part of the information (i.e., facts) in a database and to make it commercially available in the same market as the database without authorization of the database owner if certain conditions are met: the database required "substantial expenditure of financial resources" to be created; the unauthorized use "occurs in a time sensitive manner and inflicts injury on the database owner"; and unauthorized users who "free ride on the efforts" of the database owner would threaten the "incentive to produce the product" and therefore the existence of the database. Proponents of database protection bills are, for the most part, large database producers such as publishers, the National Association of Realtors, and eBay. These entities do not consider the aforementioned established protections for databases to adequately protect their works, in which, to be fair, they have invested considerable resources.

Opponents of database protection bills argue that proponents have not identified a need for such protection in the law or shown that their businesses have suffered because of the lack of such protection. They argue that such bills could create perpetual ownership in facts, in contradiction to the basic tenets of copyright law as well as the entire history of American copyright law. They argue that the proposed bill does not allow for fair use or the first sale doctrine and that the results would be a monopolistic database market and therefore increasingly inflated prices for databases. They also point to the ability under the bill for government information currently in the public domain to be protected, thereby doing away with the rights of American citizens to freely access government information granted by the First Amendment and copyright law. Although the bill does provide for limited exceptions, the language overall is ambiguous enough that it is not clear exactly what types of uses would and would not be allowed. To make matters worse, such determinations would not be made until a debate over allowable uses reached a court. And on top of that, anyone found liable in court under this proposed law could be fined triple damages.

Fair use

Another example is found in the Digital Millennium Copyright Act (DMCA). While Section 1201(c) of the Copyright Act states that nothing in the DMCA shall affect fair use, and Section 1201(d) allows certain nonprofit libraries to "gain access" to a protected work for purposes of evaluating the work for possible acquisition, Section 1201(a) prohibits the importation of equipment that allows circumvention of technologies preventing access to a copyrighted work. In other words, parts of the DMCA try to placate librarians by saying that fair use will not be affected by the act, but it goes on to prohibit the very technology that may be necessary to engage in uses that are indeed fair.

Rep. Boucher introduced the Digital Media Consumers Rights Act of 2003 in response to these concerns (undoubtedly brought to his attention by his library-supporting constituents, among others). The bill would amend the Copyright Act to allow the circumvention of copyright protection measures for any person "acting solely in furtherance of scientific research into technological protection measures." More importantly, it would also clarify that fair use includes the circumvention of technological measures when such circumvention does not result in an infringement of the work; and the manufacturing, distributing, or making noninfringing use of hardware or software products that are capable of enabling significant noninfringing use of a copyrighted work. In other words, the bill addresses some of the most substantial criticisms of the DMCA—that the anticirucumvention provisions do not accommodate fair use and, indeed, prohibit the exercise of an information user's fair use rights in the digital area. The bill was referred to committee immediately after its introduction in January of 2003 and, as of the writing of this book, was still there.

Currently, one of the most important problematic issues is the future of fair use generally. Fair use is implicated in the DMCA issues mentioned above, but the issue goes well beyond one or two specific pieces of legislation. As you know from reading Chapter 3, fair use is decided on a case-by-case basis. Behind this decision by Congress to approach fair use case by case rather than to provide specific criteria for what does or does not constitute fair use was the recognition that what qualifies as "fair" will vary from situation to situation. Congress intended the fair use analysis to be flexible to allow for this. Or course, the downside to any program set up to be flexible is that it can flex in at least two directions.

At the crux of the larger fair use issue is the question briefly mentioned in Chapter 3: Is fair use an exception to an author's exclusive right, or is it a right of information users? Naturally, those who depend on fair use, such as librarians, insist that it is a statutory right, while those who oppose extensive fair use, such as publishers, insist that it is a very narrow exception to a copyright owner's right. The Copyright Act itself is not clear. Section 107 is entitled "Limitations on exclusive rights: Fair use" (see Source A), but Section 108 refers to "the right of fair use."

In response to these threats, and again due to lobbying by library supporters, longtime and dedicated library friend Rep. Zoe Lofgren has repeatedly introduced legislation that would codify certain actions as fair uses. The Benefit Authors without Limiting Advancement for Net Consumer Expectation Act (BALANCE Act) is a reiteration of similar bills that she has introduced in previous congresses. The BALANCE Act would amend the Copyright Act to: specifically include analog or digital transmissions of a copyrighted work within fair use protections; allow the owner of a lawfully obtained or received transmission of a digital work to reproduce, store, adapt, or access the work for archival purposes or to transfer it to a preferred digital media device for purposes of effecting a nonpublic performance or display (i.e., for personal use); clarify that the first sale doctrine would also apply to digital works so long as the owner of a work does not retain a copy in retrievable form once the work is transferred; and allow circumvention of technological protection measures if necessary to enable a noninfringing use. Obviously, this bill would be valuable to information users in all walks of life. As of the writing of this book, the bill was sitting in committee. The version of this bill introduced in the 107th Congress died in committee.

Professor Ray Patterson at the University of Georgia School of Law, author of *The Nature of Copyright: A Law of Users' Rights*, feels strongly about the right versus exception debate. He believes that based on Section 107, the fair use section of the Copyright Act, which does not refer to fair use as a "right," it is nonetheless reasonable to argue that fair use is a right. In an interview with Carrie Russell, Copyright Specialist for the American Library Association Office for Information Technology Policy, Professor Patterson minces no words in characterizing the debate: "Librarians should be as aggressive in protecting the right of fair use as the publishers are in seeking to destroy it...librarians are the last line of defense against the efforts of publishers to sacrifice the right of the people to know on the altar of profit." Lest your reaction is to consider this statement a bit extreme, he goes on to explain: "This statement is not as hyperbolic as it may seem. The conduct of the publishers indicates that their goal is to do away with free lending libraries, to transform copyright into a pay-per-use right....To succeed, they must coopt librarians to be their licensing agents. Unless librarians refuse to be coopted, the publishers will succeed." (American Library Association, 2001)

How should librarians go about being aggressive and prevent being co-opted?

First and foremost, librarians need to take a stand, remembering that they are not just representatives of their institutions, but, much more importantly, representatives of their users. It is part of our professional responsibility to represent the needs and rights of users to those making decisions that affect our users. One way to do this is to get involved in legislative issues. However, your daily actions in your job also have an effect on these issues.

Why should librarians get involved in what is essentially a political issue?

As a librarian, you realize how important the Internet is to your job. Of course, there are many issues concerning the Internet other than copyright, and many legal issues affecting libraries other than those concerning the Internet. Has a thought like any of the following crossed your mind while reading this book?

- "What a mess! Why doesn't somebody with some experience and know-how get in there and clean it up?"
- "Even *I* could have done a better job deciding that case or writing that law!"
- "What's going to happen to our library services if that law doesn't change or gets decided in the wrong way in court?"
- Or, even more simply: "What a bunch of ignoramuses!"

I've certainly had all of those thoughts and more as I confront the issues set forth in this book, and others as well, like funding for libraries. But do you see what the answer to each of these questions is?

- *You* are the one with the experience and know-how to clean up the mess.
- Yes, *you* probably could have done a better job! Why? Because you know what the case or law means to libraries, library users, and Internet users.
- *You* need to see that this doesn't happen.
- Of course "they" are "ignoramuses." By definition, they don't know any better—but *you* do. Like all of us, legislators only know what they are taught, and we know that lobbyists for copyright owners are teaching legislators their take on copyright law and what it should be.

You are the key here. *You* know what libraries need, what your users need, how your users use the library and the Internet, and even how the Internet works. Most judges, lawyers, state legislators, and members of Congress know little of these things. Our system of government is a *representative* democracy. Congress relies on its constituents to tell it what they need. It is our job as information professionals to make sure that Congress knows what our users and our institutions need.

Can I really make a difference?

Let me give my favorite personal anecdote and a well-known aspect of the development of current law. During my first year as a professional librarian, I participated in the Texas Library Association's Legislative Day, in which librarians spend a day visiting their representatives in the state legislature to inform them about and discuss with them issues of concern. This was in the early 1990s, when resource sharing was just beginning to develop. A mandate had been issued by the Lieutenant Governor (the most powerful position in Texas government) that no new funds were to be given out during that session. I was lucky enough to be a part of the group who visited Lt. Gov. Bob Bullock during Legislative Day. The library association had invested a lot of time over the previous years getting to know Lt. Gov. Bullock and familiarizing him with our issues. Our big issue that year was requesting three million dollars as seed money for a statewide resource sharing project. We gave him the pitch. He asked why we needed the project. We explained, with personal stories and statistics to support our argument. He, who had just mandated that no new money be given out, turned to his aide and said, "We can find three million for these folks, can't we?" Now would that have happened if we had all been hard at work behind the reference desk, cataloging books, and teaching classes, instead of lobbying our representatives?

On a national level, it is clear that the participation of librarians and library organizations have helped tremendously in sustaining the balance in copyright law, and specifically in including exemptions for libraries in the statute. Think for a moment about how this works: How likely is it that a member of the committee working on an amendment to the copyright law would have the sudden thought, "Hey, what can we do for libraries with this bill?" We have to be there. We have to let our representatives know what we need. It is their job to try to meet our needs, but it is our job to inform them of those needs.

What do I have to do?
"But I really and truly hate public speaking/begging/politics/fill-in-the-blank." There are many ways you can get involved in the political process to help your profession. The key is to get involved.

First, you need to keep up to date on what is going on:

- The American Library Association distributes via e-mail the ALA Washington Office Newsline, a free, irregular publication that updates you on what is going on in Washington that affects libraries and tells you when response from the library community is needed. To subscribe, send an e-mail message to listproc@ala1.ala.org. Leave the subject line blank. As the first and only line of text in the message, type "subscribe ala-wo YourFirstName YourLastName" (e.g., subscribe ala-wo Melville Dewey).
- The ALA Washington Office Web site also provides information about current issues, explaining the background and why librarians should be concerned, at www.ala.org/ala/washoff/WOissues/issues.htm.

- Other library associations, including some state associations, also provide information about legislative and policy issues. Check with your organization about its legislative and policy work.
- Other Web sites with similar interests, listed in Source M, include Digital Future Coalition and Electronic Frontier Foundation.

Then, you need to get to know your representatives and keep in contact with them. ALA also provides material to help you out with this, at www.ala.org/ala/issues/issuesadvocacy.htm. This site includes online brochures such as *Library Advocacy Pocket Checklist, Effective Ways to Communicate With Legislators*, and *How to Write a Letter to Your Legislator.*

Both ALA and many state library associations sponsor legislative days, when librarians and library supporters meet with state legislators or members of Congress. In most cases, the association will organize the event and train you on the issues and how to speak to your representative. You don't have to know anything going into it except what your patrons need. The association will explain the issues and tell you how to present them in two minutes flat (legislators like short meetings!). You probably will not have to meet with a representative alone, so you will have moral support with you.

I encourage librarians to get involved in legislative days, but it is at least as important to keep in touch with your legislators via letters, e-mail, faxes, and phone calls throughout the sessions. You don't want our issues and concerns to be totally new when our group walks into a legislator's office. We need to let our legislators know that we are paying attention and that we care.

You should also keep up with what is going on in your state and your community. Talk to your state library association, your local city council, and library boards. Watch their agendas. When an issue that would effect libraries comes to the agenda, talk to your colleagues, organize a group to attend the meeting, designate someone to speak out for you.

Your libraries and your library users depend on you to represent their needs. No one else but us can do it. And there is strength in numbers. This is part of your professional duty, and many organizations and people are out there to help you. You truly can make a difference in the future of libraries, information users, and the information society.

How do I affect copyright law on a daily basis?

Although various guidelines meant to help determine whether specific uses are fair are discussed in this book (see Chapters 14–16 and Sources C–D and F–H), remember that, not only is there disagreement concerning many of these guidelines, but all are meant to be minimal standards to assist in

> ## One more reason why librarians must become activists
>
> "You must be the change you wish to see in the world." — Mahatma Ghandi

making fair use determinations. None were intended by the groups that developed them to be maximum limits. Thus, even with the use of specific guidelines, which were intended to help by giving more specific answers to fair use questions, there is no final answer as to whether a particular use will constitute fair use.

Advocates for librarians and information users believe that librarians must be assertive, as Professor Patterson stated, in exercising the fair use right. They are concerned that if librarians are conservative and limit themselves to the minimal uses put forth in guidelines, they are giving up the fight and limiting fair use forever to those standards. Being assertive means using individual judgment. It means going beyond the guidelines when it seems reasonable. Which, in turn, means asserting your rights knowledgeably, not blindly.

You will learn from this book and from many other sources how fair use decisions are made. Use this knowledge to make a determination of your own as to whether a use is fair. Work with your institution in exercising your fair use rights. More and more institutions have copyright policies for employees, faculty, and students to follow. Be aware, however, that those policies may themselves err on the side of caution and be overly conservative. Take advantage of the resources that are out there to help and support you, such as various library organizations and others listed in Source K. Get involved in legislative and advocacy activities to give a louder voice to the needs of information uses.

Above all, remember that you are responsible for standing up for the rights of information users. And remember that you are not alone. As Professor Patterson said, "librarians are the last line of defense against the efforts of publishers to sacrifice the right of the people to know." (American Library Association, 2001)

Bibliography

American Library Association. Users' Rights in Copyright: An Interview with Ray Patterson. Available: http://Copyright.ala.org [January 2001].

Patterson, L. Ray, and Stanley W. Lindberg. 1991. *The Nature of Copy-right: A Law of Users' Rights*. Athens: University of Georgia Press.

PART IV

Sourcebox

Source A

Selected excerpts from the Copyright Act of 1976 (17 U.S.C. 101 *et seq.*)

Sec. 102. Subject matter of copyright: In general

(a) Copyright protection subsists, in accordance with this title, in original works of authorship fixed in any tangible medium of expression, now known or later developed, from which they can be perceived, reproduced, or otherwise communicated, either directly or with the aid of a machine or device. Works of authorship include the following categories:

(1) literary works;
(2) musical works, including any accompanying words;
(3) dramatic works, including any accompanying music;
(4) pantomimes and choreographic works;
(5) pictorial, graphic, and sculptural works;
(6) motion pictures and other audiovisual works;
(7) sound recordings; and
(8) architectural works.

(b) In no case does copyright protection for an original work of authorship extend to any idea, procedure, process, system, method of operation, concept, principle, or discovery, regardless of the form in which it is described, explained, illustrated, or embodied in such work.

Sec. 103. Subject matter of copyright: Compilations and derivative works

(a) The subject matter of copyright as specified by section 102 includes compilations and derivative works, but protection for a work employing preexisting material in which copyright subsists does not extend to any part of the work in which such material has been used unlawfully.

(b) The copyright in a compilation or derivative work extends only to the material contributed by the author of such work, as distinguished from the preexisting material employed in the work, and does not imply any exclusive right in the preexisting material. The copyright in such work is independent of, and does not affect or enlarge the scope, duration, ownership, or subsistence of, any copyright protection in the preexisting material.

Sec. 106. Exclusive rights in copyrighted works

Subject to sections 107 through 120, the owner of copyright under this title has the exclusive rights to do and to authorize any of the following:

(1) to reproduce the copyrighted work in copies or phonorecords;

(2) to prepare derivative works based upon the copyrighted work;

(3) to distribute copies or phonorecords of the copyrighted work to the public by sale or other transfer of ownership, or by rental, lease, or lending;

(4) in the case of literary, musical, dramatic, and choreographic works, pantomimes, and motion pictures and other audiovisual works, to perform the copyrighted work publicly;

(5) in the case of literary, musical, dramatic, and choreographic works, pantomimes, and pictorial, graphic, or sculptural works, including the individual images of a motion picture or other audiovisual work, to display the copyrighted work publicly; and

(6) in the case of sound recordings, to perform the copyrighted work publicly by means of a digital audio transmission.

Sec. 107. Limitations on exclusive rights: Fair use

Notwithstanding the provisions of sections 106 and 106A, the fair use of a copyrighted work, including such use by reproduction in copies or phonorecords or by any other means specified by that section, for purposes such as criticism, comment, news reporting, teaching (including multiple copies for classroom use), scholarship, or research, is not an infringement of copyright. In determining whether the use made of a work in any particular case is a fair use the factors to be considered shall include

(1) the purpose and character of the use, including whether such use is of a commercial nature or is for nonprofit educational purposes;

(2) the nature of the copyrighted work;

(3) the amount and substantiality of the portion used in relation to the copyrighted work as a whole; and

(4) the effect of the use upon the potential market for or value of the copyrighted work. The fact that a work is unpublished shall not itself bar a finding of fair use if such finding is made upon consideration of all the above factors.

Sec. 108. Limitations on exclusive rights: Reproduction by libraries and archives

(a) Except as otherwise provided in this title and notwithstanding the provisions of section 106, it is not an infringement of copyright for a library or archives, or any of its employees acting within the scope of their employment, to reproduce no more than one copy or phonorecord of a work, except as provided in subsections (b) and (c), or to distribute such copy or phonorecord, under the conditions specified by this section, if

(1) the reproduction or distribution is made without any purpose of direct or indirect commercial advantage;

(2) the collections of the library or archives are (i) open to the public, or (ii) available not only to researchers affiliated with the library or archives or with the institution of which it is a part, but also to other persons doing research in a specialized field; and

(3) the reproduction or distribution of the work includes a notice of copyright that appears on the copy or phonorecord that is reproduced under the provisions of this section, or includes a legend stating that the work may be protected by copyright if no such notice can be found on the copy or phonorecord that is reproduced under the provisions of this section.

(b) The rights of reproduction and distribution under this section apply to three copies or phonorecords of an unpublished work duplicated solely for purposes of preservation and security or for deposit for research use in another library or archives of the type described by clause (2) of subsection (a), if

(1) the copy or phonorecord reproduced is currently in the collections of the library or archives; and

(2) any such copy or phonorecord that is reproduced in digital format is not otherwise distributed in that format and is not made available to the public in that format outside the premises of the library or archives.

(c) The right of reproduction under this section applies to three copies or phonorecords of a published work duplicated solely for the purpose of replacement of a copy or phonorecord that is damaged, deteriorating, lost, or stolen, or if the existing format in which the work is stored has become obsolete, if

(1) the library or archives has, after a reasonable effort, determined that an unused replacement cannot be obtained at a fair price; and

(2) any such copy or phonorecord that is reproduced in digital format is not made available to the public in that format outside the premises of the library or archives in lawful possession of such copy. For purposes of this subsection, a format shall be considered obsolete if the machine or device necessary to render perceptible a work stored in that format is no longer manufactured or is no longer reasonably available in the commercial marketplace.

(d) The rights of reproduction and distribution under this section apply to a copy, made from the collection of a library or archives where the user makes his or her request or from that of another library or archives, of no more than one article or other contribution to a copyrighted collection or periodical issue, or to a copy or phonorecord of a small part of any other copyrighted work, if

(1) the copy or phonorecord becomes the property of the user, and the library or archives has had no notice that the copy or phonorecord would be used for any purpose other than private study, scholarship, or research; and

(2) the library or archives displays prominently, at the place where orders are accepted, and includes on its order form, a warning of copyright in accordance with requirements that the Register of Copyrights shall prescribe by regulation.

(e) The rights of reproduction and distribution under this section apply to the entire work, or to a substantial part of it, made from the collection of a library or archives where the user makes his or her request or from that of another library or archives, if the library or archives has first determined, on the basis of a reasonable investigation, that a copy or phonorecord of the copyrighted work cannot be obtained at a fair price, if

(1) the copy or phonorecord becomes the property of the user, and the library or archives has had no notice that the copy or phonorecord would be used for any purpose other than private study, scholarship, or research; and

(2) the library or archives displays prominently, at the place where orders are accepted, and includes on its order form, a warning of copyright in accordance with requirements that the Register of Copyrights shall prescribe by regulation.

(f) Nothing in this section

(1) shall be construed to impose liability for copyright infringement upon a library or archives or its employees for the unsupervised use of reproducing equipment located on its premises: Provided, That such equipment displays a notice that the making of a copy may be subject to the copyright law;

(2) excuses a person who uses such reproducing equipment or who requests a copy or phonorecord under subsection (d) from liability for copyright infringement for any such act, or for any later use of such copy or phonorecord, if it exceeds fair use as provided by section 107;

(3) shall be construed to limit the reproduction and distribution by lending of a limited number of copies and excerpts by a library or archives of an audiovisual news program, subject to clauses (1), (2), and (3) of subsection (a); or

(4) in any way affects the right of fair use as provided by section 107, or any contractual obligations assumed at any time by the library or archives when it obtained a copy or phonorecord of a work in its collections.

(g) The rights of reproduction and distribution under this section extend to the isolated and unrelated reproduction or distribution of a single copy or phonorecord of the same material on separate occasions, but do not extend to cases where the library or archives, or its employee

(1) is aware or has substantial reason to believe that it is engaging in the related or concerted reproduction or distribution of multiple copies or phonorecords of the same material, whether made on one occasion or over a period of time, and whether intended for aggregate use by one or more individuals or for separate use by the individual members of a group; or

(2) engages in the systematic reproduction or distribution of single or multiple copies or phonorecords of material described in subsection (d): Provided, That nothing in this clause prevents a library or archives from participating in interlibrary arrangements that do not have, as their purpose or effect, that the library or archives receiving such copies or phonorecords for distribution does so in such aggregate quantities as to substitute for a subscription to or purchase of such work.

(h)

(1) For purposes of this section, during the last 20 years of any term of copyright of a published work, a library or archives, including a nonprofit educational institution that functions as such, may reproduce, distribute, display, or perform in facsimile or digital form a copy or phonorecord of such work, or portions thereof, for purposes of preservation, scholarship, or research, if such library or archives has first determined, on the basis of a reasonable investigation, that none of the conditions set forth in subparagraphs (A), (B), and (C) of paragraph (2) apply.

(2) No reproduction, distribution, display, or performance is authorized under this subsection if

(A) the work is subject to normal commercial exploitation;

(B) a copy or phonorecord of the work can be obtained at a reasonable price; or

(C) the copyright owner or its agent provides notice pursuant to regulations promulgated by the Register of Copyrights that either of the conditions set forth in subparagraphs (A) and (B) applies.

(3) The exemption provided in this subsection does not apply to any subsequent uses by users other than such library or archives.

(i) The rights of reproduction and distribution under this section do not apply to a musical work, a pictorial, graphic or sculptural work, or a motion picture or other audiovisual work other than an audiovisual work dealing with news, except that no such limitation shall apply with respect to rights granted by subsections (b) and (c), or with respect to pictorial or graphic works published as illustrations, diagrams, or similar adjuncts to works of which copies are reproduced or distributed in accordance with subsections (d) and (e).

Sec. 109. Limitations on exclusive rights: Effect of transfer of particular copy or Phonorecord

(a) Notwithstanding the provisions of section 106(3), the owner of a particular copy or phonorecord lawfully made under this title, or any person authorized by such owner, is entitled, without the authority of the copyright owner, to sell or otherwise dispose of the possession of that copy or phonorecord. Notwithstanding the preceding sentence, copies or phonorecords of works subject to restored copyright under section 104A that are manufactured before the date of restoration of copyright or, with respect to reliance parties, before publication or service of notice under section 104A(e), may be sold or otherwise disposed of without the authorization of the owner of the restored copyright for purposes of direct or indirect commercial advantage only during the 12-month period beginning on

(1) the date of the publication in the Federal Register of the notice of intent filed with the Copyright Office under section 104A(d)(2)(A), or

(2) the date of the receipt of actual notice served under section 104A(d)(2)(B), whichever occurs first.

(b)

(1)

    (A) Notwithstanding the provisions of subsection (a), unless authorized by the owners of copyright in the sound recording or the owner of copyright in a computer program (including any tape, disk, or other medium embodying such program), and in the case of a sound recording in the musical works embodied therein, neither the owner of a particular phonorecord nor any person in possession of a particular copy of a computer program (including any tape, disk, or other medium embodying such program), may, for the purposes of direct or indirect commercial advantage, dispose of, or authorize the disposal of, the possession of that phonorecord or computer program (including any tape, disk, or other medium embodying such program) by rental, lease, or lending, or by any other act or practice in the nature of rental, lease, or lending. Nothing in the preceding sentence shall apply to the rental, lease, or lending of a phonorecord for nonprofit purposes by a nonprofit library or nonprofit educational institution. The transfer of possession of a lawfully made copy of a computer program by a nonprofit educational institution to another nonprofit educational institution or to faculty, staff, and students does not constitute rental, lease, or lending for direct or indirect commercial purposes under this subsection.

    (B) This subsection does not apply to

       (i) a computer program which is embodied in a machine or product and which cannot be copied during the ordinary operation or use of the machine or product; or

      (ii) a computer program embodied in or used in conjunction with a limited purpose computer that is designed for playing video games and may be designed for other purposes.

    (C) Nothing in this subsection affects any provision of chapter 9 of this title.

(2)

    (A) Nothing in this subsection shall apply to the lending of a computer program for nonprofit purposes by a nonprofit library, if each copy of a computer program which is lent by such library has affixed to the packaging containing the program a warning of copyright in accordance with requirements that the Register of Copyrights shall prescribe by regulation.

    (B) Not later than three years after the date of the enactment of the Computer Software Rental Amendments Act of 1990, and at such times thereafter as the Register of Copyrights considers appropriate, the Register of Copyrights, after consultation with representatives of copyright owners and librarians, shall submit to the Congress a report stating whether this paragraph has achieved its intended purpose of maintaining the integrity of the copyright system while providing nonprofit libraries the capability to fulfill their function. Such report shall advise the Congress as to any information or recommendations that the Register of Copyrights considers necessary to carry out the purposes of this subsection.

(3) Nothing in this subsection shall affect any provision of the antitrust laws. For purposes of the preceding sentence, "antitrust laws" has the meaning given that term in the first section of the Clayton Act and includes section 5 of the Federal Trade Commission Act to the extent that section relates to unfair methods of competition.

(4) Any person who distributes a phonorecord or a copy of a computer program (including any tape, disk, or other medium embodying such program) in violation of paragraph (1) is an infringer of copyright under section 501 of this title and is subject to the remedies set forth in sections 502, 503, 504, 505, and 509. Such violation shall not be a criminal offense under section 506 or cause such person to be subject to the criminal penalties set forth in section 2319 of title 18.

(c) Notwithstanding the provisions of section 106(5), the owner of a particular copy lawfully made under this title, or any person authorized by such owner, is entitled, without the authority of the copyright owner, to display that copy publicly, either directly or by the projection of no more than one image at a time, to viewers present at the place where the copy is located.

(d) The privileges prescribed by subsections (a) and (c) do not, unless authorized by the copyright owner, extend to any person who has acquired possession of the copy or phonorecord from the copyright owner, by rental, lease, loan, or otherwise, without acquiring ownership of it.

(e) Notwithstanding the provisions of sections 106(4) and 106(5), in the case of an electronic audiovisual game intended for use in coin-operated equipment, the owner of a particular copy of such a game lawfully made under this title, is entitled, without the authority of the copyright owner of the game, to publicly perform or display that game in coin-operated equipment, except that this subsection shall not apply to any work of authorship embodied in the audiovisual game if the copyright owner of the electronic audiovisual game is not also the copyright owner of the work of authorship.

Sec. 110. Limitations on exclusive rights: Exemption of certain performances and displays

Notwithstanding the provisions of section 106, the following are not infringements of copyright:

(1) performance or display of a work by instructors or pupils in the course of face-to-face teaching activities of a nonprofit educational institution, in a classroom or similar place devoted to instruction, unless, in the case of a motion picture or other audiovisual work, the performance, or the display

of individual images, is given by means of a copy that was not lawfully made under this title, and that the person responsible for the performance knew or had reason to believe was not lawfully made;

(2) except with respect to a work produced or marketed primarily for performance or display as part of mediated instructional activities transmitted via digital networks, or a performance or display that is given by means of a copy or phonorecord that is not lawfully made and acquired under this title, and the transmitting government body or accredited nonprofit educational institution knew or had reason to believe was not lawfully made and acquired, the performance of a nondramatic literary or musical work or reasonable and limited portions of any other work, or display of a work in an amount comparable to that which is typically displayed in the course of a live classroom session, by or in the course of a transmission, if—

(A) the performance or display is made by, at the direction of, or under the actual supervision of an instructor as an integral part of a class session offered as a regular part of the systematic mediated instructional activities of a governmental body or an accredited nonprofit educational institution;.

(B) the performance or display is directly related and of material assistance to the teaching content of the transmission;

(C) the transmission is made solely for, and, to the extent technologically feasible, the reception of such transmission is limited to—

(i) students officially enrolled in the course for which the transmission is made; or

(ii) officers or employees of governmental bodies as a part of their official duties or employment; and

(D) the transmitting body or institution—

(i) institutes policies regarding copyright, provides informational materials to faculty, students, and relevant staff members that accurately describe, and promote compliance with, the laws of the United States relating to copyright, and provides notice to students that materials used in connection with the course may be subject to copyright protection; and

(ii) in the case of digital transmissions—

(I) applies technological measures that reasonably prevent—

(aa) retention of the work in accessible form by recipients of the transmission from the transmitting body or institution for longer than the class session; and

(bb) unauthorized further dissemination of the work in accessible form by such recipients to others; and

(II) does not engage in conduct that could reasonably be expected to interfere with technological measures used by copyright owners to prevent such retention or unauthorized further dissemination;

(3) performance of a nondramatic literary or musical work or of a dramatico musical work of a religious nature, or display of a work, in the course of services at a place of worship or other religious assembly;

(4) performance of a nondramatic literary or musical work otherwise than in a transmission to the public, without any purpose of direct or indirect commercial advantage and without payment of any fee or other compensation for the performance to any of its performers, promoters, or organizers, if-

(A) there is no direct or indirect admission charge; or

(B) the proceeds, after deducting the reasonable costs of producing the performance, are used exclusively for educational, religious, or charitable purposes and not for private financial gain, except where the copyright owner has served notice of objection to the performance under the following conditions;

(i)   the notice shall be in writing and signed by the copyright owner or such owner's duly authorized agent; and

(ii) the notice shall be served on the person responsible for the performance at least seven days before the date of the performance, and shall state the reasons for the objection; and

(iii) the notice shall comply, in form, content, and manner of service, with requirements that the Register of Copyrights shall prescribe by regulation;

Sections 110(5) – 110(1) omitted

Sec. 302. Duration of copyright: Works created on or after January 1, 1978

(a) In General. Copyright in a work created on or after January 1, 1978, subsists from its creation and, except as provided by the following subsections, endures for a term consisting of the life of the author and 70 years after the author's death.

(b) Joint Works. In the case of a joint work prepared by two or more authors who did not work for hire, the copyright endures for a term consisting of the life of the last surviving author and 70 years after such last surviving author's death.

(c) Anonymous Works, Pseudonymous Works, and Works Made for Hire. In the case of an anonymous work, a pseudonymous work, or a work made for hire, the copyright endures for a term of 95 years from the year of its first publication, or a term of 120 years from the year of its creation, whichever expires first. If, before the end of such term, the identity of one or more of the authors of an anonymous or pseudonymous work is revealed in the records of a registration made for that work under subsections (a) or (d) of section 408, or in the records provided by this subsection, the copyright in the work endures for the term specified by subsection (a) or (b), based on the life of the author or authors whose identity has been revealed. Any person having an interest in the copyright in an anonymous or pseudonymous work may at any time record, in records to be maintained by the Copyright Office for that purpose, a statement identifying one or more authors of the work; the statement shall also identify the person filing it, the nature of that person's interest, the source of the information recorded, and the particular work affected, and shall comply in form and content with requirements that the Register of Copyrights shall prescribe by regulation.

(d) Records Relating to Death of Authors. Any person having an interest in a copyright may at any time record in the Copyright Office a statement of the date of death of the author of the copyrighted work, or a statement that the author is still living on a particular date. The statement shall identify the person filing it, the nature of that person's interest, and the source of the information recorded, and shall comply in form and content with requirements that the Register of Copyrights shall prescribe by regulation. The Register shall maintain current records of information relating to the death of authors of copyrighted works, based on such recorded statements and, to the extent the Register considers practicable, on data contained in any of the records of the Copyright Office or in other reference sources.

(e) Presumption as to Author's Death. After a period of 95 years from the year of first publication of a work, or a period of 120 years from the year of its creation, whichever expires first, any person who obtains from the Copyright Office a certified report that the records provided by subsection (d) disclose nothing to indicate that the author of the work is living, or died less than 70 years before, is entitled to the benefits of a presumption that the author has been dead for at least 70 years. Reliance in good faith upon this presumption shall be a complete defense to any action for infringement under this title.

Sec. 303. Duration of copyright: Works created but not published or copyrighted before January 1, 1978

(a) Copyright in a work created before January 1, 1978, but not theretofore in the public domain or copyrighted, subsists from January 1, 1978, and endures for the term provided by section 302. In no case, however, shall the term of copyright in such a work expire before December 31, 2002; and, if the work is published on or before December 31, 2002, the term of copyright shall not expire before December 31, 2047.

(b) The distribution before January 1, 1978, of a phonorecord shall not for any purpose constitute a publication of the musical work embodied therein.

Sec. 304. Duration of copyright: Subsisting copyrights

(a) Copyrights in Their First Term on January 1, 1978. (1)(A) Any copyright, the first term of which is subsisting on January 1, 1978, shall endure for 28 years from the date it was originally secured.

(B) In the case of

(i) any posthumous work or of any periodical, cyclopedic, or other composite work upon which the copyright was originally secured by the proprietor thereof, or

(ii) any work copyrighted by a corporate body (otherwise than as assignee or licensee of the individual author) or by an employer for whom such work is made for hire, the proprietor of such copyright shall be entitled to a renewal and extension of the copyright in such work for the further term of 67 years.

(C) In the case of any other copyrighted work, including a contribution by an individual author to a periodical or to a cyclopedic or other composite work

   (i)   the author of such work, if the author is still living,

   (ii) the widow, widower, or children of the author, if the author is not living,

   (iii) the author's executors, if such author, widow, widower, or children are not living, or

   (iv) the author's next of kin, in the absence of a will of the author, shall be entitled to a renewal and extension of the copyright in such work for a further term of 67 years.

Sections 304(a)(2)(B) – 304(d) omitted.

Sec. 401. Notice of copyright: Visually perceptible copies

(a) General Provisions. Whenever a work protected under this title is published in the United States or elsewhere by authority of the copyright owner, a notice of copyright as provided by this section may be placed on publicly distributed copies from which the work can be visually perceived, either directly or with the aid of a machine or device.

(b) Form of Notice. If a notice appears on the copies, it shall consist of the following three elements:

(1) the symbol (AF) (the letter C in a circle), or the word "Copyright", or the abbreviation "'Copr."; and

(2) the year of first publication of the work; in the case of compilations, or derivative works incorporating previously published material, the year date of first publication of the compilation or derivative work is sufficient. The year date may be omitted where a pictorial, graphic, or sculptural work, with accompanying text matter, if any, is reproduced in or on greeting cards, postcards, stationery, jewelry, dolls, toys, or any useful articles; and

(3) the name of the owner of copyright in the work, or an abbreviation by which the name can be recognized, or a generally known alternative designation of the owner.

(c) Position of Notice. The notice shall be affixed to the copies in such manner and location as to give reasonable notice of the claim of copyright. The Register of Copyrights shall prescribe by regulation, as examples, specific methods of affixation and positions of the notice on various types of works that will satisfy this requirement, but these specifications shall not be considered exhaustive.

(d) Evidentiary Weight of Notice. If a notice of copyright in the form and position specified by this section appears on the published copy or copies to which a defendant in a copyright infringement suit had access, then no weight shall be given to such a defendant's interposition of a defense based on innocent infringement in mitigation of actual or statutory damages, except as provided in the last sentence of section 504(c)(2).

Sec. 501. Infringement of copyright

(a) Anyone who violates any of the exclusive rights of the copyright owner as provided by sections 106 through 118 or of the author as provided in section 106A(a), or who imports copies or phonorecords into the United States in violation of section 602, is an infringer of the copyright or right of the author, as the case may be. For purposes of this chapter (other than section 506), any reference to copyright shall be deemed to include the rights conferred by section 106A(a). As used in this subsection, the term "anyone" includes any State, any instrumentality of a State, and any officer or employee of a State or instrumentality of a State acting in his or her official capacity. Any State, and any such instrumentality, officer, or employee, shall be subject to the provisions of this title in the same manner and to the same extent as any nongovernmental entity.

(b) The legal or beneficial owner of an exclusive right under a copyright is entitled, subject to the requirements of section 411, to institute an action for any infringement of that particular right committed while he or she is the owner of it. The court may require such owner to serve written notice of the action with a copy of the complaint upon any person shown, by the records of the Copyright Office or otherwise, to have or claim an interest in the copyright, and shall require that such notice be served upon any person whose interest is likely to be affected by a decision in the case. The court may require the joinder, and shall permit the intervention, of any person having or claiming an interest in the copyright.

(c) For any secondary transmission by a cable system that embodies a performance or a display of a work which is actionable as an act of infringement under subsection (c) of section 111, a television broadcast station holding a copyright or other license to transmit or perform the same version of that work shall, for purposes of subsection (b) of this section, be treated as a legal or beneficial owner if such secondary transmission occurs within the local service area of that television station.

(d) For any secondary transmission by a cable system that is actionable as an act of infringement pursuant to section 111(c)(3), the following shall also have standing to sue:

(i)   the primary transmitter whose transmission has been altered by the cable system; and

(ii) any broadcast station within whose local service area the secondary transmission occurs.

(e) With respect to any secondary transmission that is made by a satellite carrier of a primary transmission embodying the performance or display of a work and is actionable as an act of infringement under section 119(a)(5), a network station holding a copyright or other license to transmit or perform the same version of that work shall, for purposes of subsection (b) of this section, be treated as a legal or beneficial owner if such secondary transmission occurs within the local service area of that station.

Sec. 502. Remedies for infringement: Injunctions

(a) Any court having jurisdiction of a civil action arising under this title may, subject to the provisions of section 1498 of title 28, grant temporary and final injunctions on such terms as it may deem reasonable to prevent or restrain infringement of a copyright.

(b) Any such injunction may be served anywhere in the United States on the person enjoined; it shall be operative throughout the United States and shall be enforceable, by proceedings in contempt or otherwise, by any United States court having jurisdiction of that person. The clerk of the court granting the injunction shall, when requested by any other court in which enforcement of the injunction is sought, transmit promptly to the other court a certified copy of all the papers in the case on file in such clerk's office.

Sec. 503. Remedies for infringement: Impounding and disposition of infringing articles

(a) At any time while an action under this title is pending, the court may order the impounding, on such terms as it may deem reasonable, of all copies or phonorecords claimed to have been made or used in violation of the copyright owner's exclusive rights, and of all plates, molds, matrices, masters, tapes, film negatives, or other articles by means of which such copies or phonorecords may be reproduced.

(b) As part of a final judgment or decree, the court may order the destruction or other reasonable disposition of all copies or phonorecords found to have been made or used in violation of the copyright owner's exclusive rights, and of all plates, molds, matrices, masters, tapes, film negatives, or other articles by means of which such copies or phonorecords may be reproduced.

Sec. 504. Remedies for infringement: Damages and profits

(a) In General. Except as otherwise provided by this title, an infringer of copyright is liable for either

(1) the copyright owner's actual damages and any additional profits of the infringer, as provided by subsection (b); or

(2) statutory damages, as provided by subsection (c).

(b) Actual Damages and Profits. The copyright owner is entitled to recover the actual damages suffered by him or her as a result of the infringement, and any profits of the infringer that are attributable to the infringement and are not taken into account in computing the actual damages. In establishing the infringer's profits, the copyright owner is required to present proof only of the infringer's gross revenue, and the infringer is required to prove his or her deductible expenses and the elements of profit attributable to factors other than the copyrighted work.

(c) Statutory Damages.

(1) Except as provided by clause (2) of this subsection, the copyright owner may elect, at any time before final judgment is rendered, to recover, instead of actual damages and profits, an award of statutory damages for all infringements involved in the action, with respect to any one work, for which any one infringer is liable individually, or for which any two or more infringers are liable jointly and severally, in a sum of not less than $750 or more than $30,000 as the court considers just. For the purposes of this subsection, all the parts of a compilation or derivative work constitute one work.

(2) In a case where the copyright owner sustains the burden of proving, and the court finds, that infringement was committed willfully, the court in its discretion may increase the award of statutory damages to a sum of not more than $150,000. In a case where the infringer sustains the burden of proving, and the court finds, that such infringer was not aware and had no reason to believe that his or her acts constituted an infringement of copyright, the court in its discretion may reduce the award of statutory damages to a sum of not less than $200. The court shall remit statutory damages in any case where an infringer believed and had reasonable grounds for believing that his or her use of the copyrighted work was a fair use under section 107, if the infringer was: (i) an employee or agent of a nonprofit educational institution, library, or archives acting within the scope of his or her employment who, or such institution, library, or archives itself, which infringed by reproducing the work in copies or phonorecords; or (ii) a public broadcasting entity which or a person who, as a regular part of the nonprofit activities of a public broadcasting entity (as defined in subsection (g) of section 118) infringed by performing a published nondramatic literary work or by reproducing a transmission program embodying a performance of such a work.

(d) Additional Damages in Certain Cases. In any case in which the court finds that a defendant proprietor of an establishment who claims as a defense that its activities were exempt under section 110(5) did not have reasonable grounds to believe that its use of a copyrighted work was exempt under such section, the plaintiff shall be entitled to, in addition to any award of damages under this section, an additional award of two times the amount of the license fee that the proprietor of the establishment concerned should have paid the plaintiff for such use during the preceding period of up to 3 years.

Sec. 505. Remedies for infringement: Costs and attorney's fees

In any civil action under this title, the court in its discretion may allow the recovery of full costs by or against any party other than the United States or an officer thereof. Except as otherwise provided by this title, the court may also award a reasonable attorney's fee to the prevailing party as part of the costs.

Sec. 506. Criminal offenses

(a) Criminal Infringement. Any person who infringes a copyright willfully either

(1) for purposes of commercial advantage or private financial gain, or

(2) by the reproduction or distribution, including by electronic means, during any 180-day period, of 1 or more copies or phonorecords of 1 or more copyrighted works, which have a total retail value of more than $1,000, shall be punished as provided under section 2319 of title 18, United States Code. For purposes of this subsection, evidence of reproduction or distribution of a copyrighted work, by itself, shall not be sufficient to establish willful infringement.

(b) Forfeiture and Destruction. When any person is convicted of any violation of subsection (a), the court in its judgment of conviction shall, in addition to the penalty therein prescribed, order the forfeiture and destruction or other disposition of all infringing copies or phonorecords and all implements, devices, or equipment used in the manufacture of such infringing copies or phonorecords.

(c) Fraudulent Copyright Notice. Any person who, with fraudulent intent, places on any article a notice of copyright or words of the same purport that such person knows to be false, or who, with fraudulent intent, publicly distributes or imports for public distribution any article bearing such notice or words that such person knows to be false, shall be fined not more than $2,500.

(d) Fraudulent Removal of Copyright Notice. Any person who, with fraudulent intent, removes or alters any notice of copyright appearing on a copy of a copyrighted work shall be fined not more than $2,500.

(e) False Representation. Any person who knowingly makes a false representation of a material fact in the application for copyright registration provided for by section 409, or in any written statement filed in connection with the application, shall be fined not more than $2,500.

(f) Rights of Attribution and Integrity. Nothing in this section applies to infringement of the rights conferred by section 106A(a).

Sec. 507. Limitations on actions

(a) Criminal Proceedings. Except as expressly provided otherwise in this title, no criminal proceeding shall be maintained under the provisions of this title unless it is commenced within 5 years after the cause of action arose.

(b) Civil Actions. No civil action shall be maintained under the provisions of this title unless it is commenced within three years after the claim accrued.

Sec. 509. Seizure and forfeiture

(a) All copies or phonorecords manufactured, reproduced, distributed, sold, or otherwise used, intended for use, or possessed with intent to use in violation of section 506(a), and all plates, molds, matrices, masters, tapes, film negatives, or other articles by means of which such copies or phonorecords may be reproduced, and all electronic, mechanical, or other devices for manufacturing, reproducing, or assembling such copies or phonorecords may be seized and forfeited to the United States.

Section 509(b) omitted

Sec. 511. Liability of States, Instrumentalities of States, and State officials for Infringement of Copyright

(a) In General. Any State, any instrumentality of a State, and any officer or employee of a State acting in his or her official capacity, shall not be immune, under the Eleventh Amendment of the Constitution of the United States or under any other doctrine of sovereign immunity, from suit in Federal court by any person, including any governmental or nongovernmental entity, for a violation of any of the exclusive rights of a copyright owner provided by sections 106 through 121, for importing copies of phonorecords in violation of section 602, or for any other violation under this title.

(b) Remedies. In a suit described in subsection (a) for a violation described in that subsection, remedies both at law and in equity) are available for the violation to the same extent as such remedies are available for such a violation in a suit against any public or private entity other than a State, instrumentality of a State, or officer or employee of a State acting in his or her official capacity. Such remedies include impounding and disposition of infringing articles under section 503, actual damages and profits and statutory damages under section 504, costs and attorney's fees under section 505, and the remedies provided in section 510.

Sec. 512. Limitations on liability relating to material online

(a) Transitory Digital Network Communications. A service provider shall not be liable for monetary relief, or, except as provided in subsection (j), for injunctive or other equitable relief, for infringement of copyright by reason of the provider's transmitting, routing, or providing connections for, material through a system or network controlled or operated by or for the service provider, or by reason of the intermediate and transient storage of that material in the course of such transmitting, routing, or providing connections, if

(1) the transmission of the material was initiated by or at the direction of a person other than the service provider;

(2) the transmission, routing, provision of connections, or storage is carried out through an automatic technical process without selection of the material by the service provider;

(3) the service provider does not select the recipients of the material except as an automatic response to the request of another person;

(4) no copy of the material made by the service provider in the course of such intermediate or transient storage is maintained on the system or network in a manner ordinarily accessible to anyone other than anticipated recipients, and no such copy is maintained on the system or network in a manner ordinarily accessible to such anticipated recipients for a longer period than

is reasonably necessary for the transmission, routing, or provision of connections; and

(5) the material is transmitted through the system or network without modification of its content.

(b) System Caching.

(1) Limitation on liability. A service provider shall not be liable for monetary relief, or, except as provided in subsection (j), for injunctive or other equitable relief, for infringement of copyright by reason of the intermediate and temporary storage of material on a system or network controlled or operated by or for the service provider in a case in which

(A) the material is made available online by a person other than the service provider;

(B) the material is transmitted from the person described in subparagraph (A) through the system or network to a person other than the person described in subparagraph (A) at the direction of that other person; and

(C) the storage is carried out through an automatic technical process for the purpose of making the material available to users of the system or network who, after the material is transmitted as described in subparagraph (B), request access to the material from the person described in subparagraph (A), if the conditions set forth in paragraph (2) are met.

(2) Conditions. The conditions referred to in paragraph (1) are that

(A) the material described in paragraph (1) is transmitted to the subsequent users described in paragraph (1)(C) without modification to its content from the manner in which the material was transmitted from the person described in paragraph (1)(A);

(B) the service provider described in paragraph (1) complies with rules concerning the refreshing, reloading, or other updating of the material when specified by the person making the material available online in accordance with a generally accepted industry standard data communications protocol for the system or network through which that person makes the material available, except that this subparagraph applies only if those rules are not used by the person described in paragraph (1)(A) to prevent or unreasonably impair the intermediate storage to which this subsection applies;

(C) the service provider does not interfere with the ability of technology associated with the material to return to the person described in paragraph (1)(A) the information that would have been available to that person if the material had been obtained by the subsequent users described in paragraph (1)(C) directly from that person, except that this subparagraph applies only if that technology

(i) does not significantly interfere with the performance of the provider's system or network or with the intermediate storage of the material;

(ii) is consistent with generally accepted industry standard communications protocols; and

(iii) does not extract information from the provider's system or network other than the information that would have been available to the person described in paragraph (1)(A) if the subsequent users had gained access to the material directly from that person;

(D) if the person described in paragraph (1)(A) has in effect a condition that a person must meet prior to having access to the material, such as a condition based on payment of a fee or provision of a password or other information, the service provider permits access to the stored material in significant part only to users of its system or network that have met those conditions and only in accordance with those conditions; and

(E) if the person described in paragraph (1)(A) makes that material available online without the authorization of the copyright owner of the material, the service provider responds expeditiously to remove, or disable access to, the material that is claimed to be infringing upon notification of claimed infringement as described in subsection (c)(3), except that this subparagraph applies only if

(i) the material has previously been removed from the originating site or access to it has been disabled, or a court has ordered that the material be removed from the originating site or that access to the material on the originating site be disabled; and

(ii) the party giving the notification includes in the notification a statement confirming that the material has been removed from the originating site or access to it has been disabled or that a court has ordered that the material be removed from the originating site or that access to the material on the originating site be disabled.

(c) Information Residing on Systems or Networks At Direction of Users.

(1) In general. A service provider shall not be liable for monetary relief, or, except as provided in subsection (j), for injunctive or other equitable relief, for infringement of copyright by reason of the storage at the direction of a user of material that resides on a system or network controlled or operated by or for the service provider, if the service provider

(A)

(i) does not have actual knowledge that the material or an activity using the material on the system or network is infringing;

(ii) in the absence of such actual knowledge, is not aware of facts or circumstances from which infringing activity is apparent; or

(iii) upon obtaining such knowledge or awareness, acts expeditiously to remove, or disable access to, the material;

(B) does not receive a financial benefit directly attributable to the infringing activity, in a case in which the service provider has the right and ability to control such activity; and

(C) upon notification of claimed infringement as described in paragraph (3), responds expeditiously to remove, or disable access to, the material that is claimed to be infringing or to be the subject of infringing activity.

(2) Designated agent. The limitations on liability established in this subsection apply to a service provider only if the service provider has designated an agent to receive notifications of claimed infringement described in paragraph (3), by making available through its service, including on its website in a location accessible to the public, and by providing to the Copyright Office, substantially the following information:

(A) the name, address, phone number, and electronic mail address of the agent.

(B) other contact information which the Register of Copyrights may deem appropriate. The Register of Copyrights shall maintain a current directory of agents available to the public for inspection, including through the Internet, in both electronic and hard copy formats, and may require payment of a fee by service providers to cover the costs of maintaining the directory.

(3) Elements of notification.

(A) To be effective under this subsection, a notification of claimed infringement must be a written communication provided to the designated agent of a service provider that includes substantially the following:

(i) A physical or electronic signature of a person authorized to act on behalf of the owner of an exclusive right that is allegedly infringed.

(ii) Identification of the copyrighted work claimed to have been infringed, or, if multiple copyrighted works at a single online site are covered by a single notification, a representative list of such works at that site.

(iii) Identification of the material that is claimed to be infringing or to be the subject of infringing activity and that is to be removed or access to which is to be disabled, and information reasonably sufficient to permit the service provider to locate the material.

(iv) Information reasonably sufficient to permit the service provider to contact the complaining party, such as an address, telephone number, and, if available, an electronic mail address at which the complaining party may be contacted.

(v) A statement that the complaining party has a good faith belief that use of the material in the manner complained of is not authorized by the copyright owner, its agent, or the law.

(vi) A statement that the information in the notification is accurate, and under penalty of perjury, that the complaining party is authorized to act on behalf of the owner of an exclusive right that is allegedly infringed.

(B)

   (i) Subject to clause (ii), a notification from a copyright owner or from a person authorized to act on behalf of the copyright owner that fails to comply substantially with the provisions of subparagraph (A) shall not be considered under paragraph (1)(A) in determining whether a service provider has actual knowledge or is aware of facts or circumstances from which infringing activity is apparent.

   (ii) In a case in which the notification that is provided to the service provider's designated agent fails to comply substantially with all the provisions of subparagraph (A) but substantially complies with clauses (ii), (iii), and (iv) of subparagraph (A), clause (i) of this subparagraph applies only if the service provider promptly attempts to contact the person making the notification or takes other reasonable steps to assist in the receipt of notification that substantially complies with all the provisions of subparagraph (A).

(d) Information Location Tools. A service provider shall not be liable for monetary relief, or, except as provided in subsection (j), for injunctive or other equitable relief, for infringement of copyright by reason of the provider referring or linking users to an online location containing infringing material or infringing activity, by using information location tools, including a directory, index, reference, pointer, or hypertext link, if the service provider

(1)

   (A) does not have actual knowledge that the material or activity is infringing;
   (B) in the absence of such actual knowledge, is not aware of facts or circumstances from which infringing activity is apparent; or
   (C) upon obtaining such knowledge or awareness, acts expeditiously to remove, or disable access to, the material;

(2) does not receive a financial benefit directly attributable to the infringing activity, in a case in which the service provider has the right and ability to control such activity; and

(3) upon notification of claimed infringement as described in subsection (c)(3), responds expeditiously to remove, or disable access to, the material that is claimed to be infringing or to be the subject of infringing activity, except that, for purposes of this paragraph, the information described in subsection (c)(3)(A)(iii) shall be identification of the reference or link, to material or activity claimed to be infringing, that is to be removed or access to which is to be disabled, and information reasonably sufficient to permit the service provider to locate that reference or link.

(e) Limitation on liability of nonprofit educational institutions. (1) When a public or other nonprofit institution of higher education is a service provider, and when a faculty member or graduate student who is an employee of such institution is performing a teaching or research function, for the purposes of subsections (a) and (b) such faculty member or graduate student shall be considered to be a person other than the institution, and for the purposes of subsections (c) and (d) such faculty member's or graduate student's knowledge or awareness of his or her infringing activities shall not be attributed to the institution, if

(A) such faculty member's or graduate student's infringing activities do not involve the provision of online access to instructional materials that are or were required or recommended, within the preceding 3-year period, for a course taught at the institution by such faculty member or graduate student;

(B) the institution has not, within the preceding 3-year period, received more than two notifications described in subsection (c)(3) of claimed infringement by such faculty member or graduate student, and such notifications of claimed infringement were not actionable under subsection (f); and

(C) the institution provides to all users of its system or network informational materials that accurately describe, and promote compliance with, the laws of the United States relating to copyright.

(2) Injunctions. For the purposes of this subsection, the limitations on injunctive relief contained in subsections (j)(2) and (j)(3), but not those in (j)(1), shall apply.

(f) Misrepresentations. Any person who knowingly materially mis-represents under this section

(1) that material or activity is infringing, or

(2) that material or activity was removed or disabled by mistake or misidentification, shall be liable for any damages, including costs and attorneys' fees, incurred by the alleged infringer, by any copyright owner or copyright owner's authorized licensee, or by a service provider, who is injured by such misrepresentation, as the result of the service provider relying upon such misrepresentation in removing or disabling access to the material or activity claimed to be infringing, or in replacing the removed material or ceasing to disable access to it.

(g) Replacement of Removed or Disabled Material and Limitation on Other Liability.

(1) No liability for taking down generally. Subject to paragraph (2), a service provider shall not be liable to any person for any claim based on the service provider's good faith disabling of access to, or removal of, material or activity claimed to be infringing or based on facts or circumstances from which infringing activity is apparent, regardless of whether the material or activity is ultimately determined to be infringing.

(2) Exception. Paragraph (1) shall not apply with respect to material residing at the direction of a subscriber of the service provider on a system or network controlled or operated by or for the service provider that is removed, or to which access is disabled by the service provider, pursuant to a notice provided under subsection (c)(1)(C), unless the service provider

(A) takes reasonable steps promptly to notify the subscriber that it has removed or disabled access to the material;

(B) upon receipt of a counter notification described in paragraph (3), promptly provides the person who provided the notification under subsection (c)(1)(C) with a copy of the counter notification, and informs that person that it will replace the removed material or cease disabling access to it in 10 business days; and

(C) replaces the removed material and ceases disabling access to it not less than 10, nor more than 14, business days following receipt of the counter notice, unless its designated agent first receives notice from the person who submitted the notification under subsection (c)(1)(C) that such person has filed an action seeking a court order to restrain the subscriber from engaging in infringing activity relating to the material on the service provider's system or network.

(3) Contents of counter notification. To be effective under this subsection, a counter notification must be a written communication provided to the service provider's designated agent that includes substantially the following:

(A) A physical or electronic signature of the subscriber.

(B) Identification of the material that has been removed or to which access has been disabled and the location at which the material appeared before it was removed or access to it was disabled.

(C) A statement under penalty of perjury that the subscriber has a good faith belief that the material was removed or disabled as a result of mistake or misidentification of the material to be removed or disabled.

(D) The subscriber's name, address, and telephone number, and a statement that the subscriber consents to the jurisdiction of Federal District Court for the judicial district in which the address is located, or if the subscriber's address is outside of the United States, for any judicial district in which the service provider may be found, and that the subscriber will accept service of process from the person who provided notification under subsection (c)(1)(C) or an agent of such person.

(4) Limitation on other liability. A service provider's compliance with paragraph (2) shall not subject the service provider to liability for copyright infringement with respect to the material identified in the notice provided under subsection (c)(1)(C).

(h) Subpoena To Identify Infringer.

(1) Request. A copyright owner or a person authorized to act on the owner's behalf may request the clerk of any United States district court to issue a

subpoena to a service provider for identification of an alleged infringer in accordance with this subsection.

(2) Contents of request. The request may be made by filing with the clerk

(A) a copy of a notification described in subsection (c)(3)(A);

(B) a proposed subpoena; and

(C) a sworn declaration to the effect that the purpose for which the subpoena is sought is to obtain the identity of an alleged infringer and that such information will only be used for the purpose of protecting rights under this title.

(3) Contents of subpoena. The subpoena shall authorize and order the service provider receiving the notification and the subpoena to expeditiously disclose to the copyright owner or person authorized by the copyright owner information sufficient to identify the alleged infringer of the material described in the notification to the extent such information is available to the service provider.

(4) Basis for granting subpoena. If the notification filed satisfies the provisions of subsection (c)(3)(A), the proposed subpoena is in proper form, and the accompanying declaration is properly executed, the clerk shall expeditiously issue and sign the proposed subpoena and return it to the requester for delivery to the service provider.

(5) Actions of service provider receiving subpoena. Upon receipt of the issued subpoena, either accompanying or subsequent to the receipt of a notification described in subsection (c)(3)(A), the service provider shall expeditiously disclose to the copyright owner or person authorized by the copyright owner the information required by the subpoena, notwithstanding any other provision of law and regardless of whether the service provider responds to the notification.

(6) Rules applicable to subpoena. Unless otherwise provided by this section or by applicable rules of the court, the procedure for issuance and delivery of the subpoena, and the remedies for noncompliance with the subpoena, shall be governed to the greatest extent practicable by those provisions of the Federal Rules of Civil Procedure governing the issuance, service, and enforcement of a subpoena duces tecum.

(i) Conditions for Eligibility.

(1) Accommodation of technology. The limitations on liability established by this section shall apply to a service provider only if the service provider

(A) has adopted and reasonably implemented, and informs subscribers and account holders of the service provider's system or network of, a policy that provides for the termination in appropriate circumstances of subscribers and account holders of the service provider's system or network who are repeat infringers; and

(B) accommodates and does not interfere with standard technical measures.

(2) Definition. As used in this subsection, the term "standard technical measures"

means technical measures that are used by copyright owners to identify or protect copyrighted works and

(A) have been developed pursuant to a broad consensus of copyright owners and service providers in an open, fair, voluntary, multi-industry standards process;

(B) are available to any person on reasonable and nondiscriminatory terms; and

(C) do not impose substantial costs on service providers or substantial burdens on their systems or networks.

(j) Injunctions. The following rules shall apply in the case of any application for an injunction under section 502 against a service provider that is not subject to monetary remedies under this section:

(1) Scope of relief. (A) With respect to conduct other than that which qualifies for the limitation on remedies set forth in subsection (a), the court may grant injunctive relief with respect to a service provider only in one or more of the following forms:

  (i)   An order restraining the service provider from providing access to infringing material or activity residing at a particular online site on the provider's system or network.

  (ii) An order restraining the service provider from providing access to a subscriber or account holder of the service provider's system or network who is engaging in infringing activity and is identified in the order, by terminating the accounts of the subscriber or account holder that are specified in the order.

  (iii) Such other injunctive relief as the court may consider necessary to prevent or restrain infringement of copyrighted material specified in the order of the court at a particular online location, if such relief is the least burdensome to the service provider among the forms of relief comparably effective for that purpose.

(B) If the service provider qualifies for the limitation on remedies described in subsection (a), the court may only grant injunctive relief in one or both of the following forms:

  (i)   An order restraining the service provider from providing access to a subscriber or account holder of the service provider's system or network who is using the provider's service to engage in infringing activity and is identified in the order, by terminating the accounts of the subscriber or account holder that are specified in the order.

  (ii) An order restraining the service provider from providing access, by taking reasonable steps specified in the order to block access, to a specific, identified, online location outside the United States.

(2) Considerations. The court, in considering the relevant criteria for injunctive relief under applicable law, shall consider

(A) whether such an injunction, either alone or in combination with other such injunctions issued against the same service provider under this subsection, would significantly burden either the provider or the operation of the provider's system or network;

(B) the magnitude of the harm likely to be suffered by the copyright owner in the digital network environment if steps are not taken to prevent or restrain the infringement;

(C) whether implementation of such an injunction would be technically feasible and effective, and would not interfere with access to noninfringing material at other online locations; and

(D) whether other less burdensome and comparably effective means of preventing or restraining access to the infringing material are available.

(3) Notice and Ex Parte Orders. Injunctive relief under this subsection shall be available only after notice to the service provider and an opportunity for the service provider to appear are provided, except for orders ensuring the preservation of evidence or other orders having no material adverse effect on the operation of the service provider's communications network.

(k) Definitions.

(1) Service provider. (A) As used in subsection (a), the term "service provider" means an entity offering the transmission, routing, or providing of connections for digital online communications, between or among points specified by a user, of material of the user's choosing, without modification to the content of the material as sent or received.

(B) As used in this section, other than subsection (a), the term "service provider" means a provider of online services or network access, or the operator of facilities therefor, and includes an entity described in subparagraph (A).

(2) Monetary relief. As used in this section, the term "monetary relief" means damages, costs, attorneys' fees, and any other form of monetary payment.

(l) Other Defenses Not Affected. The failure of a service provider's conduct to qualify for limitation of liability under this section shall not bear adversely upon the consideration of a defense by the service provider that the service provider's conduct is not infringing under this title or any other defense.

(m) Protection of Privacy. Nothing in this section shall be construed to condition the applicability of subsections (a) through (d) on

(1) a service provider monitoring its service or affirmatively seeking facts indicating infringing activity, except to the extent consistent with a standard technical measure complying with the provisions of subsection (i); or

(2) a service provider gaining access to, removing, or disabling access to material in cases in which such conduct is prohibited by law.

(n) Construction. Subsections (a), (b), (c), and (d) describe separate and distinct functions for purposes of applying this section. Whether a service provider qualifies for the limitation on liability in any one of those subsections shall be based solely on the criteria in that subsection, and shall not affect a determination of whether that service provider qualifies for the limitations on liability under any other such subsection.

Source B

Copyright Term Duration

Note: this is a very simplified summary of copyright terms; see Section 301 *et seq.* of the Copyright Act for the entire text.

Works created but not published before January 1, 1978 (§ 303)
(Before the 1976 Copyright Act, copyright began at publication. As a result of the 1976 act, copyright begins at the moment of creation. This section gives protection to works created but not published before the 1976 act was effective.)

- Term as indicated under£ 302 (below)
- Copyright deemed to begin January 1, 1978
- In no case shall the term expire before December 31, 2002
- If the work is published on or before December 31, 2002, the term shall not expire before December 31, 2047

Works copyrighted as of January 1, 1978 (§ 304)
(Before the 1976 Copyright Act, the term of copyright was 28 years, renewable at the end of the term for another 28 years if the author was still alive.)

Copyrights in the first term on January 1, 1978
- The first 28-year term still applies
- If the author owns the copyright, then he or his survivors, or if someone else owns the copyright then that person, is entitled to renewal for a second term of 67 years

Copyrights in their renewal term as of January 1, 1999
- Term of 95 years from original copyright date

Works created on or after January 1, 1978 (§ 302)

In general
- Copyright begins at creation
- Life plus 70

Joint authors
- Copyright begins at creation
- Life of last surviving author plus 70

Anonymous and pseudonymous works

Earliest of:

- 95 years from first publication
- 120 years from creation

Works made for hire

Earliest of:

- 95 years from first publication
- 120 years from creation

Source C

The Conference on Fair Use: Educational Fair Use Guidelines for Digital Images[1]

Table of contents:

1. Introduction.
2. Image Digitization and Use by Educational Institutions.
3. Use by Educators, Scholars, and Students.
4. Image Digitization by Educators, Scholars, and Students for Spontaneous Use.
5. Important Reminders and Fair Use Limitations Under These Guidelines.
6. Transition Period for Pre-Existing Analog Image Collections.
   Appendix A: Organizations Endorsing These Guidelines.
   Appendix B: Organizations Participating in Development of These Guidelines.

1. Introduction:

1.1 Preamble.

Fair use is a legal principle that provides certain limitations on the exclusive rights[2] of copyright holders. The purpose of these guidelines is to provide guidance on the application of fair use principles by educational institutions, educators, scholars, and students who wish to digitize copyrighted visual images under fair use rather than by seeking authorization from the copyright owners for non-commercial educational purposes. These guidelines apply to fair use only in the context of copyright.

There is no simple test to determine what is fair use. Section 107 of the Copyright Act[3] sets forth the four fair use factors which should be assessed in each instance, based on the particular facts of a given case, to determine whether a use is a "fair use": (1) the purpose and character of the use, including whether such use is of a commercial nature or is for nonprofit educational purposes, (2) the nature of the copyrighted work, (3) the amount and substantiality of the portion used in relation to the copyrighted work as a whole, and (4) the effect of the use upon the potential market for or value of the copyrighted work. While only the courts can authoritatively determine whether a particular use is fair use, these guidelines represent the endorsers' consensus of conditions under which fair use should generally apply and examples of when permission is required. Uses that exceed these guidelines may or may not be fair use. The endorsers also agree that the more one exceeds these guidelines, the greater the risk that fair use does not apply.

The limitations and conditions set forth in these guidelines do not apply to works in the public domain—such as U.S. government works or works on which copyright has expired for which there are no copyright restrictions—or to works for which the individual or institution has obtained permission for the particular use. Also, license agreements may govern the uses of some works and users should refer to the applicable license terms for guidance.

The participants who developed these guidelines met for an extended period of time and the result represents their collective understanding in this complex area. Because digital technology is in a dynamic phase, there may come a time when it is necessary to review the guidelines. Nothing in these guidelines should be construed to apply to the fair use privilege in any context outside of educational and scholarly uses of digital images. These guidelines do not cover non-educational or commercial digitization or use at any time, even by non-profit educational institutions. These guidelines are not intended to cover fair use of copyrighted works in other educational contexts such as educational multimedia projects,[4] distance education, or electronic reserves, which may be addressed in other fair use guidelines.

This Preamble is an integral part of these guidelines and should be included whenever the guidelines are reprinted or adopted by organizations and educational institutions. Users are encouraged to reproduce and distribute these guidelines freely without permission; no copyright protection of these guidelines is claimed by any person or entity.

1.2 Background: Rights in visual images.

As photographic and electronic technology has advanced, the making of high-quality reproductions of visual images has become easier, cheaper, and more widely accessible. However, the fact that images may be easily available does not automatically mean they can be reproduced and reused without permission. Confusion regarding intellectual property rights in visual images arises from the many ways that images are created and the many sources that may be related to any particular image. Clearing permission, when necessary, requires identifying the holder of the applicable rights. Determining all the holders of the rights connected with an image requires an understanding of the source of the image, the content portrayed, and the creation of the image, both for original visual images and for reproductions of images.

Visual images can be original works or reproductions of other works; in some cases, original works may incorporate reproductions of other works as well. Often, a digital image is several generations removed from the visual image it reproduces. For example, a digital image of a painting may have been scanned from a slide, which was copied from a published book that contained a printed reproduction of the work of art; this reproduction may have been made from a color transparency photographed directly from the original painting. There may be intellectual property rights in the original painting, and each additional stage of reproduction in this chain may involve another layer of rights.

A digital image can be an original visual image, a reproduction, a published reproduction, or a copy of a published reproduction. An original visual image is a work of art or an original work of authorship (or a part of a work), fixed in digital or analog form and expressed in a visual medium. Examples include graphic, sculptural, and architectural works, as well as stills from motion pictures or other audio-visual works. A reproduction is a copy of an original visual image in digital or analog form. The most common forms of reproductions are photographic, including prints, 35mm slides, and color transparencies. The original visual image shown in a reproduction is often referred to as the "underlying work." Digital images can be reproductions of either original visual images or of other reproductions. A published reproduction is a reproduction of an original visual image appearing in a work distributed in copies and made available to the public by sale or other transfer of ownership, or by rental, lease, or lending. Examples include a plate in an exhibition catalog that reproduces a work of art, and a digital image appearing in a CD-ROM or online. A copy of a published reproduction is a subsequent copy made of a published reproduction of an original visual image, for example, a 35mm slide which is a copy of an image in a book.

The rights in images in each of these layers may be held by different rightsholders; obtaining rights to one does not automatically grant rights to use another, and therefore all must be considered when analyzing the rights connected with an image. Rights to use images will vary depending not only on the identities of the layers of rightsholders, but also on other factors such as the terms of any bequest or applicable license.

1.3 Applicability of these guidelines.

These guidelines apply to the creation of digital images and their use for educational purposes. The guidelines cover (1) pre-existing analog image collections and (2) newly acquired analog visual images. These guidelines do not apply to images acquired in digital form, or to images in the public domain, or to works for which the user has obtained the relevant and necessary rights for the particular use.

Only lawfully acquired copyrighted analog images (including original visual images, reproductions, published reproductions, and copies of published reproductions) may be digitized pursuant to these guidelines. These guidelines apply only to educational institutions, educators, scholars, students, and image collection curators engaging in instructional, research, or scholarly activities at educational institutions for educational purposes.

1.4 Definitions.

Educational institutions are defined as nonprofit organizations whose primary purpose is supporting the nonprofit instructional, research, and scholarly activities of educators, scholars, and students. Examples of educational institutions include K-12 schools, colleges, and universities; libraries, museums, hospitals, and other nonprofit institutions also are considered educational institutions under this definition when they engage in nonprofit instructional, research, or scholarly activities for educational purposes. **Educational purposes** are defined as non-commercial instruction or curriculum-based teaching by educators to students at nonprofit educational institutions, and **research and scholarly activities**, defined as planned non-commercial study or investigation directed toward making a contribution to a field of knowledge and non-commercial presentation of research findings at peer conferences, workshops, or seminars.

Educators are faculty, teachers, instructors, curators, librarians, archivists, or professional staff who engage in instructional, research, or scholarly activities for educational purposes as their assigned responsibilities at educational institutions; independent scholars also are considered educators under this definition when they offer courses at educational institutions. **Students** are participants in instructional, research, or scholarly activities for educational purposes at educational institutions.

A **digital image** is a visual work stored in binary code (bits and bytes). Examples include bitmapped images (encoded as a series of bits and bytes each representing a particular pixel or part of the image) and vector graphics (encoded as equations and/ or algorithms representing lines and curves). An **analog image collection** is an assemblage of analog visual images systematically maintained by an educational institution for educational purposes in the form of slides, photographs, or other stand-alone visual media. A **pre-existing analog image collection** is one in existence as of [December 31, 1996]. A **newly acquired analog visual image** is one added to an institution's collection after [December 31, 1996].

A **visual online catalog** is a database consisting of thumbnail images of an institution's lawfully acquired image collection, together with any descriptive text including, for example, provenance and rights information that is searchable by a number of fields, such as source. A **thumbnail image**, as used in a visual online catalog or image browsing display to enable visual identification of records in an educational institution's image collection, is a small scale, typically low resolution, digital reproduction which has no intrinsic commercial or reproductive value.

2. Image digitization and use by educational institutions:

This Section covers digitization by educational institutions of newly acquired analog visual images and Section 6 covers digitization of pre-existing analog image collections. Refer to the applicable section depending on whether you are digitizing newly acquired or pre-existing analog visual works.

2.1 Digitizing by institutions: Newly acquired analog visual images.

An educational institution may digitize newly, lawfully, acquired analog visual images to support the permitted educational uses under these guidelines unless such images are readily available in usable digital form for purchase or license at a fair price. Images that are readily available in usable digital form for purchase or license at a fair price should not be digitized for addition to an institutional image collection without permission.

2.2 Creating thumbnail images.

An educational institution may create thumbnail images of lawfully acquired images for inclusion in a visual catalog for use at the institution. These thumbnail images may be combined with descriptive text in a visual catalog that is searchable by a number of fields, such as the source.

2.3 Access, display, and distribution on an institution's secure electronic network.

Subject to the time limitations in Section 2.4, an educational institution may display and provide access to images digitized under these guidelines through its own secure electronic network. When displaying digital images on such networks, an educational institution should implement technological controls and institutional policies to protect the rights of copyright owners, and use best efforts to make users aware of those rights. In addition, the educational institution must provide notice stating that digital images on its secure electronic network shall not be downloaded, copied, retained, printed, shared, modified, or otherwise used, except as provided for in the permitted educational uses under these guidelines.

2.3.1 Visual online catalog: An educational institution may display a visual online catalog, which includes the thumbnail images created as part of the institution's digitization process, on the institution's secure electronic network, and may provide access to such catalog by educators, scholars, and students affiliated with the educational institution.

2.3.2 Course compilations of digital images: An educational institution may display an educator's compilation of digital images (see also Section 3.1.2) on the institution's secure electronic network for classroom use, after-class review, or directed study, provided that there are technological limitations (such as a password or PIN) restricting access only to students enrolled in the course. The institution may display such images on its secure electronic network only during the semester or term in which that academic course is given.

2.3.3 Access, display, and distribution beyond the institution's secure electronic network: Electronic access to, or display or distribution of, images digitized under these guidelines, including the thumbnail images in the institution's visual online catalog, is not permitted beyond the institution's own electronic network, even for educational purposes. However, those portions of the visual online catalog which do not contain images digitized under these guidelines, such as public domain images and text, may be accessed, displayed, or distributed beyond the institution's own secure electronic network.

2.4 Time Limitations for Use of Images Digitized by Institutions from Newly Acquired Analog Visual Images.

An educational institution may use and retain in digital image collections images which are digitized from newly acquired analog visual images under these guidelines, as long as the retention and use comply with the following conditions:

2.4.1 Images digitized from a known source and not readily available in usable digital form for purchase or license at a fair price may be used for one academic term and may be retained in digital form while permission is being sought. Permission is required for uses beyond the initial use; if permission is not received, any use is outside the scope of these guidelines and subject to the four-factor fair use analysis (see Section 1.1).

2.4.2 Where the rightsholder of an image is unknown, a digitized image may be used for up to 3 years from first use, provided that a reasonable inquiry (see Section 5.2) is conducted by the institution seeking permission to digitize, retain, and reuse the digitized image. If, after 3 years, the educational institution is unable to identify sufficient information to seek permission, any further use of the image is outside the scope of these guidelines and subject to the four-factor fair use analysis (see Section 1.1).

3. Use by educators, scholars, and students:

Subject to the time limitations in Section 2.4, images digitized under these guidelines may be used by educators, scholars, and students as follows:

3.1 Educator use of images digitized under these guidelines.

3.1.1 An educator may display digital images for educational purposes, including face-to-face teaching of curriculum-based courses, and research and scholarly activities at a non-profit educational institution.

3.1.2 An educator may compile digital images for display on the institution's secure electronic network (see also Section 2.3.2) to students enrolled in a course given by that educator for classroom use, after-class review, or directed study, during the semester or term in which the educator's related course is given.

3.2 Use of images for peer conferences.

Educators, scholars, and students may use or display digital images in connection with lectures or presentations in their fields, including uses at non-commercial professional development seminars, workshops, and conferences where educators meet to discuss issues relevant to their disciplines or present works they created for educational purposes in the course of research, study, or teaching.

3.3 Use of images for publications.

These guidelines do not cover reproducing and publishing images in publications, including scholarly publications in print or digital form, for which permission is generally required. Before publishing any images under fair use, even for scholarly and critical purposes, scholars and scholarly publishers should conduct the four-factor fair use analysis (see Section 1.1).

3.4 Student use of images digitized under these guidelines.
Students may:

- Use digital images in an academic course assignment such as a term paper or thesis, or in fulfillment of degree requirements.
- Publicly display their academic work incorporating digital images in courses for which they are registered and during formal critiques at a nonprofit educational institution.
- Retain their academic work in their personal portfolios for later uses such as graduate school and employment applications.

Other student uses are outside the scope of these guidelines and are subject to the four-factor fair use analysis (see Section 1.1).

4. Image digitization by educators, scholars, and students for spontaneous use:
Educators, scholars, and students may digitize lawfully acquired images to support the permitted educational uses under these guidelines if the inspiration and decision to use the work and the moment of its use for maximum teaching effectiveness are so close in time that it would be unreasonable to expect a timely reply to a request for permission. Images digitized for spontaneous use do not automatically become part of the institution's image collection. Permission must be sought for any reuse of such digitized images or their addition to the institution's image collection.

5. Important reminders and fair use limitations under these guidelines:

5.1 Creation of digital image collections.
When digitizing copyrighted images, as permitted under these guidelines, an educational institution should simultaneously conduct the process of seeking permission to retain and use the images.

Where the rightsholder is unknown, the institution should pursue and is encouraged to keep records of its reasonable inquiry (see Section 5.2). Rightsholders and others who are contacted are encouraged to respond promptly to inquiries.

5.2 Reasonable inquiry.
A reasonable inquiry by an institution for the purpose of clearing rights to digitize and use digital images includes, but is not limited to, conducting each of the following steps: (1) checking any information within the control of the educational institution, including slide catalogs and logs, regarding the source of the image; (2) asking

relevant faculty, departmental staff, and librarians, including visual resource collections administrators, for any information regarding the source of the image; (3) consulting standard reference publications and databases for information regarding the source of the image; and (4) consulting rights reproduction collectives and/or major professional associations representing image creators in the appropriate medium.

5.3 Attribution and acknowledgment.

Educators, scholars, and students should credit the sources and display the copyright notice(s) with any copyright ownership information shown in the original source, for all images digitized by educators, scholars, and students, including those digitized under fair use. Crediting the source means adequately identifying the source of the work, giving a full bibliographic description where available (including the creator/author, title, publisher, and place and date of publication) or citing the electronic address if the work is from a network source. Educators, scholars, and students should retain any copyright notice or other proprietary rights notice placed by the copyright owner or image archive or collection on the digital image, unless they know that the work has entered the public domain or that the copyright ownership has changed. In those cases when source credits and copyright ownership information cannot be displayed on the screen with the image for educational reasons (e.g., during examinations), this information should still be linked to the image.

5.4 Licenses and contracts.

Institutions should determine whether specific images are subject to a license or contract; a license or contract may limit the uses of those images.

5.5 Portions from single sources such as published compilations or motion pictures.

When digitizing and using individual images from a single source such as a published compilation (including but not limited to books, slide sets, and digital image collections), or individual frames from motion pictures or other audiovisual works, institutions and individuals should be aware that fair use limits the number and substantiality of the images that may be used from a single source. In addition, a separate copyright in a compilation may exist. Further, fair use requires consideration of the effect of the use on the potential market for or value of the copyrighted work. The greater the number and substantiality of images taken from a single source, the greater the risk that the use will not be fair use.

5.6 Portions of individual images.

Although the use of entire works is usually not permitted under fair use, it is generally appropriate to use images in their entirety in order to respect the integrity of the original visual image, as long as the limitations on use under these guidelines are in place. For purposes of electronic display, however, portions of an image may be used to highlight certain details of the work for educational purposes as long as the full image is displayed or linked to the portion.

5.7 Integrity of images: alterations.

In order to maintain the integrity of copyrighted works, educators, scholars, and students are advised to exercise care when making any alterations in a work under fair use for educational purposes such as criticism, comment, teaching, scholarship, and research. Furthermore, educators, scholars, and students should note the nature of any changes they make to original visual images when producing their own digital images.

5.8 Caution in downloading images from other electronic sources.

Educators, scholars, and students are advised to exercise caution in using digital images downloaded from other sources, such as the Internet. Such digital environments contain a mix of works protected by copyright and works in the public domain, and some copyrighted works may have been posted to the Internet without authorization of the copyright holder.

6. Transition period for pre-existing analog image collections:

6.1 Context.

Pre-existing visual resource collections in educational institutions (referred to in these guidelines as "pre-existing analog image collections") often consist of tens of thousands of images which have been acquired from a wide variety of sources over a period of many years. Many pre-existing collections lack adequate source information for older images and standards for accession practices are still evolving. In addition, publishers and vendors may no longer be in business, and information about specific images may no longer be available. For many images there may also be several layers of rightsholders: the rights in an original visual image are separate from rights in a reproduction of that image and may be held by different rightsholders. All these factors complicate the process of locating rightsholders, and seeking permissions for pre-existing collections will be painstaking and time consuming.

However, there are significant educational benefits to be gained if pre-existing analog image collections can be digitized uniformly and systematically. Digitization will allow educators to employ new technologies using the varied and numerous images necessary in their current curricula. At the same time, rightsholders and educational institutions have concerns that images in some collections may have been acquired without permission or may be subject to restricted uses. In either case, there may be rightsholders whose rights and interests are affected by digitization and other uses.

The approach agreed upon by the representatives who developed these guidelines is to permit educational institutions to digitize lawfully acquired images as a collection and to begin using such images for educational purposes. At the same time, educational institutions should begin to identify the rightsholders and seek permission to retain and use the digitized images for future educational purposes. Continued use depends on the institutions' making a reasonable inquiry (see Section 5.2) to clear the rights in the digitized image. This approach seeks to strike a reasonable balance and workable solution for copyright holders and users who otherwise may not agree on precisely what constitutes fair use in the digital era.

6.2 Digitizing by institutions: images in pre-existing analog image collections.

6.2.1 Educational institutions may digitize images from pre-existing analog image collections during a reasonable transition period of 7 years (the approximate useful life of a slide) from [December 31, 1996]. In addition, educators, scholars, and students may begin to use those digitized images during the transition period to support the educational uses under these guidelines. When digitizing images during the transition period, institutions should simultaneously begin seeking the permission to digitize, retain, and reuse all such digitized images.

6.2.2 Digitization from pre-existing analog image collections is subject to limitations on portions from single sources such as published compilations or motion pictures (see Section 5.5). Section 6 of these guidelines should not be interpreted to permit the systematic digitization of images from an educational institution's collections of books, films, or periodicals as part of any methodical process of digitizing images from the institution's pre-existing analog image collection during the transition period.

6.2.3 If, after a reasonable inquiry (see Section 5.2), an educational institution is unable to identify sufficient information to seek appropriate permission during the transition period, continued retention and use is outside the scope of these guidelines and subject to the four-factor fair use analysis (see Section 1.1). Similarly, digitization and use of such collections after the expiration of the transition period is outside the scope of these guidelines and subject to the four-factor fair use analysis (see Section 1.1).

Notes

1. These guidelines shall not be read to supersede other pre-existing educational use guidelines that deal with the 1976 Copyright Act.
2. *See* Section 106 of the Copyright Act.
3. The Copyright Act of 1976, as amended, is codified at 17 U.S.C. Sec. 101 et seq.
4. In general, multimedia projects are stand-alone, interactive programs incorporating both original and pre-existing copyrighted works in various media formats, while visual image archives are databases of individual visual images from which images intended for educational uses may be selected for display.

Source D

The Conference on Fair Use: Fair Use Guidelines for Electronic Reserve Systems*

Revised: March 5, 1996

Introduction

Many college, university, and school libraries have established reserve operations for readings and other materials that support the instructional requirements of specific courses. Some educational institutions are now providing electronic reserve systems that allow storage of electronic versions of materials that students may retrieve on a computer screen, and from which they may print a copy for their personal study. When materials are included as a matter of fair use, electronic reserve systems should constitute an ad hoc or supplemental source of information for students, beyond a textbook or other materials. If included with permission from the copyright owner, however, the scope and range of materials is potentially unlimited, depending upon the permission granted. Although fair use is determined on a case-by-case basis, the following guidelines identify an understanding of fair use for the reproduction, distribution, display, and performance of materials in the context of creating and using an electronic reserve system.

Making materials accessible through electronic reserve systems raises significant copyright issues. Electronic reserve operations include the making of a digital version of text, the distribution and display of that version at workstations, and downloading and printing of copies. The complexities of the electronic environment, and the growing potential for implicating copyright infringements, raise the need for a fresh understanding of fair use. These guidelines are not intended to burden the facilitation of reserves unduly, but instead offer a workable path that educators and librarians may follow in order to exercise a meaningful application of fair use, while also acknowledging and respecting the interests of copyright owners.

These guidelines focus generally on the traditional domain of reserve rooms, particularly copies of journal articles and book chapters, and their accompanying graphics. Nevertheless, they are not meant to apply exclusively to textual materials

* Note: These guidelines were written during the Conference on Fair Use process. However, the working group was unable to reach consensus on the guidelines and thus decided that they would not be disseminated as a part of the CONFU Report.

and may be instructive for the fair use of other media. The guidelines also focus on the use of the complete article or the entire book chapter. Using only brief excerpts from such works would most likely also be fair use, possibly without all of the restrictions or conditions set forth in these guidelines. Operators of reserve systems should also provide safeguards for the integrity of the text and the author's reputation, including verification that the text is correctly scanned.

The guidelines address only those materials protected by copyright and for which the institution has not obtained permission before including them in an electronic reserve system. The Limitations and conditions set forth in these guidelines need not apply to materials in the public domain—such as works of the U.S. government or works on which copyright has expired—or to works for which the institution has obtained permission for inclusion in the electronic reserve system. License agreements may govern the uses of some materials. Persons responsible for electronic reserve systems should refer to applicable license terms for guidance. If an instructor arranges for students to acquire a work by some means that includes permission from the copyright owner, the instructor should not include that same work on an electronic reserve system as a matter of fair use.

These guidelines are the outgrowth of negotiations among diverse parties attending the Conference on Fair Use ("CONFU") meetings sponsored by the Information Infrastructure Task Force's Working Group on Intellectual Property Rights. While endorsements of any guidelines by all conference participants is unlikely, these guidelines have been endorsed by the organizations whose names appear at the end. These guidelines are in furtherance of the Working Group's objective of encouraging negotiated guidelines of fair use.

This introduction is an integral part of these guidelines and should be included with the guidelines wherever they may be reprinted or adopted by a library, academic institution, or other organization or association. No copyright protection of these guidelines is claimed by any person or entity, and anyone is free to reproduce and distribute this document without permission.

A. Scope of material

1. In accordance with fair use (Section 107 of the U.S. Copyright Act), electronic reserve systems may include copyrighted materials at the request of a course instructor.

2. Electronic reserve systems may include short items (such as an article from a journal, a chapter from a book or conference proceedings, or a poem from a collected work) or excerpts from longer items. "Longer items" may include articles, chapters, poems, and other works that are of such length as to constitute a substantial portion of a book, journal, or other work of which they may be a part. "Short items" may include articles, chapters, poems, and other works of a customary length and structure as to be a small part of a book, journal, or other work, even if that work may be marketed individually.

3. Electronic reserve systems should not include any material unless the instructor, the library, or another unit of the educational institution possesses a lawfully obtained copy.
4. The total amount of material included in electronic reserve systems for a specific course as a matter of fair use should be a small proportion of the total assigned reading for a particular course.

B. Notices and attributions

1. On a preliminary or introductory screen, electronic reserve systems should display a notice, consistent with the notice described in Section 108(f)(1) of the Copyright Act. The notice should include additional language cautioning against further electronic distribution of the digital work.
2. If a notice of copyright appears on the copy of a work that is included in an electronic reserve system, the following statement shall appear at some place where users will likely see it in connection with access to the particular work: "The work from which this copy is made includes this notice: [restate the elements of the statutory copyright notice: e.g., Copyright 1996, XXX Corp.]"
3. Materials included in electronic reserve systems should include appropriate citations or attributions to their sources.

C. Access and use

1. Electronic reserve systems should be structured to limit access to students registered in the course for which the items have been placed on reserve, and to instructors and staff responsible for the course or the electronic system.
2. The appropriate methods for limiting access will depend on available technology. Solely to suggest and not to prescribe options for implementation, possible methods for limiting access may include one or more of the following or other appropriate methods:
    (a) individual password controls or verification of a student's registration status; or
    (b) password system for each class; or
    (c) retrieval of works by course number or instructor name, but not by author or title of the work; or
    (d) access limited to workstations that are ordinarily used by, or are accessible to, only enrolled students or appropriate staff or faculty.
3. Students should not be charged specifically or directly for access to electronic reserve systems.

D. Storage and reuse

1. Permission from the copyright holder is required if the item is to be reused in a subsequent academic term for the same course offered by the same instructor, or if the item is a standard assigned or optional reading for an individual course taught in multiple sections by many instructors.
2. Material may be retained in electronic form while permission is being sought

or until the next academic term in which the material might be used, but in no event for more than three calendar years, including the year in which the materials are last used.

3. Short-term access to materials included on electronic reserve systems in previous academic terms may be provided to students who have not completed the course.

Source E

Code of Ethics of the American Library Association

As members of the American Library Association, we recognize the importance of codifying and making known to the profession and to the general public the ethical principles that guide the work of librarians, other professionals providing information services, library trustees and library staffs.

Ethical dilemmas occur when values are in conflict. The American Library Association Code of Ethics states the values to which we are committed, and embodies the ethical responsibilities of the profession in this changing information environment.

We significantly influence or control the selection, organization, preservation, and dissemination of information. In a political system grounded in an informed citizenry, we are members of a profession explicitly committed to intellectual freedom and the freedom of access to information. We have a special obligation to ensure the free flow of information and ideas to present and future generations.

The principles of this Code are expressed in broad statements to guide ethical decision making. These statements provide a framework; they cannot and do not dictate conduct to cover particular situations.

I. We provide the highest level of service to all library users through appropriate and usefully organized resources; equitable service policies; equitable access; and accurate, unbiased, and courteous responses to all requests.

II. We uphold the principles of intellectual freedom and resist all efforts to censor library resources.

III. We protect each library user's right to privacy and confidentiality with respect to information sought or received and resources consulted, borrowed, acquired or transmitted.

IV. We recognize and respect intellectual property rights.

V. We treat co-workers and other colleagues with respect, fairness and good faith, and advocate conditions of employment that safeguard the rights and welfare of all employees of our institutions.

VI. We do not advance private interests at the expense of library users, colleagues, or our employing institutions.

VII. We distinguish between our personal convictions and professional duties and do not allow our personal beliefs to interfere with fair representation of the aims of our institutions or the provision of access to their information resources.

VIII. We strive for excellence in the profession by maintaining and enhancing our own knowledge and skills, by encouraging the professional development of co-workers, and by fostering the aspirations of potential members of the profession.

Adopted by the ALA Council
June 28, 1995

Source F

The Conference on Fair Use: Fair Use Guidelines for Educational Multimedia*

Table of Contents

1. Introduction
2. Preparation of Educational Multimedia Projects Under These Guidelines
3. Permitted Educational Uses for Multimedia Projects Under These Guidelines
4. Limitations
5. Examples of When Permission is Required
6. Important Reminders
Appendix A: Organizations Endorsing These Guidelines
Appendix B: Organizations Participating in Development of These Guidelines

1. Introduction

1.1 Preamble

Fair use is a legal principle that defines the limitations on the exclusive rights[2] of copyright holders. The purpose of these guidelines is to provide guidance on the application of fair use principles by educators, scholars and students who develop multimedia projects using portions of copyrighted works under fair use rather than by seeking authorization for non-commercial educational uses. These guidelines apply only to fair use in the context of copyright and to no other rights.

There is no simple test to determine what is fair use. Section 107 of the Copyright Act[3] sets forth the four fair use factors which should be considered in each instance, based on particular facts of a given case, to determine whether a use is a "fair use": (1) the purpose and character of use, including whether such use is of a commercial nature or is for nonprofit educational purposes, (2) the nature of the copyrighted work, (3) the amount and substantiality of the portion used in relation to the

---

*   Note: These Guidelines were written during the Conference on Fair Use process and disseminated as part of the final CONFU Report. However, no general consensus regarding these Guidelines was reached among CONFU participants, especially representatives of some academic and educational institutions and representatives of library concerns.[1]

copyrighted work as a whole, and (4) the effect of the use upon the potential market for or value of the copyrighted work.

While only the courts can authoritatively determine whether a particular use is fair use, these guidelines represent the participants[4] consensus of conditions under which fair use should generally apply and examples of when permission is required. Uses that exceed these guidelines may nor may not be fair use. The participants also agree that the more one exceeds these guidelines, the greater the risk that fair use does not apply.

The limitations and conditions set forth in these guidelines do not apply to works in the public domain—such as U.S. Government works or works on which copyright has expired for which there are no copyright restrictions—or to works for which the individual or institution has obtained permission for the particular use. Also, license agreements may govern the uses of some works and users should refer to the applicable license terms for guidance.

The participants who developed these guidelines met for an extended period of time and the result represents their collective understanding in this complex area. Because digital technology is in a dynamic phase, there may come a time when it is necessary to review the guidelines. Nothing in these guidelines shall be construed to apply to the fair use privilege in any context outside of educational and scholarly uses of educational multimedia projects.

This Preamble is an integral part of these guidelines and should be included whenever the guidelines are reprinted or adopted by organizations and educational institutions. Users are encouraged to reproduce and distribute these guidelines freely without permission; no copyright protection of these guidelines is claimed by any person or entity.

1.2 Background

These guidelines clarify the application of fair use of copyrighted works as teaching methods are adapted to new learning environments. Educators have traditionally brought copyrighted books, videos, slides, sound recordings and other media into the classroom, along with accompanying projection and playback equipment. Multimedia creators integrated these individual instructional resources with their own original works in a meaningful way, providing compact educational tools that allow great flexibility in teaching and learning. Material is stored so that it may be retrieved in a nonlinear fashion, depending on the needs or interests of learners. Educators can use multimedia projects to respond spontaneously to students' questions by referring quickly to relevant portions. In addition, students can use multimedia projects to pursue independent study according to their needs or at a pace appropriate to their capabilities. Educators and students want guidance about the application of fair use principles when creating their own multimedia projects to meet specific instructional objectives.

1.3 Applicability of these guidelines

(Certain basic terms used throughout these guidelines are identified in bold and defined in this section.)

These guidelines apply to the use, without permission, of portions of lawfully acquired copyrighted works in educational multimedia projects which are created by educators or students as part of a systematic learning activity by nonprint educational institutions.

Educational multimedia projects created under these guidelines incorporate students' or educators' original material, such as course notes or commentary, together with various copyrighted media formats including but not limited to, motion media, music, text material, graphics, illustrations, photographs and digital software which are combined into an integrated presentation. Educational institutions are defined as nonprofit organizations whose primary focus is supporting research and instructional activities of educators and students for noncommercial purposes.

For the purposes of the guidelines, educators include faculty, teachers, instructors, and others who engage in scholarly, research and instructional activities for educational institutions. The copyrighted works used under these guidelines are lawfully acquired if obtained by the institution or individual through lawful means such as purchase, gift or license agreement but not pirated copies. Educational multimedia projects which incorporate portions of copyrighted works under these guidelines may be used only for educational purposes in systematic learning activities including use in connection with non-commercial curriculum-based learning and teaching activities by educators to students enrolled in courses at nonprofit educational institutions or otherwise permitted under Section 3. While these guidelines refer to the creation and use of educational multimedia projects, readers are advised that in some instances other fair use guidelines such as those for off-air taping may be relevant.

2. Preparation of educational multimedia projects using portions of copyrighted works

These uses are subject to the Portion Limitations listed in Section 4. They should include proper attribution and citation as defined in Sections 6.2.

2.1 By students:

Students may incorporate portions of lawfully acquired copyrighted works when producing their own educational multimedia projects for a specific course.

2.2 By educators for curriculum-based instruction:

Educators may incorporate portions of lawfully acquired copyrighted works when producing their own educational multimedia programs for their own teaching tools in support of curriculum-based instructional activities at educational institutions.

3. Permitted uses of educational multimedia programs created under these guidelines

Uses of educational multimedia projects created under these guidelines are subject to the Time, Portion, Copying and Distribution Limitations listed in Section 4.

3.1 Student use:

Students may perform and display their own educational multimedia projects created under Section 2 of these guidelines for educational uses in the course for which they were created and may use them in their own portfolios as examples of their academic work for later personal uses such as job and graduate school interviews

3.2 Educator use for curriculum-based instruction:

Educators may perform and display their own educational multimedia projects created under Section 2 for curriculum-based instruction to students in the following situations:

3.2.1 for face-to-face instruction,

3.2.2 assigned to students for directed self-study,

3.2.3 for remote instruction to students enrolled in curriculum-based courses and located at remote sites, provided over the educational institution's secure electronic network in real-time, or for after class review or directed self-study, provided there are technological limitations on access to the network and educational multimedia project (such as a password or PIN) and provided further that the technology prevents the making of copies of copyrighted material.

If the educational institution's network or technology used to access the educational multimedia project created under Section 2 of these guidelines cannot prevent duplication of copyrighted material, students or educators may use the multimedia educational projects over an otherwise secure network for a period of only 15 days after its initial real-time remote use in the course of instruction or 15 days after its assignment for directed self-study. After that period, one of the two use copies of the educational multimedia project may be placed on reserve in a learning resource center, library or similar facility for on-site use by students enrolled in the course. Students shall be advised that they are not permitted to make their own copies of the multimedia project.

3.3 Educator use for peer conferences:

Educators may perform or display their own multimedia projects created under Section 2 of these guidelines in presentations to their peers, for example, at workshops and conferences.

3.4 Educator use for professional portfolio

Educators may retain educational multimedia projects created under Section 2 of these guidelines in their personal portfolios for later personal uses such as tenure review or job interviews.

4. Limitations—time, portion, copying and distribution

The preparation of educational multimedia projects incorporating copyrighted works under Section 2, and the use of such projects under Section 3, are subject to the limitations noted below.

4.1 Time limitations

Educators may use their educational multimedia projects created for educational purposes under Section 2 of these guidelines for teaching courses, for a period of up to two years after the first instructional use with a class. Use beyond that time period, even for educational purposes, requires permission for each copyrighted portion incorporated in the production. Students may use their educational multimedia projects as noted in Section 3.1.

4.2 Portion limitations

Portion limitations mean the amount of a copyrighted work that can reasonably be used in educational multimedia projects under these guidelines regardless of the original medium from which the copyrighted works are taken. In the aggregate means the total amount of copyrighted material from a single copyrighted work that is permitted to be used in an educational multimedia project without permission under these guidelines. These limits apply cumulatively to each educator's or student's multimedia project(s) for the same academic semester, cycle or term. All students should be instructed about the reasons for copyright protection and the need to follow these guidelines. It is understood, however, that students in kindergarten through grade six may not be able to adhere rigidly to the portion limitations in this section in their independent development of educational multimedia projects. In any event, each such project retained under Sections 3.1 and 4.3 should comply with the portion limitaitons in this section.

4.2.1 Motion media

Up to 10% or 3 minutes, whichever is less, in the aggregate of a copyrighted motion media work may be reproduced or otherwise incorporated as part of a multimedia project created under Section 2 of these guidelines.

4.2.2 Text material

Up to 10% or 1000 words, whichever is less, in the aggregate of a copyrighted work consisting of text material may be reproduced or otherwise incorporated as part of a multimedia project created under Section 2 of these guidelines. An entire poem of less than 250 words may be used, but no more than three poems by one poet, or five poems by different poets from any anthology may be used. For poems of greater length, 250 words may be used but no more than three excerpts by a poet, or five excerpts by different poets from a single anthology may be used.

4.2.3 Music, lyrics, and music video

Up to 10%, but in no event more than 30 seconds, of the music and lyrics from an individual musical work (or in the aggregate of extracts from an individual work), whether the musical work is embodied in copies, or audio or audiovisual works, may be reproduced or otherwise incorporated as a part of a multimedia project created under Section 2. Any alterations to a musical work shall not change the basic melody or the fundamental character of the work.

4.2.4 Illustrations and photographs

The reproduction or incorporation of photographs and illustrations is more difficult to define with regard to fair use because fair use usually precludes the use of an entire work. Under these guidelines a photograph or illustration may be used in its entirety but no more than 5 images by an artist or photographer may be reproduced or otherwise incorporated as part of an educational multimedia project created under Section 2. When using photographs and illustrations from a published collective work, not more than 10% or 15 images, whichever is less, may be reproduced or otherwise incorporated as part of an educational multimedia project created under Section 2.

4.2.5 Numerical data sets

Up to 10% or 2500 fields or cell entries, whichever is less, from a copyrighted database or data table may be reproduced or otherwise incorporated as part of a educational multimedia project created under Section 2 of these guidelines. A field entry is defined as a specific item of information, such as a name or Social Security number, in a record of a database file. A cell entry is defined as the intersection where a row and a column meet on a spreadsheet.

4.3 Copying and distribution limitations

Only a limited number of copies, including the original, may be made of an educator's educational multimedia project. For all of the uses permitted by Section 3, there may be no more than two use copies only one of which may be placed on reserve as described in Section 3.2.3.

An additional copy may be made for preservation purposes but may only be used or copied to replace a use copy that has been lost, stolen, or damaged. In the case of a jointly created educational multimedia project, each principal creator may retain one copy but only for the purposes described in Sections 3.3 and 3.4 for educators and Section 3.1 for students.

5. Examples of when permission is required

5.1 Using multimedia projects for non-educational or commercial purposes

Educators and students must seek individual permissions (licenses) before using copyrighted works in educational multimedia projects for commercial reproduction and distribution.

5.2 Duplication of multimedia projects beyond limitations listed in these guidelines

Even for educational uses, educators and students must seek individual permissions for all copyrighted works incorporated in their personally created educational multimedia projects before replicating or distributing beyond the limitations listed in Section 4.3.

5.3 Distribution of multimedia projects beyond limitations listed in these guidelines

Educators and students may not use their personally created educational multimedia projects over electronic networks, except for uses as described in Section 3.2.3, without obtaining permissions for all copyrighted works incorporated in the program.

6. Important reminders

6.1 Caution in downloading material from the internet

Educators and students are advised to exercise caution in using digital material downloaded from the Internet in producing their own educational multimedia projects, because there is a mix of works protected by copyright and works in the public domain on the network. Access to works on the Internet does not automatically mean that these can be reproduced and reused without permission or royalty payment and, furthermore, some copyrighted works may have been posted to the Internet without authorization of the copyright holder.

6.2 Attribution and acknowledgment

Educators and students are reminded to credit the sources and display the copyright notice © and copyright ownership information if this is shown in the original source, for all works incorporated as part of the educational multimedia projects prepared by educators and students, including those prepared under fair use. Crediting the source must adequately identify the source of the work, giving a full bibliographic description where available (including author, title, publisher, and place and date of publication). The copyright ownership information includes the copyright notice (©, year of first publication and name of the copyright holder).

The credit and copyright notice information may be combined and shown in a separate section of the educational multimedia project (e.g. credit section) except for images incorporated into the project for the uses described in Section 3.2.3. In such cases, the copyright notice and the name of the creator of the image must be incorporated into the image when, and to the extent, such information is reasonably available; credit and copyright notice information is considered "incorporated" if it is attached to the image file and appears on the screen when the image is viewed. In those cases when displaying source credits and copyright ownership information on the screen with the image would be mutually exclusive with an instructional objective (e.g. during examinations in which the source credits and/or copyright information would be relevant to the examination questions), those images may be displayed without such information being simultaneously displayed on the screen. In such cases, this information should be linked to the image in a manner compatible with such instructional ≠objectives.

6.3 Notice of use restrictions

Educators and students are advised that they must include on the opening screen of their multimedia program and any accompanying print material a notice that certain materials are included under the fair use exemption of the U.S. Copyright Law and have been prepared according to the multimedia fair use guidelines and are restricted from further use.

6.4 Future uses beyond fair use

Educators and students are advised to note that if there is a possibility that their own educational multimedia project incorporating copyrighted works under fair use could later result in broader dissemination, whether or not as commercial product, it is strongly recommended that they take steps to obtain permissions during the development process for all copyrighted portions rather than waiting until after completion of the project.

6.5 Integrity of copyrighted works: alterations

Educators and students may make alterations in the portions of the copyrighted works they incorporate as part of an educational multimedia project only if the alterations support specific instructional objectives. Educators and students are advised to note that alterations have been made.

6.6 Reproduction or decompilation of copyrighted computer programs

Educators and students should be aware that reproduction or decompilation of copyrighted computer programs and portions thereof, for example the transfer of underlying code or control mechanisms, even for educational uses, are outside the scope of these guidelines.

6.7 Licenses and contracts

Educators and students should determine whether specific copyrighted works, or other data or information are subject to a license or contract. Fair use and these guidelines shall not preempt or supersede licenses and contractual obligations.

Notes

1. These Guidelines shall not be read to supersede other preexisting education fair use guidelines that deal with the Copyright Act of 1976.
2. See Section 106 of the Copyright Act.
3. The Copyright Act of 1976, as amended, is codified at 17 U.S.C. Sec.101 et seq.

4. The names of the various organizations participating in this dialog appear at the end of these guidelines and clearly indicate the variety of interest groups involved, both from the standpoint of the users of copyrighted material and also from the standpoint of the copyright owners.

Source G

American Library Association Model Policy Concerning College and University Photocopying for Classroom, Research and Library Reserve Use

(Permission granted by the American Library Association, 2001)

This model policy, another in a series of copyright advisory documents developed by the American Library Association (ALA), is intended for the guidance and use of academic librarians, faculty, administrators, and legal counsel in response to implementation of the rights and responsibilities provisions of Public Law 94–553, General Revision of the Copyright Law, which took effect on January 1, 1978.

Prepared by ALA Legal Counsel Mary Hutchings of the law firm Sidley & Austin, with advise and assistance from the Copyright Subcommittee (ad hoc) of ALA's Legislation Committee, Association of College and Research Libraries (ACRL) Copyright Committee, Association of Research Libraries (ARL) and other academic librarians and copyright attorneys, the model policy outlines "fair use" rights in the academic environment for classroom teaching, research activities and library services. Please note that it does not address other library photocopying which may be permitted under other sections of the Copyright Law, e.g.,§ 108 (Reproduction by Libraries and Archives).

Too often, members of the academic community have been reluctant or hesitant to exercise their rights of fair use under the law for fear of courting an infringement suit. It is important to understand that in U.S. law, copyright is a limited statutory monopoly and the public's right to use materials must be protected. Safeguards have been written into the legislative history accompanying the new copyright law protecting librarians, teachers, researchers and scholars and guaranteeing their rights of access to information as they carry out their responsibilities for educating or conducting research. It is, therefore, important to heed the advise of a former U.S. Register of Copyrights: "If you don't use fair use, you will lose it!"

I. The copyright act and photocopying

From time to time, the faculty and staff of this University [College] may use photocopied materials to supplement research and teaching. In many cases, photocopying can facilitate the University's [College's] mission; that is, the development and transmission of information. However, the photocopying of copyrighted materials is a right granted under the copyright law's doctrine of "fair use" which must not be abused. This report will explain the University's [College's] policy concerning the photocopying of copyrighted materials by faculty and library staff. Please note that this policy does not address other library photocopying which may be permitted under sections of the copyright law, e.g., 17 U.S.C.§ 108.

Copyright is a constitutionally conceived property right which is designed to promote the progress of science and the useful arts by securing for an author the benefits of his or her original work of authorship for a limited time. U.S. Constitution, Art. I, Sec. 8. The Copyright statute, 17 U.S.C.§ 101 et seq., implements this policy by balancing the author's interest against the public interest in the dissemination of information affecting areas of universal concern, such as art, science, history and business. The grand design of this delicate balance is to foster the creation and dissemination of intellectual works for the general public.

The Copyright Act defines the rights of a copyright holder and how they may be enforced against an infringer. Included within the Copyright Act is the "fair use" doctrine which allows, under certain conditions, the copying of copyrighted material. While the Act lists general factors under the heading of "fair use" it provides little in the way of specific directions for what constitutes fair use. The law states:

17 U.S.C.§ 107. Limitations on exclusive rights: Fair use

Notwithstanding the provisions of section 106, the fair use of a copyrighted work, including such use by reproduction in copies or phonorecords or by any other means specified by that section, for purposes such as criticism, comment, news reporting, teaching (including multiple copies for classroom use), scholarship, or research, is not an infringement of copyright. In determining whether the use made of a work in any particular case is a fair use the factors to be considered shall include

(1) the purpose and character of the use, including whether such use is of a commercial nature or is for nonprofit educational purposes;

(2) the nature of copyrighted work;

(3) the amount and substantiality of the portion used in relation to the copyrighted work as a whole; and

(4) the effect of the use upon the potential market for or value of the copyrighted work.

The purpose of this report is to provide you, the faculty and staff of this University [College], with an explanation of when the photocopying of copyrighted material in our opinion is permitted under the fair use doctrine. Where possible, common examples of research, classroom, and library reserve photocopying have been included to illustrate what we believe to be the reach and limits of fair use.

Please note that the copyright law applies to all forms of photocopying, whether it is undertaken at a commercial copying center, at the University's [College's] central or departmental copying facilities or at a self-service machine. While you are free to use the services of a commercial establishment, you should be prepared to provide documentation of permission from the publisher (if such permission is necessary under this policy), since many commercial copiers will require such proof.

We hope this report will give you an appreciation of the factors which weight in favor of fair use and those factors which weigh against fair use, but faculty members must determine for themselves which works will be photocopied. This University [College] does not condone a policy of photocopying instead of purchasing copyrighted works where such photocopying would constitute an infringement under the Copyright law, but it does encourage faculty members to exercise good judgment in serving the best interests of students in an efficient manner.

Instructions for securing permission to photocopy copyrighted works when such copying is beyond the limits of fair use appear at the end of this report. It is the policy of this University that the user (faculty, staff or librarian) secure such permission whenever it is legally necessary.

II. Unrestricted photocopying

A. Uncopyrighted published works

Writing published before January 1, 1978 which have never been copyrighted may be photocopied without restriction. Copies of works protected by copyright must bear a copyright notice, which consists of the letter "c" in a circle, or the word "Copyright", or the abbreviation "Copr.", plus the year of first publication, plus the name of the copyright owner. 17 U.S.C.§ 401. As to works published before January 1, 1978, in the case of a book, the notice must be placed on the title page or the reverse side of the title page. In the case of a periodical the notice must be placed either on the title page, the first page of text, or in the masthead. A pre-1978 failure to comply with the notice requirements results in the work being injected into the public domain, i.e., unprotected. Copyright notice requirements have been relaxed since 1978, so that the absence of notice on copies of a work published after January 1, 1978 does not necessarily mean the work in the public domain. 17 U.S.C.§ 405 (a) and (c). However, you will not be liable for damages for copyright infringement of works published after that date, if, after normal inspection, you photocopy a work on which you cannot find a copyright symbol and you have not received actual notice of the fact the work is copyrighted. 17 U.S.C.§ 405(b).

However, a copyright owner who found out about your photocopying would have the right to prevent further distribution of the copies if in fact the work were copyrighted and the copies are infringing. 17 U.S.C.§ 405(b).

B. Published works with expired copyrights

Writings with expired copyrights may be photocopied without restriction. All copyrights prior to 1906 have expired. 17 U.S.C.§ 304(b). Copyrights granted after 1906 may have been renewed; however the writing will probably not contain notice of the renewal. Therefore, it should be assumed all writings dated 1906 or later are covered by a valid copyright, unless information to the contrary is obtained from the owner or the U.S. Copyright Office (see Copyright Office Circular 15t).

Copyright Office Circular R22 explains how to investigate the copyright status of a work. One way is to use the Catalog of Copyright Entries published by the Copyright Office and available in [the University Library] many libraries. Alternatively you may request the Copyright Office to conduct a search of its registration and/or assignment records. The Office charges an hourly fee for this service. You will need to submit as much information as you have concerning the work in which you are interested, such as the title, author, approximate date of publication, the type of work or any available copyright data. The Copyright Office does caution that its searches are not conclusive; for instance, if a work obtained copyright less than 28 years ago, it may be fully protected although there has been no registration or deposit.

C. Unpublished works

Unpublished works, such as theses and dissertations, may be protected by copyright. If such a work was created before January 1, 1978 and has not been copyrighted or published without copyright notice, the work is protected under the new Act for the life of the author plus fifty years, 17 U.S.C.§ 303, but in no case earlier than December 31, 2002. If such a work is published on or before that date, the copyright will not expire before December 31, 2027. Works created after January 1, 1978 and not published enjoy copyright protection for the life of the author plus fifty years. 17 U.S.C.§ 302.

D. U.S. government publications

All U.S. Government publications with the possible exception of some National Technical Information Service Publications less than five years old may be photocopied without restrictions, except to the extent they contain copyrighted materials from other sources. 17 U.S.C.§ 105. U.S. Government publications are documents prepared by an official or employee of the government in an official capacity. 17 U.S.C.§ 101.

Government publications include the opinions of courts in legal cases, Congressional Reports on proposed bills, testimony offered at Congressional hearings and the works of government employees in their official capacities. Works prepared by outside authors on contract to the government may or may not be protected by copyright, depending on the specifics of the contract. In the absence of copyright notice on such works, it would be reasonable to assume they are government works in the public domain. It should be noted that state government works may be protected by copyright. See, 17 U.S.C.§ 105. However, the opinions of state courts are not protected.

III. Permissible photocopying of copyrighted works

The Copyright Act allows anyone to photocopy copyrighted works without securing permission from the copyright owner when the photocopying amounts to a "fair use" of the material. 17 U.S.C.§ 107. The guidelines in this report discuss the boundaries for fair use of photocopied material used in research or the classroom or in a library reserve operation. Fair use cannot always be expressed in numbers—either the number of pages copied or the number of copies distributed. Therefore, you should wight the various factors listed in the Act and judge whether the intended use of photocopied, copyrighted material is within the spirit of the fair use doctrine. Any serious questions concerning whether a particular photocopying constitutes fair use should be directed to University [College] counsel.

A. Research uses

At the very least, instructors may make a single copy of any of the following for scholarly research or use in teaching or preparing to teach a class:

1. a chapter from a book;
2. an article from a periodical or newspaper;
3. a short story, short essay, or short poem, whether or not from a collective work;
4. a chart, diagram, graph, drawing, cartoon or picture from a book, periodical, or newspaper.

These examples reflect the most conservative guidelines for fair use. They do not represent inviolate ceilings for the amount of copyrighted material which can be photocopied within the boundaries of fair use. When exceeding these minimum levels, however, you again should consider the four factors listed in Section 107 of the Copyright Act to make sure that any additional photocopying is justified. The following demonstrate situations where increased levels of photocopying would continue to remain within the ambit of fair use:

1. the inability to obtain another copy of the work because it is not available from another library or source cannot be obtained within your time constraints;
2. the intention to photocopy the material only once and not to distribute the material to others;
3. the ability to keep the amount of material photocopied within a reasonable proportion to the entire work (the larger the work, the greater amount of material which may be photocopied).

Most single-copy photocopying for your personal use in research—even when it involves a substantial portion of a work—may well constitute fair use.

B. Classroom uses

Primary and secondary school educators have, with publishers, developed the following guidelines, which allow a teacher to distribute photocopied material to students in a class without the publisher's prior permission, under the following conditions:

1. the distribution of the same photocopied material does not occur every semester;
2. only one copy is distributed for each student which copy must become the student's property;
3. the material includes a copyright notice on the first page of the portion of material photocopied;
4. the students are not assessed any fee beyond the actual cost of the photocopying.

In addition, the educators agreed that the amount of material distributed should not exceed certain brevity standards. Under those guidelines, a prose work may be reproduced in its entirety if it is less than 2500 words in length. If the work exceeds such length, the excerpt reproduced may not exceed 1000 words, or 10% of the work, whichever is less. In the case of poetry, 250 words is the maximum permitted.

These minimum standards normally would not be realistic in the University setting. Faculty members needing to exceed these limits for college education should not feel hampered by these guidelines, although they should attempt a "selective and sparing" use of photocopied, copyrighted material.

The photocopying practices of an instructor should not have a significant detrimental impact on the market for the copyrighted work. 17 U.S.C.§ 107(4). To guard against this effect, you usually should restrict use of an item of photocopied material to one course and you should not repeatedly photocopy excepts from one periodical or author without the permission of the copyright owner.

C. Library reserve uses

At the request of a faculty member, a library may photocopy and place on reserve excerpts from copyrighted works in its collection in accordance with guidelines similar to those governing formal classroom distribution for face-to-face teaching discussed above. This University [College] believes that these guidelines apply to the library reserve shelf to the extent it functions as an extension of classroom readings or reflects an individual student's right to photocopy for his personal scholastic use under the doctrine of fair use. In general, librarians may photocopy materials for reserve room use for the convenience of students both in preparing class assignments and in pursuing informal educational activities which higher education requires, such as advanced independent study and research.

If the request calls for only one copy to be placed on reserve, the library may photocopy an entire article, or an entire chapter from a book, or an entire poem. Requests for multiple copies on reserve should meet the following guidelines:

1. the amount of material should be reasonable in relation to the total amount of material assigned for one term of a course taking into account the nature of the course, its subject matter and level, 17 U.S.C.§ 107(1) and (3);
2. the number of copies should be reasonable in light of the number of students enrolled, the difficulty and timing of assignments, and the number of other courses which may assign the same material, 17 U.S.C.§ 107(1) and (3);

3. the material should contain a notice of copyright, see 17 U.S.C.§ 401;

4. the effect of photocopying the material should not be detrimental to the market for the work. (In general, the library should own at least one copy of the work.) 17 U.S.C.§ 107(4).

For example, a professor may place on reserve as a supplement to the course textbook a reasonable number of copies of article from academic journals or chapters from trade books. A reasonable number of copies will in most instances be less than six, but factors such as the length or difficulty of the assignment, the number of enrolled students and the length of time allowed for completion of the assignment may permit more in unusual circumstances.

In addition, a faculty member may also request that multiple copies of photocopied, copyrighted material be placed on the reserve shelf if there is insufficient time to obtain permission from the copyright owner. For example, a professor may place on reserve several photocopies of an entire article from a recent issue of *Time* magazine or the *New York Times* in lieu of distributing a copy to each member of the class. If you are in doubt as to whether a particular instance of photocopying is fair use in the reserve reading room, you should waive any fee for such a use.

D. Uses of photocopied material requiring permission

1. repetitive copying: The classroom or reserve use of photocopied materials in multiple courses or successive years will normally require advance permission from the owner of the copyright, 17 U.S.C.§ 107(3).

2. copying for profit: Faculty should not charge students more than the actual cost of photocopying the material, 17 U.S.C.§ 107(1).

3. consumable works: The duplication of works that are consumed in the classroom, such as standardized tests, exercises, and workbooks, normally requires permission from the copyright owner, 17 U.S.C.§ 107(4).

4. creation of anthologies as basic text material for a course: Creation of a collective work or anthology by photocopying a number of copyrighted articles and excerpts to be purchased and used together as the basic text for a course will in most instances require the permission of the copyrighted owners. Such photocopying of a book and thus less likely to be deemed fair use, 17 U.S.C.§ 107(4).

E. How to obtain permission

When a use of photocopied material requires that you request permission, you should communicate complete and accurate information to the copyright owner. The American Association of Publishers suggests that the following information be included in a permission request letter in order to expedite the process:

1. Title, author and/or editor, and edition of materials to be duplicated.

2. Exact material to be used, giving amount, page numbers, chapters and, if possible, a photocopy of the material.

3. Number of copies to be made.

4. Use to be made of duplicated materials.
5. Form of distribution (classroom, newsletter, etc.).
6. Whether or not the material is to be sold.
7. Type of reprint (ditto, photography, offset, typeset).

The request should be sent, together with a self-addressed return envelope, to the permissions department of the publisher in question. If the address of the publisher does not appear at the front of the material, it may be readily obtained in a publication entitled *The Literary Marketplace*, published by the R. R. Bowker Company and available in all libraries.

The process of granting permission requires time for the publisher to check the status of the copyright and to evaluate the nature of the request. It is advisable, therefore, to allow enough lead time to obtain permission before the materials are needed. In some instances, the publisher may assess a fee for the permission. It is not inappropriate to pass this fee on to the student who receive copies of the photocopied material.

The Copyright Clearance Center also has the right to grant permission and collect fees for photocopying rights for certain publications. Libraries may copy from any journal which is registered with the CCC and report the copying beyond fair use to CCC and pay the set fee. A list of publications for which the CCC handles fees and permissions is available from CCC, 310 Madison Avenue, New York, N.Y. 10017.

Source H

Agreement on Guidelines for Classroom Copying in Not-for-Profit Educational Institutions

(From the House Committee on the Judiciary, Report on the Copyright Act of 1976.)

With respect to books and periodicals

The purpose of the following guidelines is to state the minimum standards of educational fair use under Section 107 of H.R. 2223. The parties agree that the conditions determining the extent of permissible copying for educational purposes may change in the future; that certain types of copying permitted under these guidelines may not be permissible in the future; and conversely that in the future other types of copying not permitted under these guidelines may be permissible under revised guidelines.

Moreover, the following statement of guidelines is not intended to limit the types of copying permitted under the standards of fair use under judicial decision and which are stated in Section 107 of the Copyright Revision Bill. There may be instances in which copying which does not fall within the guidelines stated below may nonetheless be permitted under the criteria of fair use.

Guidelines

I. Single copying for teachers

A single copy may be made of any of the following by or for a teacher at his or her individual request for his or her scholarly research or use in teaching or preparation to teach a class:

A. A chapter from a book;
B. An article from a periodical or newspaper;
C. A short story, short essay or short poem, whether or not from a collective work;
D. A chart, graph, diagram, drawing, cartoon or picture from a book, periodical, or newspaper.

II. Multiple copies for classroom use

Multiple copies (not to exceed in any event more than one copy per pupil in a course) may be made by or for the teacher giving the course for classroom use or discussion; provided that:

A. The copying meets the tests of brevity and spontaneity as defined below; and,

B. Meets the cumulative effect test as defined below; and,

C. Each copy includes a notice of copyright.

Definitions

Brevity

(*i*) Poetry: (a) A complete poem if less than 250 words and if printed on not more than two pages or, (b) from a longer poem, an excerpt of not more than 250 words.

(*ii*) Prose: (a) Either a complete article, story or essay of less than 2,500 words, or (b) an excerpt from any prose work of not more than 1,000 words or 10% of the work, whichever is less, but in any event a minimum of 500 words.

[Each of the numerical limits stated in "i" and "ii" above may be expanded to permit the completion of an unfinished line of a poem or of an unfinished prose paragraph.]

(*iii*) Illustration: one chart, graph, diagram, drawing, cartoon or picture per book or per periodical issue.

(*iv*) "Special" works: Certain works in poetry, prose or in "poetic prose" which often combine language with illustrations and which are intended sometimes for children and at other times for a more general audience fall short of 2,500 words in their entirety. Paragraph "ii" above notwithstanding such "special works" may not be reproduced in their entirety; however, an excerpt comprising not more than two of the published pages of such special work and containing not more than 10% of the words found in the text thereof, may be reproduced.

Spontaneity

(*i*) The copying is at the instance and inspiration of the individual teacher, and

(*ii*) The inspiration and decision to use the work and the moment of its use for maximum teaching effectiveness are so close in time that it would be unreasonable to expect a timely reply to a request for permission.

Cumulative effect

(*i*) The copying of the material is for only one course in the school in which the copies are made.

(*ii*) Not more than one short poem, article, story, essay or two excerpts may be copied from the same author, nor more than three from the same collective work or periodical volume during one class term.

(*iii*) There shall not be more than nine instances of such multiple copying for one course during one class term.

[The limitations stated in "ii" and "iii" above shall not apply to current news periodicals and newspapers and current news sections of other periodicals.]

III. Prohibitions as to I and II above

Notwithstanding any of the above, the following shall be prohibited:

(A) Copying shall not be used to create or to replace or substitute for anthologies, compilations or collective works. Such replacement or substitution may occur whether copies of various works or excerpts therefrom are accumulated or reproduced and used separately.

(B) There shall be no copying of or from works intended to be "consumable" in the course of study or of teaching. These include workbooks, exercises, standardized tests and test booklets and answer sheets and like consumable material.

(C) Copying shall not:
   (a) substitute for the purchase of books, publishers' reprints or periodicals;
   (b) be directed by higher authority;
   (c) be repeated with respect to the same item by the same teacher from term to term.

(D) No charge shall be made to the student beyond the actual cost of the photocopying.

Source I

How to get permission to use copyrighted material

During the process of writing the 1976 Copyright Act, Congress at some point realized that there was no centralized, easily accessible method of gaining permission to use a copyrighted work. In an effort to make it easier for libraries and others to enjoy legal uses of works that did not fall under any of the exceptions, such as that for library photocopying, the Senate recommended that "workable clearance and licensing procedures be developed." At the time, one of the main concerns was library photocopying. Now, of course, the Internet introduces an entirely new area of need. The Copyright Clearance Center (CCC), established in response to the 1976 act, provides licensing services for the reproduction and distribution of copyrighted materials in both print and electronic formats internationally. The CCC, however, cannot cover everything ever published, and the Internet makes this more true than ever.

Of course, the Internet presents some challenges not seen in the photocopying arena, namely self-publishing. With so much material available on the Internet, and so much of it not related to any formal publishing organization, not to mention the speed with which pages change, it is more difficult for collective licensing organizations to establish relations with owners of copyright in Web pages than in published books. Nonetheless, many collective licensing organizations have expanded their services to included licensing of Web pages.

If you want to seek permission to use material on a Web page then, you have a few avenues to pursue. First, many commercial copyright owners will allow *limited* use of their works for nonprofit educational purposes, though remember that this is the owner's option, unless your use is a fair use. If you believe your use falls into this category, you should contact the "publisher" of the page directly. The copyright owner will probably want a description of exactly what material you wish to use and how. If your use does not fall into this category, the path you choose first might depend on whether the page is authored by an individual, corporation, institution, or other large entity. Note that if your own pages do not fall into the nonprofit, educational category, you should be prepared to pay for your use. If the author is an individual, it might be easiest to send a letter to the copyright owner asking for permission and describing how you intend to use the information. Letters with original signatures from the copyright owner are preferable to emails, which may or may not be recognized by the courts. Be sure to keep records of your communications and to abide by any agreement you reach with the copyright owner.

If you wish to use information from a site where the copyright is owned by an institution—say you want to include a picture of the new electric car from Ford Motor Company's Web pages on your pages about alternative energy—you still have a few options. First, look over the pages to see if they provide contact information for seeking copyright permission. If not, you might contact the organization directly, but it might be quicker and easier to use a licensing organization, namely the CCC. Keep in mind that you may not find a licensing organization that will work with the entity in which you are interested. The Copyright Clearance Center may be reached at:

www.copyright.com
(978) 750–8400
info@copyright.com

Source J

How to protect your work

Registering for copyright[1]

Keep in mind that a work is protected by copyright the minute it is "fixed in a tangible medium." You do *not* need to register your work with the Copyright Office in order to ensure copyright protection. However, several benefits inure to registered works:

- Registration establishes a public record of the copyright claim.
- In order to file a claim of infringement, the work in question must be registered.
- Registration made within five years of publication establishes prima facie evidence of the validity of the copyright. This means that if your work is registered, the other guy in the battle has the burden of proving your copyright to be invalid, rather than you having to prove its validity.
- If a work is registered within three months of publication, or prior to an infringement of the work, you as the injured copyright owner may recover statutory damages and attorney's fees. If the work is not registered until after the infringement occurs, you may receive only actual damages and profits as awards in a suit against an infringer.
- Registration provides the U.S. Customs Service with the information they need to protect against the importation of infringing copies of your work.

A major benefit also inures to the Library of Congress (LC) from copyright registrations. The registration process requires the author to submit two copies of his work. These copies are sent to the Library of Congress. Registration is, in part, meant to ensure and build the LC's collection. As you might imagine, this is a controversial practice for various reasons.

Registering a work is quite simple and inexpensive. As the author, you must file with the Copyright Office a completed registration form, submit a fee of $30 (as of winter 2004), and deposit two copies of the work with the office. Different forms are filed for different types of work, but they are all quite simple to complete. Remember, the Copyright Office is trying to encourage registration, so they want to make it as painless as possible. In some cases, different requirements for the deposit of copies exist as well, depending on the type of work.

The Copyright Office publishes a wide range of pamphlets, called "circulars," which are very good at explaining the why's and how's of copyright law and registration. The circulars, as well as registration forms, are all available on the Copyright Office's Web site, in text, PDF, or HTML format: *www.loc.gov/copyright/*

Making it easy for others to respect your rights

Keep in mind that, especially in the cyberworld, many infringers have no idea that they are doing anything wrong. Some may assume that copyright does not apply in cyberspace at all. Others may assume that if a work does not have a copyright statement on it, it is up for grabs. Either way, you may prevent ignorant infringements by making it easy for users to see that your page is copyrighted and to contact you for permissions. Place a copyright notice on every page. Your notice should consist of the © symbol, the word "copyrighted," or the abbreviation "copr."; *and* the year of publication of the work; *and* the name of the copyright owner. Thus, appropriate statements would look like:

> © Gretchen McCord Hoffmann, 2005
> copyright Gretchen McCord Hoffmann, 2005
> copr. Gretchen McCord Hoffmann, 2005

An additional benefit of placing notices on your pages is that a defendant cannot then claim innocent infringement, which a court may consider in awarding damages.

You might also include statements giving your position on others' use of your page. If you are happy to allow others to use your page if they simply note that they have received permission, say so. If you are willing to allow certain uses, such as for educational or nonprofit uses, say so. Otherwise, a statement such as, "Copyright owner may be contacted to seek permission for use of this page at . . . ," in addition to being a courtesy, may reinforce the fact that no one can legally use your page without your permission.

Using technology to protect your digital works

Technology may be used to protect your online works to some extent. Such measures include marking a page as your own, so that if someone tries to download print, or copy the page, your mark comes through as a "watermark." You may have seen similar watermarks on some paper when you attempt to photocopy it. For example, some college transcripts will produce photocopies with a huge watermark proclaiming the fact that "this is a photocopy, not an original." Other means might enable you to limit access to your online works, allowing users to read a Web page but not download or print it. These technologies are in their infancy, but expect to see a rapid growth in availability over the next few years, due in part to the strong protection given by the Digital Millennium Copyright Act.

Monitoring infringement of your work on the web

Registration doesn't prevent someone from infringing your work; instead, it puts you in a stronger position and gives you more options should an infringer come along. Even technological tricks are no guarantee that your work won't be infringed. If a surefire means of preventing infringement existed, we wouldn't be having this conversation. Perhaps the better question is: How do you know when someone infringes your work?

If you are seriously concerned about infringement, you should use a combination of methods to combat it, including registering your work, placing notices on every page, and implementing some technological protections. You may also consider investing the time to monitor potential infringements on the Web. This involves setting aside time on a regular basis to search the Web for your pages, or parts thereof, on someone else's server.

"But that's ridiculous," you're saying. "How can I search for each phrase on each of my pages every month?" Practically speaking, it would be impossible to literally search for any infringement of any portion of your pages. But you can use tricks that may make your searching a little easier.

Keep in mind that many people who infringe on the Internet are simply ignorant of copyright laws and don't realize that they are doing something illegal. Thus, they probably won't take the time to "doctor" up a page to make it less identifiable as the original. One of my friends, an instruction librarian, identified an infringer who fell in this category by using metatags. (Metatags are discussed in Chapter 11) Metatags are extremely easy to insert in your HTML code and are not seen by those viewing your page. You might include in metatags copyright statements or inventive words that are unlikely to be used by other Web pages, so that you can use search engines to search for "copyright University of America Library, 2000" or "Supercalifragilistic-expialidocious," or simply your name, none of which are likely to turn up on too many pages other than your own. Should someone stealing your page realize that she is stealing, she can easily remove the metatags, however, so this is certainly not foolproof.

The bottom line is that there is no certain way to prevent infringement or to detect every infringement. This was true long before the Internet existed, as well. For this reason, the more techniques you use in combination, the more likely you will be able to both prevent and detect infringements.

Responding to an infringement

The first thing you should do if you discover someone infringing a work you have created as part of your job is to contact your institution's legal counsel with the information of what is being infringed, how or how much, and the URLs of the infringing pages. Discuss with your legal counsel whether she or you should contact the infringer to request that he stop his infringing actions. Keep monitoring the infringing page, and if the material is not removed, keep in touch with your counsel about pursuing the matter.

If you believe that your personal pages, in which you own the copyright, have been infringed, you might contact the infringer yourself to explain what you believe he is doing wrong and why. If you are willing for him to use your material as long as he includes a permission statement or to enter into some other compromise, let him know that. If not, ask him to take down the material and let him know that you will be talking to an attorney if he does not. You might ask your institution's legal counsel for a suggestion of attorneys to contact for help.

As a practical matter, the same path is usually taken in most infringement cases that are not major commercial infringements. First, a cease-and-desist letter is sent to the infringer. Usually, that's the end of it. If not, he will be notified that further legal action will be pursued should he not respond immediately to your request. Then, your legal counsel would file a complaint in court. Often, that will persuade the infringer to cease and desist. Seldom will such a case actually go to trial.

The main things for you to keep in mind are that you should always be in touch with legal counsel and you should keep records of all your communications with that person and the infringer, should you have any direct contact, as well as records of the infringing acts and the dates on which you discovered them.

Note

1. Should you wish to register works that you have created as part of your job, such as your library's Web pages, chences are those works will be considered "works for hire," which means that your employer owns the copyright, not you. If you are uncertain, clear this up before registering a work.

Source K

Resources: organizations

United States Copyright Office
U.S. Copyright Office
Library of Congress
101 Independence Avenue, S.E.
Washington, DC 20559–6000
(202) 707–3000
www.loc.gov/copyright

American Library Association Washington Office
1301 Pennsylvania Avenue, N.W.
Suite 403
Washington, DC 20004
(202) 628–8419
www.ala.org/washoff

American Library Association Office for Information Technology Policy
1301 Pennsylvania Avenue, N.W.
Suite 403
Washington, DC 20004
(202) 628–8424
www.ala.org/oitp

Copyright Clearance Center
222 Rosewood Drive
Danvers, MA 01923
(978) 750–8400
info@copyright.com

Electronic Frontier Foundation
1550 Bryant Street, Suite 725
San Francisco CA 94103
(415) 436–9333
www.eff.org

Source L

Resources: publications

Bielefield, Arlene, and Lawrence Cheeseman. 1993. *Libraries and Copyright Law.* New York: Neal-Schuman Publishers, Inc.

Bruwelheide, Janis H. 1995. *The Copyright Primer for Librarians and Educators.* 2nd ed. Chicago: American Library Association.

Fishman, Stephen. 1994. *The Copyright Handbook: How to Protect and Use Written Works.* 2nd ed. Berkeley: Nolo Press.

Gasaway, Laura N., ed. 1997. *Growing Pains: Adapting Copyright for Libraries, Education, and Society.* Littleton, Co. Fred B. Rothman & Co.

Gasaway, Laura N., and Sarah K. Wiant. 1994. *Libraries and Copyright: A Guide to Copyright Law in the 1990s.* Washington, D.C.: Special Libraries Association.

Hayes, David L. "Advanced Copyright Issues on the Internet," *Texas Intellectual Property Law Journal* 7, no. 1, (Fall 1998): 2.

Leaffer, Marshall. 1995. *Understanding Copyright Law.* 2nd ed. New York: Matthew Bender & Co., Inc.

Lehman, Bruce A. 1998. *The Conference on Fair Use: Final Report to the Commissioner on the Conclusion of the Conference on Fair Use.* Washington, D.C.: U.S. Patent and Trademark Office.

———. 1995. *Intellectual Property and the National Information Infrastructure: The Report of the Working Group on Intellectual Property Rights.* Washington, D.C.: U.S. Patent and Trademark Office.

Patterson, L. Ray, and Stanley W. Lindberg. 1991. *The Nature of Copyright: A Law of Users' Rights.* Athens: University of Georgia Press.

Source M

Resources: Web pages

American Library Association
www.ala.org

American Library Association Washington Office
www.ala.org/washoff

American Library Association Washington Office Copyright Education Program
copyright.ala.org

Association of Research Libraries
arl.cni.org/info/frn/copy/copytoc.html

Brinson, J. Dianne and Mark F. Radcliffe. *An Intellectual Property Law Primer for Multimedia and Web Developers.* Cyberspace and New Media Law Center, 1998. www2.viaweb.com/lib/laderapress/primer.html

CONFU: The Conference on Fair Use
www.utsystem.edu/ogc/intellectualproperty/confu.htm

Copyright Clearance Center, Inc.
www.copyright.com

Copyright on the Internet, Franklin Pierce Law Center
www.fplc.edu/tfield/copynet.htm

Cyberlaw Encyclopedia
www.gahtan.com/cyberlaw/Copyright_Law/

Daily IP News
www.ipmag.com

Digital Future Coalition
www.dfc.org

Electronic Frontier Foundation
www.eff.org

FindLaw: Copyright
www.findlaw.com/01topics/23intellectprop/01copyright/index.html

Harper, Georgia. *Copyright Crash Course.*
www.utsystem.edu/ogc/intellectualproperty/cprtindx.htm

Intellectual Property Reference Library
www.servtech.com/~mbobb/

Internet Law News
http:///bna.com/ilaw (can also subscribe to receive free via daily e-mail)

Legal Information Institute
www.law.cornell.edu/topics/copyright.html

Liblicense
www.library.yale.edu/~llicense/index.shtml

Licensing Electronic Resources: Strategic and Practical Considerations for Signing
Electronic Information Delivery Agreements
www.arl.org/scomm/licensing/licbooklet.html

Lutzker, Arnold P. *Primer on the Digital Millennium: What the Digital Millennium
Copyright Act and the Copyright Term Extension Act Mean for the Library Community*
www.ala.org/washoff/primer.html

Principles for Licensing Electronic Resources
www.arl.org/scomm/licensing/principles.html

Stanford University Libraries. *Copyright and Fair Use.*
http://fairuse.stanford.edu/

United States Copyright Office
http://lcweb.loc.gov/copyright/

United States Copyright Act
www.law.cornell.edu/uscode/17/

Source N

Glossary

Amicus Brief (also Amicus Curiae) — Literally, "friend of the court"; a brief filed by someone not a party to a lawsuit on behalf of a party to the suit and for the purpose of attempting to sway the court on an issue that is a focus of the lawsuit.

Assign — To transfer ownership.

Audiovisual Work — A work that consists of a series of related images that are intrinsically intended to be shown by the use of machines or devices such as projectors, viewers, or electronic equipment, together with accompanying sounds, if any.

Berne Convention — International treaty titled the Berne Convention for the Protection of Literary and Artistic Works. The effective date of U.S. membership is March 1, 1989. The Berne Convention required modifications to the U.S. Copyright Act regarding requirements to register a work before bringing suit for infringement and eliminated the requirement to display a copyright notice on protected works.

Case Law — Law established by reported cases and the interpretation of statutory law. Compare *statute*.

Caching — Storage of data in a temporary memory buffer.

Circumvention — As used in the *Copyright Act*, descrambling a scrambled work, decrypting an encrypted work, or otherwise avoiding, bypassing, removing, deactivating, or impairing a technological measure taken to control access to or copying of a work in electronic format.

Codify — To incorporate into the official body of statutory law. For example, the fair use doctrine was originated by the courts in case law and was codified when it was written into the Copyright Act of 1976.

Commercial Use — Not defined by statute; some courts have stated that a commercial use is a use in which commercial advantage attaches to the immediate commercial motivation behind the reproduction or distribution of a work and not to the ultimate profit-making motivation behind the entity in which a library is located. Part of the analysis of the first fair use factor.

Contributory Infringement — Knowingly inducing, causing, or contributing to another party's direct infringement. See also *innocent infringement* and *vicarious infringement.*

Copies — Material objects other than phonorecords in which a work is fixed and can be perceived, reproduced, or otherwise communicated.

Copyright Act of 1976 — Current statute governing U.S. copyright law. The Copyright Act became effective as of January 1, 1978, and has been amended periodically since. The previous statute was the Copyright Act of 1909.

Copyright Clearance Center — An entity that acts as an intermediary between copyright owners and users of protected works and that licenses limited uses of such works.

Damages — In a legal context, the amount of compensation or award given to the prevailing party in a lawsuit.

Derivative Work — A work based upon one or more preexisting works, such as a translation, sequel, or a movie version of a book, or any other form in which a work may be recast, transformed, or adapted.

Digital Millennium Copyright Act of 1998 — The primary provisions of interest to libraries in the DMCA address limitations on liability for Internet service providers and anti circumvention technology. While the ISP liability provisions may benefit libraries, the anti circumvention technology provisions (Section 1201 of the Copyright Act) have been highly criticized as restricting fair uses.

Direct Infringement — See *infringement.*

Display — To show a copy of a work either directly or by means of any device or process.

Fair Use — A defense to a claim of infringement; determined on a case-by-case basis by the application of four factors as delineated in Section 107 of the Copyright Act.

File-Sharing — Commonly used to refer to the copying and/or distribution of files via peer-to-peer networks. Also *file-swapping.*

File-Swapping — Commonly used to refer to the copying and/or distribution of files via peer-to-peer networks. Also *file-sharing.*

First Sale Doctrine — Allows the owner of a particular lawfully made copy of a work to dispose of that copy however he or she wishes and to publicly display the copy without the need to obtain permission of the copyright owner.

Fixation — The fundamental concept in copyright law that, in order to be protected by copyright, a work must be fixed in a *tangible medium of expression* in a manner sufficiently permanent or stable to permit it to be perceived, reproduced, or otherwise communicated for a period of more than transitory duration.

Framing — An inline link that displays the outside file within a frame.

Idea/Expression Dichotomy — The fundamental concept in copyright law that ideas cannot be protected by copyright, but the expression of the idea may be.

Implied License — A license formed by implications based on the actions of the parties, in contrast to an express license, in which the parties specifically agree to the content of a license.

Infringement (also "Direct Infringement") — To violate the exclusive rights of a copyright owner under the Copyright Act by making use of a copyrighted work without permission of the copyright owner where such use does not constitute an exemption. See also *contributory infringement, innocent infringement,* and *vicarious infringement.*

Inline Link — A link that pulls into the linking page an image or other file residing on a separate Web page; compare *framing.*

Innocent Infringement — A misnomer; the defendant has infringed but was not aware and had no reason to believe that his or her act constituted an act of copyright infringement. Note that innocent infringement may not be claimed if the infringed work contains a copyright notice. (See also *contributory infringement* and *vicarious infringement*).

Intellectual Property — Refers to the legal protection of various types of intangible property. Intellectual property is generally broker into three categories, all of which are protected by federal law: copyright, trademark, and patents. A fourth category, trade secrets, is subject to state laws.

ISP — Internet Service Provider.

John Doe Summons — An order of the court to appear in a proceeding, issued to someone whose name is unknown. The true name of the defendant is substituted when it becomes known.

Licensing — The granting by a copyright owner of the right to limited uses of protected works without transferring ownership either of copyrights in the work or of an actual copy of the work.

MP3 — A file extension alternative name for MPEG files, which are relatively small-sized digital compression files used for audio and/or video; the smaller size makes them practical for Internet transmission and personal storage.

Musical Work — The written embodiment of a composition, such as a score. Compare *sound recording*.

Original Work — Refers to the requirement that, to be protected by copyright, a work must be created by the author claiming copyright, as opposed to being copied from a preexisting work.

Outlink — A hyperlink that connects to a site outside of the originating, or linking, site.

P2P — *See* Peer-to-Peer Network.

Packet Switching — A process in Internet transmission in which messages or files are broken into individual packets before being transmitted and then reassembled into the original file upon arrival at the final destination.

Peer-to-Peer Network — A network that allows individuals to copy files residing on each other's computers; also P2P.

Perform — To recite, render, play, dance, or act a work either directly or by means of any device or process.

Phonorecord — A material object in which sounds other than accompanying an audiovisual work are fixed and can be perceived, reproduced, or otherwise communicated.

Piracy — Technically, any unlawful reproduction and distribution of copyrighted works, but generally used to refer to such acts done on a large scale and purely for profit.

Public Domain — The aggregate of works not protected by copyright. If a work is "in the public domain," it is not subject to the restrictions of copyright law and therefore free for anyone to use. Once a work is in the public domain, it can never obtain copyright protection again (unless subject to the Sonny Bono Act).

Publication — The distribution of copies of a work to the public by sale or other transfer of ownership or by rental, lease, or lending, or the offering to a group of persons to do the same. Part of the analysis of the second fair use factor.

Publicly — To perform or display a work publicly is to do so (1) at a place open to the public or at any place where a substantial number of persons outside of the normal circle of a family and its social acquaintances is gathered; or (2) to transmit or otherwise communicate a performance or display of a work to such a place, or to the public, by means of any device or process, whether the members of the public capable of receiving the performance or display receive it in the same place or in separate places or whether they receive it at the same time or at different times.

RAM — Random access memory; temporary storage in a computer.

RIAA — Recording Industry Association of America; the RIAA has taken an extremely aggressive approach in policing its copyrights.

Sound Recording — A work that results from a fixation of a series of musical, spoken, or other sounds. Compare *musical work*.

Spider — A software program that collects specific information from web pages. Also known as *Webcrawler*.

Sonny Bono Act — Sonny Bono Copyright Term Extension Act of 1998; extended the term of copyright from life-plus-50 to life-plus-70 or, in the case of corporate authorship, from 75 years to 95 years.

Statute — Official codification of law by a legislative body, for example the U.S. Code. Compare *case law*.

Statute of Anne — First modern copyright law, passed by British Parliament in 1710.

Strict Liability Law — Law that imposes liability on the defendant without the need to prove bad intent or sometimes even knowledge; all that is necessary is that the defendant engaged in the bad behavior.

Subpoena — A command either to appear in court to give testimony or to produce certain documents to a court.

Taken/Taking — In the context of copyright law, refers to the use being made of a protected work. For example, if one copies a paragraph from a protected work, one has "taken" that paragraph.

TEACH Act — Technology, Education, and Copyright Harmonization Act of 2002; exempts from copyright protection certain public performances and displays made in the course of providing distance education.

Technological Measure — As used in the *Copyright Act*, any technological means of protecting access to or use of a copyrighted work.

Term of Copyright — The duration of copyright protection.

Trademark — Any word, name, symbol, device, or combination thereof that is used to identify and distinguish a good or service from that produced or sold by others by identifying the source of the good or service.

Transformative — A use that changes the original work to the extent that it adds something new, with a further purpose or a different character, altering the original with new expression, meaning, or message, as opposed to simply superseding the original work. Part of the analysis of the first fair use factor.

Treaty — An agreement entered into by multiple nations and often dictating consistency in the laws of the signatory countries. For example, when the United States acceded to the *Berne Convention*, an international treaty on the protection of Intellectual Property, the *Copyright Act* had to be amended to remove the requirement that a work must display a copyright notice in order to be protected by copyright.

TRIPS — International treaty titled Agreement on Trade-Related Aspects of Intellectual Property Rights. The U.S. acceded to TRIPS in 1994. TRIPS required amendments to the U.S. Copyright Act addressing anticircumvention of technological protection measures for copyrighted works, resulting in Section 1201 of the Copyright Act, and implemented as part of the *Digital Millennium Copyright Act*.

Vicarious Infringement — Having the right and ability to control the infringing activity of another party and having an obvious and direct financial interest in the infringing activity. See also *contributory infringement* and *innocent infringement*.

Webcrawler — *See* Spider.

Willful Infringement — To knowingly, deliberately, or intentionally infringe.

Work-made-for-hire — (1) A work performed by an employee within the scope of his or her employment; or (2) if the parties expressly agree in a written instrument signed by both that the work is to be considered a work-made-for-hire: a work specially ordered or commissioned for use as (a) a contribution to a collective work; (b) a part of a motion picture or other audiovisual work; (c) a translation; (d) a supplementary work; (e) a compilation; (f) an instructional text; (g) a test; (h) answer material for a test; or (i) an atlas.

Index

A

access, copyright owner's right to
  control, 94, 98–99
advocacy, 169
Agreement on Trade-Related Aspects of
  Intellectual Property Rights (TRIPS),
  10
Aimster, 102–105
amount and substantiality of the portion
  used, fair use factor, 32–33, 35
anti-circumvention, 55, 94, 96–99
archival purposes, copying allowed for,
  31, 55, 89–90
archiving, 38–39

B

balance in copyright law, 3–4, 5
Berne Convention for the Protection of
  Literary and Artistic Works, 10
browse-wrap license, 79
browsing, 69, 76–79
  as public display or performance,
    76–79
  fair use, 78–79
  implied license, 77–78
  Web, 69, 76–79

C

caching, 48, 69
circumvention, 93–94, 96–99
classroom copying, 36–37, 135–144
  ALA guidelines, 142–143
  classroom copying guidelines, 139–
    142
click-wrap license, 79

clip art, 82–83
conditions of use, 158
CONFU guidelines, 36–37, 143–144
  cumulative effect of copying, 37
  exceptions to performances and
    display rights, 138
  fair use, 135–138
contributory infringement, 24, 71–72,
  103–104
  peer-to-peer networks, 103–104
copies, defining, 46
Copyright Clearance Center, 35–36, 144
copyright infringement. *See* infringement.
copyright management information, 55
copyright management technology, 94,
  96–99
copyright notice, 19, 81, 83
copyright policy, 163–167
  content, 165
  DMCA, 164–165
  TEACH Act, 165
copyright exclusive rights, 21
creativity, 16–17

D

damages for copyright infringement, 19,
  24–25
databases, copyright protection for,
  172–173
deep linking, 63–64
derivative works, 30, 75–76
Digital Millennium Copyright Act
  (DMCA), 54–55, 95–99, 105, 173–
  175

effect on copyright owner's exclusive rights, 96
effect on fair use, 96–99, 173–175
First Amendment implications, 95–99
ISP safe harbor, 122–125
privacy issues, 95–96, 105
digitizing print works, 31, 89–90
preservation purposes, 89–90
distance education, 55–56, 85–86, 150–153
CONFU guidelines, 152
licensing, 152–153
public performance and display exception, 148–152
TEACH Act, 150–152
Web pages, 85–86
DMCA. *See* Digital Millennium Copyright Act.
downloading from the Web, 73–75, 81, 82–85
fair use, 82, 83
restrictions on use, 84–85
duration of copyright protection, 22, 51–54, 170–172

E

educational uses, 34
effect on the potential market for the work, 33–34, 35
electronic reserves, 135–144
ALA guidelines, 142–144
classroom copying guidelines, 139–143
CONFU guidelines, 137, 143–144
exceptions to performances and display rights, 138
fair use, 135–138
e-mail, 17–19
employees as authors, 20, 166
exceptions to copyright owner's exclusive rights, 18–19, 29, 37–42
display, 29

distributions, 29
factors, 29–36
public performance, 18–19
types of uses, 29
exclusive rights of copyright owner, 21
expression, 15, 17

F

facts, 31
protection of, 16–17, 172–173
factual works, 31
fair use, 27–36, 37, 78–79, 173–175
amount and substantiality of the portion used (factor), 32–33, 35
four factors, 29–36
linking, 78–79
nature of the work factor (factor), 30–32
potential effect on the marketplace factor (factor), 33–34
purpose and character of the use (factor), 29–30, 34
threats to, 173–175
types of uses, 29
file-sharing, 101–106
file-swapping, 101–106
first sale doctrine, 23, 29, 39–42, 127, 140
reserves, 140
fixation, 17–19, 71
framing, 49, 60, 64–66

G

government documents, 23
Grokster, 102–105

H

"heart" of the work, 32–33
hyperlinking, 48, 59–68
as infringement, 60–61, 66–68
images as links, 61
logos and trademarks as links, 62

I

idea/expression dichotomy, 15
independent contractors as authors, 20–21
infringement, 19, 24–25, 121–122
    contributory, 24–25, 122
    damages, 19, 24–25
    "innocent," 24–25
    vicarious, 24–25, 122
    willful, 24–25
inline links, 48, 59–60, 65–66
innocent infringement, 24
interlibrary loans (ILL), 38–39, 127–133
    CONFU guidelines for electronic ILL, 130–132
    CONTU guidelines for print ILL, 129–130
    limitation on exclusive rights of copyright owner, 127–129
international copyright laws, 10, 22
Internet service providers (ISPs), 93, 122–125
    liability for copyright infringement, 54–55, 93, 122–125
    libraries as ISPs, 122–125
    subject to subpoena, 95

L

liability for copyright infringement, 113–117
    criminal liability, 115
    damages, 114, 116
    impoundment, 114
    injunction, 113–114
    state immunity, 116–117
library instruction, 147–152
    classroom copying guideline, 148–152
    CONFU guideline, 148–152
    licensing, 148–149
    public performance and display exception, 148–152

library photocopying, 38
linking. *See* hyperlinking.
lobbing, 175–178

N

Napster, 102–105
nature of the copyrighted work (fair use factor), 30–32, 35
network, 43
non-profit institutions, 18
non-profit use, 34

O

online service provider (OSP). *See* Internet service providers.
original work of authorship, 16
out links, 48, 60–64
out-of-print books, 21
ownership of copyright, 20–21

P

packet-switching, 44–45
parodies, 30
patents, 11
peer-to-peer (P2P) networks, 101–106
    copyright infringement, 102–104
    fair use, 102–103
photocopying, library exception, 55
plagiarism, 16
preservation
    copying allowed for, 31, 38, 55, 89–100
    digitizing print works, 89–100
printing, 73–75
publication, significance of, 7, 9, 31–32
public display, 76–79
    first sale doctrine exception, 76
public domain, 21, 23, 25, 166–168
public performance, 17–19, 76–79
purpose and character of the use (fair use factor), 34
purpose of copyright, 3–4, 5, 16

R

RAM, 45–48, 70, 78
RAM copies, 46
registration of copyright, 7, 19
requirements for obtaining copyright
   protection, 19
Recording Industry Association of
   America (RIAA), 95–96, 102–105
   and peer-to-peer networks, 102–105
   use of DMCA subpoena provision,
      95–96, 105
resource sharing, 127–133
RIAA. *See* Recording Industry Association of America.
rights protected by copyright, 21

S

Sonny Bono Copyright Extension Act,
   51–54, 170–172
subject matter of copyright protection, 15

T

tangible medium of expression, 17–19
Technology, Education, and Copyright
   Harmonization Act (TEACH Act),
   55–58, 85–86, 138–139, 146
   classroom Web pages, 138–139
   electronic reserves, 138–139
   Web pages, 85–86

Term of copyright protection. *See*
   Duration of copyright protection.
terms of use, 158
trademark, 11, 107–112
   dilution, 109–112
   infringement, 109–112
   links, 111–112
   metatags, 110–111
   URLs, 109–110
   Web pages, 109–112
transformative use, 30

V

vicarious infringement, 24, 103–104
   peer-to-peer networks, 103–104
video, public performance of, 17–19

W

Web pages, 81–90, 135
   class-based, 135
   creating, 81–90
   distribution right, 86–88
   incorporating others' works, 88–89
   public display, 84–85
   public performance, 84–85
   TEACH Act, 85
willful infringement, 24
work-made-for-hire doctrine, 20–21,
   166

About the author

Gretchen McCord Hoffmann is a second-generation librarian on both sides of the family (with both parents now retired librarians) and currently a practicing attorney. She practiced as an academic librarian for six years, first as a reference librarian at the University of Texas at San Antonio Library and then as Coordinator of Library Instruction at the University of Houston Libraries. After becoming increasingly interested in and concerned with legal issues surrounding the Internet and digital information, she decided to attend law school and is currently an Associate Attorney in the Intellectual Property & Technology Section of the Austin office of Fulbright & Jaworski L.L.P. Her practice focuses on copyright and trademark issues, with a little privacy law in the mix.

Gretchen received her BA from Rice University and MSIS from the University of North Texas. She received her JD from the University of Texas School of Law in 2001 and is licensed to practice law in the State of Texas. While in law school, Gretchen served as Chief Articles Editor of the Texas Intellectual Property Law Journal and Co-Editor-in-Chief of the Texas Journal of Women and the Law. She received the 1999–2000 Sidley Austin Best Student Note Award for her paper, "Arguments for the Need for Statutory Solutions to the Copyright Problem Presented by RAM Copies Made During Web Browsing." During law school, she interned for the Texas Supreme Court and the Senate Jurisprudence Committee of the Texas Legislature and worked for the Texas Library Association as a legislative assistant.

Gretchen is currently the President-Elect of the Texas Library Association (also second generation) and will serve as President in 2005–2006. Also in T.L.A., she is currently Lead Singer for the Doo-Wop Intergalactic Round Table and a member of the Legislative Committee. She is also an alumna of both the Snowbird Leadership Institute and the TALL Texans Leadership Institute. Gretchen is a member of the Board of Directors of Library Partners, Inc. In the Texas State Bar, she is currently chair of the Texas Intellectual Property Law Journal Committee and a member of the Copyright Committee.

During both her library and legal careers, Gretchen has written and spoken extensively on copyright issues of concern to librarians. Although she thoroughly enjoys her legal practice, she greatly misses working with librarians on a daily basis and looks forward to every opportunity to present a copyright workshop or program to librarians.

After plotting unsuccessfully for years to leave Texas, Gretchen and her husband, an architect, moved to Austin for Gretchen to attend law school. In less than three months, they fell madly in love with Austin and currently enjoy life there in their newly built home.

DATE DUE

DEC 0 9 2010	
MAR 0 2 2011	